THE CITY & GUILDS TEXTBOOK

LEVEL 1 DIPLOMA IN
PAINTING AND
DECORATING

THE CITY & GUILDS TEXTBOOK

LEVEL 1 DIPLOMA IN PAINTING AND DECORATING

ANN COOK

COLIN FEARN

STEVE WALTER

BARRIE YARDE

SERIES TECHNICAL EDITOR
MARTIN BURDFIELD

About City & Guilds

City & Guilds is the UK's leading provider of vocational qualifications, offering over 500 awards across a wide range of industries, and progressing from entry level to the highest levels of professional achievement. With over 8500 centres in 100 countries, City & Guilds is recognised by employers worldwide for providing qualifications that offer proof of the skills they need to get the job done.

Equal opportunities

City & Guilds fully supports the principle of equal opportunities and we are committed to satisfying this principle in all our activities and published material. A copy of our equal opportunities policy statement is available on the City & Guilds website.

First edition 2014
Reprinted 2014

ISBN 978-0-85193-295-8

Publisher Fiona McGlade
Development Editor Frankie Jones
Production Editor Lauren Cubbage

Cover design by Design Deluxe
Illustrations by Barking Dog Art and Saxon Graphics Ltd
Typeset by Saxon Graphics Ltd, Derby
Printed in the UK by Cambrian Printers Ltd

British Library Cataloguing in Publication Data

A catalogue record for this book is available from the British Library.

Publications

For information about or to order City & Guilds support materials, contact 0844 534 0000 or centresupport@cityandguilds.com. You can find more information about the materials we have available at www.cityandguilds.com/publications.

Every effort has been made to ensure that the information contained in this publication is true and correct at the time of going to press. However, City & Guilds' products and services are subject to continuous development and improvement and the right is reserved to change products and services from time to time. City & Guilds cannot accept liability for loss or damage arising from the use of information in this publication.

City & Guilds
1 Giltspur Street
London EC1A 9DD

T 0844 543 0033

www.cityandguilds.com

publishingfeedback@cityandguilds.com

CONTENTS

FOREWORD

Whether in good times or in a difficult job market, I think one of the most important things for young people is to learn a skill. There will always be a demand for talented and skilled individuals who have knowledge and experience. That's why I'm such an avid supporter of vocational training. Vocational courses provide a unique opportunity for young people to learn from people in the industry, who know their trade inside out.

Careers rarely turn out as you plan them. You never know what opportunity is going to come your way. However, my personal experience has shown that if you haven't rigorously learned skills and gained knowledge, you are unlikely to be best placed to capitalise on opportunities that do come your way.

When I left school, I went straight to work in a butcher's shop, which was a fantastic experience. It may not be the industry I ended up making my career in, but being in the butcher's shop, working my way up to management level and learning from the people around me was something that taught me a lot about business and about the working environment.

Later, once I trained in the construction industry and was embarking on my career as a builder, these commercial principles were vital in my success and helped me to go on to set up my own business. The skills I had learned gave me an advantage and I was therefore able to make the most of my opportunities.

Later still, I could never have imagined that my career would take another turn into television. Of course, I recognise that I have had lucky breaks in my career, but when people say you make your own luck, I think there is definitely more than a grain of truth in that. People often ask me what my most life-changing moment has been, expecting me to say winning the first series of *Big Brother*. However, I always answer that my most life-changing moment was deciding to make the effort to learn the construction skills that I still use every day. That's why I was passionate about helping to set up a construction academy in the North West, helping other people to acquire skills and experience that will stay with them for their whole lives.

After all, an appearance on a reality TV show might have given me a degree of celebrity, but it is the skills that I learned as a builder that have kept me in demand as a presenter of DIY and building shows, and I have always continued to run my construction business. The truth is, you can never predict the way your life will turn out, but if you have learned a skill from experts in the field, you'll always be able to take advantage of the opportunities that come your way.

Craig Phillips

City & Guilds qualified bricklayer, owner of a successful construction business and television presenter of numerous construction and DIY shows

ABOUT THE AUTHORS

ANN COOK

CHAPTER 7

I started my painting and decorating career as a mature student, achieving the City & Guilds Bronze Medal for Advanced Craft, and progressed from self-employment to teaching between 1989 and 1998. I then became a City & Guilds External Verifier for Construction.

In 2002 I started my own assessment centre, delivering NVQs for experienced practitioners and CPD for college lecturers. I have also developed NVQ portfolios for 18 construction occupations, used by centres across the UK.

I am a member and past president of the Association of Painting Craft Teachers, and was a member of the committee for the Young Decorator of the Year competition for a number of years.

Since 2003, I have been a member of the National Working Group for Painting and Decorating, setting the National Occupational Standards. I have also written training programmes for apprentices, and I deliver training and assessment in the painting and decorating heritage sector.

COLIN FEARN

CHAPTERS 1 AND 2

I was born, grew up and continue to live in Cornwall with my wife, three children and Staffordshire bull terrier.

As a qualified carpenter and joiner, I have worked for many years on sites and in several joinery shops.

I won the National Wood Award for joinery work and am also a Fellow of the Institute of Carpenters, holder of the Master Craft certificate and have a BA in Education and Training.

I was until recently a full-time lecturer at Cornwall College, teaching both full-time students and apprentices.

I now work full-time as a writer for construction qualifications, practical assessments, questions and teaching materials for UK and Caribbean qualifications.

In my spare time I enjoy walks, small antiques and 'keeping my hand in' with various building projects.

STEVE WALTER
CHAPTERS 4 AND 5

I was born in London and on leaving school in 1967 was apprenticed to a large decorating company, attending Brixton School of Building part time.

In those days the apprenticeship lasted for five years, with an extra two years as an improver. I specialised in decorative finishes and wall coverings and worked in prestigious buildings for the rich and famous all over London.

I took a break from decorating for three years to train and work as a steeplejack, before returning to my first love to set up my own decorating firm.

I moved to the Sussex coast in 1995, and was soon employed full time while also studying to gain an educational qualification and degree. By 2012 I was head of department and lead Internal Verifier for Sussex Downs College. I am now semi-retired, but I still do consultancy work, building and painting of stage sets and enjoy keeping up with the decorating at home.

BARRIE YARDE
CHAPTERS 3 AND 6

I have been very fortunate to have had a long career in construction, and in particular as a painter and decorator. I was trained as an apprentice by an 'old master', who helped me gain the skills that have given me such a wonderful career.

It was very much a case of practice and more practice, until I was able to demonstrate mastery of the skills that I had been shown.

I later went into teaching, and the years spent teaching in college have, I believe, delivered the right result – many of my learners have developed into fine craftspeople themselves.

I hope I can continue to encourage others to follow a worthwhile career in construction. I have been inspired by many others – too numerous to mention – and so I hope that this textbook will provide inspiration for you, encouraging you to study and learn the skills of painting and decorating.

MARTIN BURDFIELD
SERIES TECHNICAL EDITOR

I come from a long line of builders and strongly believe that you will find a career in the construction industry a very rewarding one. Be proud of the work you produce; it will be there for others to admire for many years.

As an apprentice I enjoyed acquiring new knowledge and learning new skills. I achieved the C&G Silver Medal for the highest marks in the Advanced Craft Certificate and won the UK's first Gold Medal in Joinery at the World Skills Competition. My career took me on from foreman, to estimator and then works manager with a number of large joinery companies, where I had the privilege of working on some prestigious projects.

Concurrent with this I began working in education. I have now worked in further education for over 35 years enjoying watching learners' skills improve during their training. For 10 years I ran the Skillbuild Joinery competitions and was the UK Training Manager and Chief Expert Elect at the World Skills Competition, training the UK's second Gold Medallist in Joinery.

Working with City & Guilds in various roles over the past 25 years has been very rewarding.

I believe that if you work and study hard anything is possible.

HOW TO USE THIS TEXTBOOK

Welcome to your City & Guilds Level 1 Diploma in Painting and Decorating textbook. It is designed to guide you through your Level 1 qualification and be a useful reference for you throughout your career. Each chapter covers a unit from the 6707 Level 1 qualification, and covers everything you will need to understand in order to complete your written or online tests and prepare for your practical assessments.

Please note that not all of the chapters will cover the learning outcomes in order. They have been put into a logical sequence as used within the industry and to cover all skills and techniques required.

Throughout this textbook you will see the following features:

Skeleton gun

Sealants, caulk and mastic tubes are inserted into a metal frame called a skeleton gun in order to dispense them directly onto a surface.

Regional variation: cage, mastic gun

Trade dictionary – This feature lists the key terms and tools that you will pick up from reading this book.

Substrate

The building material, (eg plaster, timber) or surface on which decorative materials are applied

Useful words – Words in bold in the text are explained in the margin to help your understanding.

INDUSTRY TIP

Never use paint directly from the manufacturer's container as any contamination can ruin the whole batch of paint.

Industry tips – Useful hints and tips related to working in the painting and decorating industry.

ACTIVITY

What PPE is necessary when preparing surfaces for painting? Use the internet to find examples of a decorator's PPE and list four pieces of equipment and the hazards that they will protect you from.

Activities – These are suggested activities for you to complete.

Step-by-steps – These steps illustrate techniques and procedures that you will need to learn in order to carry out painting and decorating tasks.

STEP 1 Apply the first application of coating to the surface using the cross-hatch method. Work in areas of approximately 300mm square along the surface and then continue down or across the surface.

STEP 2 Lay off the applied paint in the short direction, overlapping each brush stroke by a third of the width of the brush. The paint will flow into itself and make an invisible join.

Case Study: Lucy and Tomas

Lucy and Tomas decided to set up their own decorating business, so they put an advertisement in the newspaper. They were soon asked to price up decorating a living room for Mrs Khan. They visited the site and made a rough estimate, without measuring, of what materials they would need and guessed that it would take three days. Mrs Khan accepted the price.

Case Studies – Each chapter ends with a case study of an operative who has faced a common problem in the industry. Some of these will reveal the solution and others provide you with the opportunity to solve the problem.

At the end of every chapter are some 'Test your knowledge' questions. These questions are designed to test your understanding of what you have learnt in that chapter. This can help with identifying further training or revision needed. You will find the answers at the end of the book.

INTRODUCTION

This book has been written to support students studying painting and decorating at Level 1. By studying this book, you should receive a thorough grounding in the skills and knowledge you will need to complete your course and either progress to Level 2, or enter the workforce. You will learn about the wider construction industry and how it works, as well as the skills and techniques you will need in order to work as a painter and decorator. You will be able to work safely on site and in domestic settings, using the correct tools and equipment to prepare, paint and wallpaper surfaces to produce a professional finish.

The features mentioned on the previous page are there to help you retain the information you will need to become a painter and decorator. The large trade dictionary included in this textbook is a list of important industry terms, techniques and tools. Use this for reference in class and in the workshop. Become familiar with the terms and techniques, and pay attention to the skills you need to master. If you put in the effort, you will be rewarded with a satisfying and successful career in painting and decorating.

ACKNOWLEDGEMENTS

I wish to thank my family and colleagues, particularly Tom Little, for their support and encouragement during the writing of this book.

Ann Cook

I would like to thank my dear wife Helen for her support in writing for this book. I dedicate my work to Matt, Tasha and Daisy, and not forgetting Floyd and Mrs Dusty.

Colin Fearn

I dedicate this to the trade I have been passionate about since I first held a paint brush and I hope that this will inspire future generations of decorators to have pride in their work. I would like to thank my partner, Wendy Dovey, for her support as proofreader, scribe and computer wizard! She taught me grown-up words and political correctness.

Steve Walter

I would like to thank in particular my wife, Becky, for her patience and understanding throughout this project. I would like also to pay tribute to Dick Fouracre, who set me on the way as a decorator; and to Albert Allen, my great friend and teaching mentor who set me on my way into teaching. We have all shared a passion for the craft of decoration and it has served us well.

Barrie Yarde

To my gorgeous wife Clare, without whose constant support, understanding and patience I would not have been able to continue. To Matthew and Eleanor, for not being there on too many occasions: normal service will be resumed. Finally, my parents, to whom I will always be grateful.

Martin Burdfield

City & Guilds would like to sincerely thank the following:

For invaluable painting and decorating expertise

Alan Phelan and Elaine Bentley.

For their help with photoshoots

Jules Selmes (photographer), Adam Giles (photographer's assistant), Steve Lammas, Gary Thoirs, Casie Bedwell, Hamed Bamba, Lee Farrell, Luke Kalavashoti, Jade Keen, Stefan Kuhl, Andrew Maughan, Ismail Mohamud, Kris O'Neill, Abdul Qaffar, Mohammed Sanusi-Omosanya, Alan Saxton, James Shiels and Billy Snowball.

For supplying pictures for the book cover

Jules Selmes: © City & Guilds

TRADE DICTIONARY

Industry term	Definition and regional variations
Abrade	To scratch the surface with a coarse material to provide a 'key', which will help coatings adhere.
Absorbent	An absorbent surface that soaks up liquids, eg bare plaster, bare timber. The more liquid a material can soak up, the more absorbent it is.
Access equipment	Equipment that will enable you to gain access to work at a higher level than you can reach from the floor.
Adhere	To stick to a substance or surface.
Adhesive	In decorating and particularly paperhanging terms, adhesive is a material sometimes referred to as paste that can stick paper to ceiling and wall surfaces.

Industry term	Definition and regional variations
Approved Code of Practice (ACoP)  	An ACoP gives practical advice for those involved in the construction industry on complying with health and safety legislation, such as using machinery safely. It has a special legal status and employers and employees are expected to work within its guidelines.
Architect 	A trained professional who designs a structure and represents the client who wants the structure built. They are responsible for the production of the working drawings. They supervise the construction of buildings or other large structures.
Architectural technician 	A draftsperson who works in an architectural practice. They usually prepare the drawings for a building.
Architraves 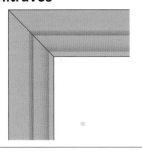	The moulded frames around doors or windows.
Arris	A sharp external edge, such as the edge of a door.
Asbestos 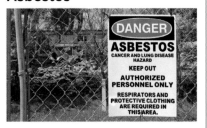	A naturally occurring mineral that was commonly used for a variety of purposes, including: insulation, fire protection, roofing and guttering. It is extremely hazardous and can cause a serious lung disease known as asbestosis.

Industry term	Definition and regional variations
Barrier cream 	Cream used to protect you from contact dermatitis and against irritation. It should be used before carrying out any painting and decorating task.
Bill of quantities 	Produced by a quantity surveyor and describes everything that is required for the job based on the drawings, specification and schedules. It is sent out to contractors and ensures that all the contractors are pricing for the job using the same information.
Block brush 	Useful for brushing down rough surfaces such as cement rendering and brickwork and for applying cement-based paints. *Regional variation: cement paint brush*
British Standards Institute (BSI)	The authority that develops and publishes standards in the UK.
Brush marks 	A defect in the paint finish where visible heavy brush marks are left by the brush filling/bristles, even after laying off has been completed. *Regional variation: ladders*
Building Regulations	A series of documents that set out legal requirements for the standards of building work.
Butt joint	Edges of lengths of paper that touch without a gap or overlap.
Centring	Setting out a wall to create a balanced or even effect for the pattern. Working out from the centre should enable this.

Industry term	Definition and regional variations
Chalk and line 	A tool for marking chalk lines when setting out for wallpapering. The image on the left shows the self-chalking type of line, although it is possible to use a piece of string and chalk sticks.
Cherry pickers 	A motor vehicle which has an extendable boom with a cage that operatives can stand in when painting high points/areas on buildings/bridges, etc.
Chisel knife 	A narrow bladed scraper, usually of 25mm width, used to access areas into which a normal scraper cannot reach.
Claw hammer	A hammer used mainly for removing projecting nails from a surface. It can be used in conjunction with a nail punch to drive in projecting nails in new joinery.
Coalesce	In painting and decorating terms, where particles merge to form a film, particularly in water-borne coatings – the drying process is also known as coalescence.
Concrete 	Material made up of cement, sand and stones of varying sizes and in varying proportions. It is mixed with water.

Industry term	Definition and regional variations
Consistency	Related directly to the viscosity of a coating, which can be altered by the addition of thinners or solvents.
Contact dermititis 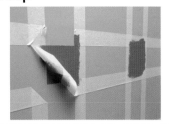	A type of eczema that can cause red, itchy and scaly skin, and sometimes burning and stinging. It leads to skin becoming blistered, dry and cracked, and can affect any part of the body, but most commonly the hands.
Creep 	Where masking tape has not been securely fixed to a surface and some scumble or paint seeps beneath it – this will result in there not being a sharp edge to the broken colour effect.
Curtains 	Heavy build-up of paint/coating sliding down a surface.
Cutting in 	The process of producing a sharp neat paint line between two structural components in a room, such as a wall/ceiling, architrave/wall, etc.
Dado 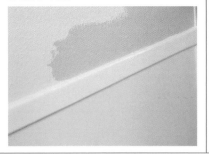	An area of wall immediately above the skirting in a room, and separated from the wall filling by a timber, plaster or plastic strip secured to the wall.
Dado rail	A rail secured to the wall that produces two individual areas in a room; the upper walls are normally much larger in area.

Industry term	Definition and regional variations
Damp proof course (DPC) 	A layer or strip of watertight material placed in a joint of a wall to prevent the passage of water. Fixed at a minimum of 150mm above finished ground level.
Datum point 	A fixed point or height from which to take reference levels. They may be permanent Ordnance bench marks (OBMs) or temporary bench marks (TBMs, pictured here). The datum point is used to transfer levels across a building site. It represents the finished floor level (FFL) on a dwelling.
Decant	To transfer a liquid by pouring from one container into another.
Door furniture 	Anything attached to the door, eg handles, knobs, locks, letterboxes, fingerplates and hinges. *Regional variation: ironmongery*
Drop sheets 	Most commonly these large sheets are made from cotton twill (although they can also be plastic), which are designed to prevent preparation debris and paint from causing damage to the floor and/or furnishings.
Dusting brush 	A dusting brush is used to remove dust, debris and other particles from a surface before painting.
Efflorescence	A white crystalline deposit which may form on the surface of plaster, cement or new bricks if the substrate contains a high proportion of soluble mineral salts.

Industry term	Definition and regional variations
Fall protection system 	Safety equipment designed to prevent or arrest falls. Examples include guard-rail systems, safety net systems, positioning-device systems and personal fall-restraint systems (PFAS).
Ferrous 	Containing iron.
Filling board 	A filling board is used for transferring filler from where it is mixed to the workstation. A decorator may make their own to suit their needs. It is very similar to a plasterer's hawk.
Filling knife 	A knife used to apply filler to open-grain work on timber, holes, cracks or any defect on a surface. It looks very much like a stripping knife but the blade is more flexible as it is made of a thinner-gauge metal.
First fix	The main elements of construction. First fix carpentry relates to fixing roofing timbers, building frames, etc.
Fitch brush 	Used for fine detailed work in areas that are difficult to reach with a paint brush. They are available with pure bristle or synthetic filling, which is usually white and set in a round or flat ferrule.

Industry term	Definition and regional variations
Flashing	A defect that occurs in flat and eggshell finishes and looks like glossy streaks or patches. One cause is losing the wet edge during application.
Flash point	The temperature at which a material gives off a vapour that will ignite if exposed to flame. Chemicals with a low flash point are labelled as highly flammable.
Flat wall brush 	Used to apply emulsion to large flat areas such as ceilings and walls, and may also be used to apply adhesive to wallpaper. Available in a wide range of varying qualities, and may be either man-made or pure bristle.
Flush	When two surfaces are even, on the same level with no raised edges.
Folding rule 	Used for measuring lengths of wallpaper before cutting and widths of cuts. It is typically 1m long. It folds into four to make it easy to store in the pocket of overalls.
Foundation 	Used to spread the load of a building to the subsoil.
Fungicidal wash	When preparing a surface for decoration, this product is used to treat a surface that has become infected with mould, mildew or other fungal infestations. If it isn't used, the stains will show through the final finish and the fungi will continue to grow.
Graining 	Applying and manipulating an appropriately coloured scumble to imitate the appearance of a specific timber.
Grounding out	Applying the ground coat for painted decorative work.

Industry term	Definition and regional variations
Hacking knife 	Used to remove old putty from a window frame.
Hair stipple brush 	Used to remove all traces of brush marks and leave a smooth, even finish. *Regional variations: hair stippler, stippler*
Handrail 	Used with access equipment to reduce the risk of falling.
Hard dry 	Describing a paint film that is hard enough to be worked on without damaging its finish.
Hatchings Brickwork	Patterns used on a drawing to identify different materials to meet the standard BS 1192.
Health and Safety Executive (HSE)	The national independent watchdog for work-related health, safety and illness. Its mission is to prevent death, injury and ill-health in Great Britain's workplaces.

Industry term	Definition and regional variations
Hop-up	Small podium scaffold which can be collapsed down when not in use.
Hot air gun	A hot air gun is used to remove paint from a surface by heating the coating to a temperature where it softens; it can then be removed by using a scraper, shavehook, etc. *Regional variation: stripper*
Improvement notice	Issued by an HSE or local authority inspector to formally notify a company that improvements are needed to the way it is working.
Industrial Standards	Minimum standards of quality of completed work universally adopted within an industry.
Inertia-operated anchor device	A safety device attached to a safety line that operates in the same way as car seat belts.
Key	The condition of a surface to receive paint which will help adhesion of the coating. A 'key' can be provided by natural porosity, or by abrading the surface.
Kinetic lifting	This is a method of lifting items where the main force is provided by the operative's own muscular strength. Using the recognised technique will avoid injury.
Kitemark	Confirms that the product that carries it conforms to the relevant British Standards.
Knot	A natural defect in timber, which occurs where branches formed during the growth of a tree. Most often very resinous, and require the application of knotting to seal them.

Industry term	Definition and regional variations
Knotting solution 	A quick drying spirit based sealer, used to prevent the resin in knots causing discolouration of applied paint. It can also be used to seal small areas of other surface contaminants, ie felt tip pen, during preparation.
Laser level 	Using a laser level can be an extremely accurate method of producing both vertical and horizontal lines, eg for paperhanging, etc. Accuracy of lines will depend on correctly setting up the equipment.
Ladders 	Ladders can be made from wood, aluminium, steel or fibreglass. Ladder types include pole ladders, standing ladders, double and treble extending ladders and roof ladders.
Laying off 	Finishing off an area of paintwork with very light strokes of the brush in order to eliminate brush marks.
Liquid paint remover (LPR) 	A chemical-based type of paint stripper for removing old paint systems.

Industry term	Definition and regional variations
Making good 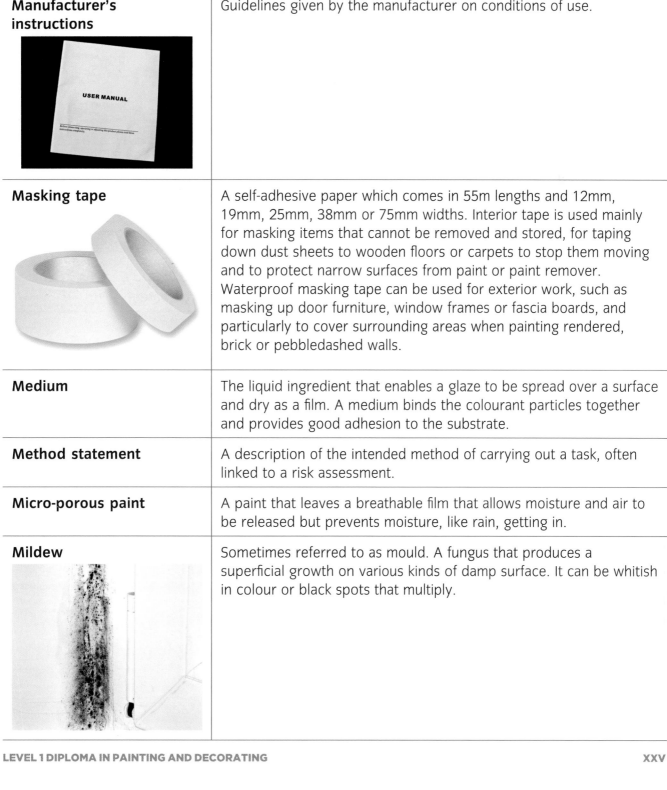	Typically to fill holes and defects in the surface. Repairing a defective area to produce a sound, level finish.
Manufacturer's instructions 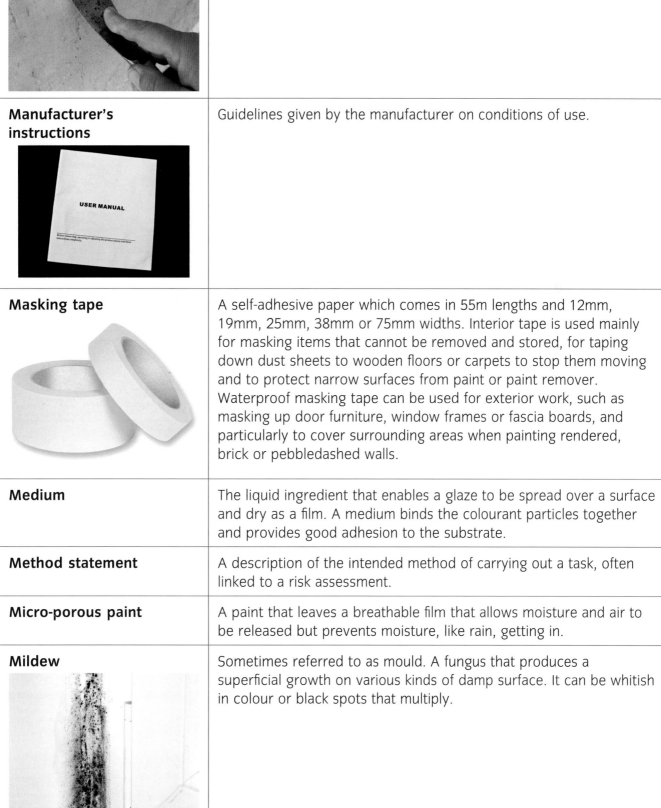	Guidelines given by the manufacturer on conditions of use.
Masking tape 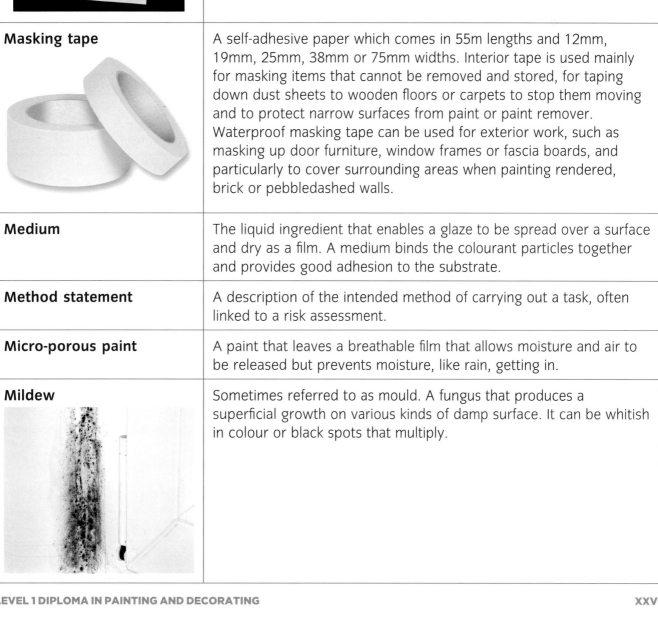	A self-adhesive paper which comes in 55m lengths and 12mm, 19mm, 25mm, 38mm or 75mm widths. Interior tape is used mainly for masking items that cannot be removed and stored, for taping down dust sheets to wooden floors or carpets to stop them moving and to protect narrow surfaces from paint or paint remover. Waterproof masking tape can be used for exterior work, such as masking up door furniture, window frames or fascia boards, and particularly to cover surrounding areas when painting rendered, brick or pebbledashed walls.
Medium	The liquid ingredient that enables a glaze to be spread over a surface and dry as a film. A medium binds the colourant particles together and provides good adhesion to the substrate.
Method statement	A description of the intended method of carrying out a task, often linked to a risk assessment.
Micro-porous paint	A paint that leaves a breathable film that allows moisture and air to be released but prevents moisture, like rain, getting in.
Mildew	Sometimes referred to as mould. A fungus that produces a superficial growth on various kinds of damp surface. It can be whitish in colour or black spots that multiply.

Industry term	Definition and regional variations
Mould growth	Mould is a general term for types of fungi, made up of airborne spores that can multiply and feed on organic matter, for example in pastes (starch pastes contain organic products such as wheat). It may vary in colour depending on the species of fungus, ie black, green, pink, etc.
Nail punch	This is a metal tool used with a hammer, to knock protruding nails below a timber surface.
Nibs	Small particles of foreign matter, such as paint skin or grit, that have dried in the film of a coating and which cause it to feel rough.
Opacity	The ability of the pigment in paint to obliterate or hide the existing surface colour.
Opaque	Not transmitting light – the opposite of transparent.
Outrigger	Stabilisers on mobile tower scaffolds.
Overalls	Protective clothing worn when painting and decorating. If the overalls have a bib they will enable you to carry a small number of tools, particularly a hanging brush and shears, in the pockets, making them efficient and easy to use.

Industry term	Definition and regional variations
Paint kettle 	These are made from either plastic or metal and are used to decant paint for use. Plastic is generally used for water-borne paint and metal for oil based paint. *Regional variation: paint pot*
Paint stirrer 	These are used to ensure that all the ingredients in a paint container are dispersed evenly and that the coating is of a smooth consistency.
Paint strainer 	Ideally, paint strainers are only useful for removing contaminants from those surface coatings whose viscosity will allow them to pass through the gauze. Searching paint from containers to which unused material has been returned is the main use for this piece of equipment, but even new unused materials can contain 'bits'.
Paperhanging brush 	This is used to apply papers to walls to ensure that all air pockets are removed and that the paper lies flat without creases. *Regional variation: smoothing brush*
Paperhanging shears 	These are used to cut lengths of wallpaper, and also for trimming around obstacles. *Regional variations: scissors, paperhanging scissors*
Paste brush 	This is a 125mm or 150mm flat wall brush used to apply paste or adhesive to wall or surface coverings. It is also used to apply size to absorbent wall and ceiling surfaces before hanging papers.

Industry term	Definition and regional variations
Paste table 	This is used to lay out wallpapers for measuring, cutting, matching and pasting. It is usually made from wood or plastic, and is typically 1.8m long and 560mm wide.
Pasting machine 	This is used to apply paste to papers. This method can be extremely quick and ensures that the correct amount of paste is applied when correctly set up.
Perimeter 2.2m 4.2m	The distance around an object or room.
Personal protective equipment (PPE) 	This is defined in the Personal Protective Equipment at Work Regulations 1992 as 'all equipment (including clothing affording protection against the weather) which is intended to be worn or held by a person at work and which protects against one or more risks to a person's health or safety.' For example, safety helmets, gloves, eye protection, high-visibility clothing, safety footwear and safety harnesses.
Pin hammer 	Small hand-held hammer used with nail punches and when placing sprigs in window frames, etc. *Regional variation: ball-pein hammer*
Plumb bob 	This is used for ensuring that first and subsequent lengths of wallpaper are hung vertically. It is a small weight, usually made from steel, suspended from a length of cord.

Industry term	Definition and regional variations
Podium steps	A low-level access platform with adjustable height and guard rail. The steps may be tubular, self-erecting or folded prior to erection, to enable them to pass through standard doors and corridors.
Porosity	The state of being porous – when small spaces or voids in a solid material mean that it can absorb liquids.
Prime	To apply the first coat of paint to a surface. Most often the paint will be thinned to increase absorption, which will provide increased adhesion, particularly on a porous surface.
Programme of work	A series of events where the order of activities and the amount of time involved has been planned out. This is usually shown in the form of a bar or Gantt chart. *Regional variation: work schedule*
Prohibition notice	Issued by an HSE or local authority inspector when there is an immediate risk of personal injury. Receiving one means you are breaking health and safety regulations.
Putty knife	Used to fill small nail holes and cracks and also for applying putty to traditional wood and metal windows when replacing glass. *Regional variation: stopping knife*
Radiator brush	Used to apply paint to areas that are difficult to reach with a paintbrush, particularly behind pipes, radiators and columns. These have a bristle filling attached to a long wooden handle, or a wire handle that can be bent to fit into awkward areas.

Industry term	Definition and regional variations
Registration marks 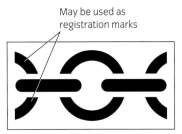 May be used as registration marks	Marks (or a very small cut-out section) made on a stencil which are lined up with chalk lines on the surface, and/or part of a previously applied stencil if using a multi-plate stencil, to ensure correct positioning before applying paint.
Rendering	A sand and cement mix covering to brickwork.
Risk assessment 	An assessment of the hazards and risks associated with an activity and the reduction and monitoring of them.
Roller 	The standard type of roller used by decorators is a cylinder roller, which consists of a straight cylinder with a fabric cover called a sleeve. The choice of roller will depend on the type of coating being used and the type of substrate to be painted. There are many types, including very smooth rollers for applying finishing paints to flat doors and lambswool rollers for applying paint to a textured surface such as pebbledash.
Ropiness 	Another surface finish defect similar to brush marks, but where the marks are much heavier and coarser; being more pronounced, they are highly visible and unsightly. Usually due to poor brush application because paint has thickened and has not been adequately brushed out or laid off. *Regional variations: ribbiness, tramlines*
Rubbing block 	A tool used when abrading surfaces, particularly applied filler. Rubber types can be used when rubbing down wet, and have pins which can be used to hold the abrasive in place whilst the block is in use. *Regional variation: sanding block*
Scaffold boards	Planks used to provide a working platform on trestles and tubular scaffolds.

Industry term	Definition and regional variations
Scale  Scale: 1:1250	This is the ratio in size of an item in a drawing in relation to its actual size. On site, scale rulers are used to determine the actual size of the item in a structure.
Scumble 	A glaze (translucent product that will retain a design), to which a colourant has been added.
Scuttle 	A type of bucket used with a roller and filled with paste to speed up the process of pasting papers on the paste table. They are also useful for the types of papers that require the wall to be pasted instead of the back of the paper.
Seam roller 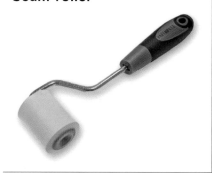	A small roller made from boxwood or plastic, used to apply localised pressure to wallpaper seams and/or internal corners that may not be adhering well. Care should be taken in their use.
Second fix	The final finish, the construction work following plastering, ie when a carpenter fixes architraves, skirtings, doors, etc.
Services 	The energy and water facilities which are supplied to properties from the 'mains' supplies, and also the drainage systems to remove waste from a building.

Industry term	Definition and regional variations
Set out	To put in a specified position or location – following a drawing, written specification or verbal instructions.
Shavehooks	These are hand tools used when removing coatings in conjunction with hot air or paint removers, particularly from surfaces that have intricate mouldings. They can have triangular, combination, or pear-shaped heads.
Shellac	A natural resin found mainly in India, made of secretions from insects. When dissolved in spirit it forms the basis of French polish, knotting and sealers.
Sinking	Reduction in the sheen of a paint film. This may occur where a section of making good has not been spot-primed and the film former has been partly absorbed by the porous filler.
Sizing	Applying a thin coat of glue size or thinned paste to an absorbent surface before hanging wallpaper.
Skeleton gun	Sealants, caulk and mastic tubes are inserted into a metal frame called a skeleton gun in order to dispense them directly onto a surface. *Regional variations: cage, mastic gun, caulking gun, caulk gun*
Skid marks	This is a defect caused by poor application techniques, normally occurring when applying too much pressure during the roller application of paint or the production of broken colour effects. It leaves marks which appear as 'streaks' on the surface.

Industry term	Definition and regional variations
Specification	A contract document that gives information about the quality of materials and standards of workmanship required.
Spirit level	A tool used to make sure the work is level (horizontal) and plumb (vertical).
Spot-prime	To apply appropriate primer to sections of surface area that have been made good, to prevent the next coat from sinking into the filler.
Stencil brush	Used when producing stencils. This is a round brush with a filling of short, stiff bristles set in a metal ferrule on a short handle. Stencil brushes are available in a range of diameter sizes from 6mm to 38mm, and the size selected should be appropriate for the area of colour to be applied.
Straight edge	Used by some decorators, particularly for trimming waste paper when up against straight edges such as skirtings, door frames and ceiling edges. They can come with a handle or without and are typically 600mm in length.
Stripping knife	Knife used to remove wallpaper, loose or flaking paint and other debris or nibs in the making good process. *Regional variation: scraper*
Substrate	The building material (eg plaster, timber) or surface on which decorative materials are applied.

Industry term	Definition and regional variations
Sustainability 	The ability to continue to do something with minimal long-term effects on the environment. Materials that can be 'replaced' by regrowth in the future will be sustainable.
Swingback 	This is the name given to the rear frame of a pair of swingback steps. A framed back support is hinged to the back of the steps to provide support and to enable the steps to be set at the correct angle.
Tack rag 	A cotton gauze textile, impregnated with a non-drying resin that makes it 'sticky'. It is used to remove fine residual dust from a surface before any paint is applied. *Regional variation: tack cloth*
Tape measure 	A measuring tool used to set out and check dimensions. A range of tape measures in various sizes is required when setting out a structure or for the application of decorative finishes. Tape measures vary in range from 3m to 30m.
Toe board 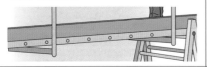	Attached to access equipment for extra safety and to stop items being kicked off the platform.
Tower scaffold 	A static or mobile working platform.

Industry term	Definition and regional variations
Translucent	Allows light to pass through, but prevents images from being seen clearly.
Transparent	Easily seen through, like clear glass.
Trestle 	A type of working platform. Used with scaffold boards or lightweight stagings to form a working platform.
Trimming knife 	Some decorators like to use trimming knives when wallpapering, when they need to cut around obstacles.
Two-knot brush 	Used to apply water-thinned paints to rough surfaces such as cement, rendering and brickwork. They are also used to apply cement-based paints, as the bristles are not attacked by the alkali in the cement, and for washing down surfaces when using a cleaning agent such as sugar soap.
UV light	Ultraviolet rays from the sun, which can cause health problems (for example with the skin or eyes) and damage to materials.
Viscosity	The ability of a liquid or coating to flow; the more viscous it is, the slower it flows.
Volatile organic compound (VOC) 	Materials that evaporate readily from many sources; an example of which is the solvents used in the manufacture of many coatings. The measurement of volatile organic compounds shows how much pollution a product will emit into the air when in use.

Industry term	Definition and regional variations
Washing-down brush 	These are relatively cheap two-knot brushes, available in one size only, and used for washing down with sugar soap or detergent.
Wet and dry (abrasive paper) 	Wet and dry abrasive paper, made from silicon carbide, may be used either dry or with water, which reduces clogging. The process of using wet and dry abrasive paper with water as a lubricant is known as 'wet flatting'. This process may be used to keep the atmosphere and surrounding area free from dust pollution.
Whiting 	Chalk (calcium carbonate) prepared by drying and grinding, as used in whitewash and sometimes as an extender in paint.
Wire brush 	Used for removing loose rust and corrosion from metalwork.
Wood ingrain 	Wood ingrain paper is a pulp paper made up of two layers between which small chips of wood are sandwiched. It usually comes in 10m long by 530mm wide rolls and can be supplied in different grades of texture: fine, medium or coarse. Wood ingrain is usually coated with water-borne paints, or sometimes oil based paints, after hanging. It tends to mask irregularities in the underlying surface due to the pronounced texture of the woodchip appearance. *Regional variation: woodchip*
Work at height	Any work that, without the proper precautions in place, could result in a fall. This can include work at ground level with the risk of falling into an opening in a floor or hole in the ground.

Chapter 1
Unit 201: Health, safety and welfare in construction

A career in the building industry can be a very rewarding one, both personally and financially. However, building sites and workshops are potentially very dangerous places; there are many potential hazards in the construction industry. Many construction operatives (workers) are injured each year, some fatally. Regulations have been brought in over the years to reduce accidents and improve working conditions.

By reading this chapter you will know about:

1 The health and safety regulations, roles and responsibilities.

2 Accident and emergency reporting procedures and documentation.

3 Identifying hazards in the workplace.

4 Health and welfare in the workplace.

5 Handling materials and equipment safely.

6 Access equipment and working at heights.

7 Working with electrical equipment in the workplace.

8 Using personal protective equipment (PPE).

9 The cause of fire and fire emergency procedures.

HEALTH AND SAFETY LEGISLATION

According to the Health and Safety Executive (HSE) figures, in 2011/12:

- Forty-nine construction operatives were fatally injured. Twenty-three of these operatives were self-employed. This compares with an average of 59 fatalities over the previous five years, of which an average of 19 fatally injured construction operatives were self-employed.

- The rate of fatal injury per 100,000 construction operatives was 2.3, compared with a five-year average of 2.5.

- Construction industry operatives were involved in 28% of fatal injuries across all industry sectors and it accounts for the greatest number of fatal injuries in any industry sector.

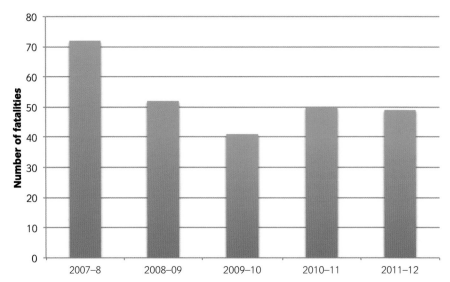

Number and rate of fatal injuries to workers in construction (RIDDOR)

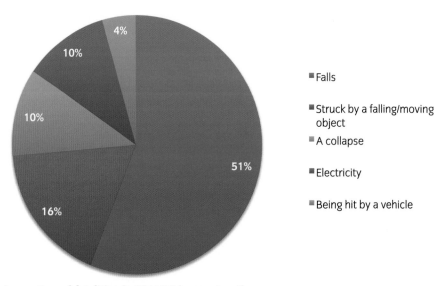

Proportion of fatalities in 2011/12 in construction

Health and safety legislation and great efforts made by the industry have made workplaces much safer in recent years. It is the responsibility of everyone involved in the building industry to continue to make it safer. Statistics are not just meaningless numbers – they represent injuries to real people. Many people believe that an accident will never happen to them, but it can. Accidents can:

- have a devastating effect on lives and families

- cost a lot financially in injury claims

- result in prosecution

- lead to job loss if an employee broke their company's safety policy.

Employers have an additional duty to ensure operatives have access to welfare facilities, eg drinking water, first aid and toilets, which will be discussed later in this chapter.

If everyone who works in the building industry pays close attention to health, safety and welfare, all operatives – including you – have every chance of enjoying a long, injury-free career.

UK HEALTH AND SAFETY REGULATIONS, ROLES AND RESPONSIBILITIES

In the UK there are many laws (legislation) that have been put into place to make sure that those working on construction sites, and members of the public, are kept healthy and safe. If these laws and regulations are not obeyed then prosecutions can take place. Worse still, there is a greater risk of injury and damage to your health and the health of those around you.

Standard construction safety equipment

The principal legislation that relates to health, safety and welfare in construction is:

- Health and Safety at Work Act (HASAWA) 1974

- Control of Substances Hazardous to Health (COSHH) Regulations 2002

- Reporting of Injuries, Diseases and Dangerous Occurrences Regulations (RIDDOR) 2013

- Construction, Design and Management (CDM) Regulations 2007

- Provision and Use of Work Equipment Regulations (PUWER) 1998

- Manual Handling Operations Regulations 1992

- Personal Protective Equipment (PPE) at Work Regulations 1992

- Work at Height Regulations 2005 (as amended)

- Lifting Operations and Lifting Equipment Regulations (LOLER) 1998

- Control of Noise at Work Regulations 2005

- Control of Vibration at Work Regulations 2005.

HEALTH AND SAFETY AT WORK ACT (HASAWA) 1974

The Health and Safety at Work Act (HASAWA) 1974 applies to all workplaces. Everyone who works on a building site or in a workshop is covered by this legislation. This includes employed and self-employed operatives, subcontractors, the employer and those delivering goods to the site. It not only protects those working, it also ensures the safety of anyone else who might be nearby.

KEY EMPLOYER RESPONSIBILITIES

The key employer health and safety responsibilities under HASAWA are to:

- provide a safe working environment

- provide safe access (entrance) and egress (exit) to the work area

- provide adequate staff training

- have a written health and safety policy in place

- provide health and safety information and display the appropriate signs

- carry out risk assessments

- provide safe machinery and equipment and to ensure it is well-maintained and in a safe condition

- provide adequate supervision to ensure safe practices are carried out

- involve trade union safety representatives, where appointed, in matters relating to health and safety

- provide personal protective equipment (**PPE**) free of charge, ensure the appropriate PPE is used whenever needed, and that operatives are properly supervised

- ensure materials and substances are transported, used and stored safely.

PPE

This is defined in the Personal Protective Equipment at Work Regulations 1992 as 'all equipment (including clothing affording protection against the weather) which is intended to be worn or held by a person at work and which protects against one or more risks to a person's health or safety.'

Risk assessments and method statements

The HASAWA requires that employers must carry out regular **risk assessments** to make sure that there are minimal dangers to their employees in a workplace.

Risk assessment

An assessment of the hazards and risks associated with an activity and the reduction and monitoring of them

Risk Assessment

Activity / Workplace assessed: Return to work after accident
Persons consulted / involved in risk assessment
Date:
Reviewed on:

Location:
Risk assessment reference number:
Review date:
Review by:

Significant hazard	**People at risk and what is the risk** Describe the harm that is likely to result from the hazard (eg cut, broken leg, chemical burn, etc) and who could be harmed (eg employees, contractors, visitors, etc)	**Existing control measure** What is currently in place to control the risk?	**Risk rating** Use matrix identified in guidance note Likelihood (L) Severity (S) Multiply (L) * (S) to produce risk rating (RR)				**Further action required** What is required to bring the risk down to an acceptable level? Use hierarchy of control described in guidance note when considering the controls needed	**Actioned to:** Who will complete the action?	**Due date:** When will the action be completed by?	**Completion date:** Initial and date once the action has been completed
			L	S	RR	L/M/H				
Uneven floors	Operatives	Verbal warning and supervision	2	1	2	m	None applicable	Site supervisor	Active now	Ongoing
Steps	Operatives	Verbal warning	2	1	2	m	None applicable	Site supervisor	Active now	Ongoing
Staircases	Operatives	Verbal warning	2	2	4	m	None applicable	Site supervisor	Active now	Ongoing

		Likelihood		
		1 Unlikely	**2 Possible**	**3 Very likely**
Severity	1 Slight/minor injuries/minor damage	**1**	**2**	**3**
	2 Medium injuries/significant damage	**2**	**4**	**6**
	3 Major injury/extensive damage	**3**	**6**	**9**

Likelihood
3 – Very likely
2 – Possible
1 – Unlikely

Severity
3 – Major injury/extensive damage
2 – Medium injury/significant damage
1 – Slight/minor damage

1 – Low risk, action should be taken to reduce the risk if reasonably practicable
2, 3, 4 – Medium risk, is a significant risk and would require an appropriate level of resource
6 & 9 – High risk, may require considerable resource to mitigate. Control should focus on elimination of risk, if not possible control should be obtained by following the hierarchy of control

123 type risk assessment

A risk assessment is a legally required tool used by employers to:

- identify work hazards
- assess the risk of harm arising from these hazards
- adequately control the risk.

Risk assessments are carried out as follows:

1 Identify the hazards. Consider the environment in which the job will be done. Which tools and materials will be used?

2 Identify who might be at risk. Think about operatives, visitors and members of the public.

3 Evaluate the risk. How severe is the potential injury? How likely is it to happen? A severe injury may be possible but may also be very improbable. On the other hand a minor injury might be very likely.

4 If there is an unacceptable risk, can the job be changed? Could different tools or materials be used instead?

5 If the risk is acceptable, what measures can be taken to reduce the risk? This could be training, special equipment and using PPE.

6 Keep good records. Explain the findings of the risk assessment to the operatives involved. Update the risk assessment as required – there may be new machinery, materials or staff. Even adverse weather can bring additional risks.

A **method statement** is required by law and is a useful way of recording the hazards involved in a specific task. It is used to communicate the risk and precautions required to all those involved in the work. It should be clear, uncomplicated and easy to understand as it is for the benefit of those carrying out the work (and their immediate supervisors).

Inductions and tool box talks

Any new visitors to and operatives on a site will be given an induction. This will explain:

- the layout of the site

- any hazards of which they need to be aware

- the location of welfare facilities

- the assembly areas in case of emergency

- site rules.

Tool box talks are short talks given at regular intervals. They give timely safety reminders and outline any new hazards that may have arisen because construction sites change as they develop. Weather conditions such as extreme heat, wind or rain may create new hazards.

KEY EMPLOYEE RESPONSIBILITIES

The HASAWA covers the responsibilities of employees and subcontractors:

- You must work in a safe manner and take care at all times.

- You must make sure you do not put yourself or others at risk by your actions or inactions.

Method statement

A description of the intended method of carrying out a task, often linked to a risk assessment

INDUSTRY TIP

The Construction Skills Certification Scheme (CSCS) was set up in the mid-90s with the aim of improving site operatives' competence to reduce accidents and drive up on-site efficiency. Card holders must take a health and safety test. The colour of card depends on level of qualification held and job role. For more information see www.cscs.uk.com

ACTIVITY

Think back to your induction. Write down what was discussed. Did you understand everything? Do you need any further information? If you have not had an induction, write a list of the things you think you need to know.

INDUSTRY TIP

Remember, if you are unsure about any health and safety issue always seek help and advice.

- You must co-operate with your employer in regard to health and safety. If you do not you risk injury (to yourself or others), prosecution, a fine and loss of employment. Do not take part in practical jokes and horseplay.

- You must use any equipment and safeguards provided by your employer. For example, you must wear, look after and report any damage to the PPE that your employer provides.

- You must not interfere or tamper with any safety equipment.

- You must not misuse or interfere with anything that is provided for employees' safety.

FIRST AID AND FIRST-AID KITS

First aid should only be applied by someone trained in first aid. Even a minor injury could become infected and therefore should be cleaned and a dressing applied. If any cut or injury shows signs of infection, becomes inflamed or painful seek medical attention. An employer's first-aid needs should be assessed to indicate whether a first-aider (someone trained in first aid) is necessary. The minimum requirement is to appoint a person to take charge of first-aid arrangements. The role of this appointed person includes looking after the first-aid equipment and facilities and calling the emergency services when required.

First-aid kits vary according to the size of the workforce. First-aid boxes should not contain tablets or medicines.

INDUSTRY TIP

The key employee health and safety responsibilities are to:
- work safely
- work in partnership with your employer
- report hazards and accidents as per company policy.

INDUSTRY TIP

Employees must not be charged for anything given to them or done for them by the employer in relation to safety.

INDUSTRY TIP

In the event of an accident, first aid will be carried out by a qualified first aider. First aid is designed to stabilise a patient for later treatment if required. The casualty may be taken to hospital or an ambulance may be called. In the event of an emergency you should raise the alarm.

ACTIVITY

Your place of work or training will have an appointed first-aider who deals with first aid. Find out who they are and how to make contact with them.

ACTIVITY

Find the first-aid kit in your workplace or place of training. What is inside it? Is there anything missing?

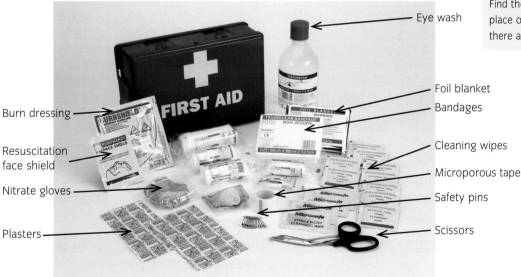

Eye wash

Foil blanket

Bandages

Cleaning wipes

Microporous tape

Safety pins

Scissors

Burn dressing

Resuscitation face shield

Nitrate gloves

Plasters

First-aid kit

SOURCES OF HEALTH AND SAFETY INFORMATION

Source	How they can help
Health and Safety Executive (HSE)	A government body that oversees health and safety in the workplace. It produces health and safety literature such as the **Approved Code of Practice** (ACoP).
Construction Skills	The construction industry training body produces literature and is directly involved with construction training.
The Royal Society for the Prevention of Accidents (ROSPA)	It produces literature and gives advice.
The Royal Society for Public Health	An independent, multi-disciplinary charity that is dedicated to the promotion and protection of collective human health and wellbeing.
Institution of Occupational Safety and Health (IOSH)	A chartered body for health and safety practitioners. The world's largest health and safety professional membership organisation.
The British Safety Council	It helps businesses with their health, safety and environmental management.

HEALTH AND SAFETY EXECUTIVE (HSE)

The HSE is a body set up by the government. The HSE ensures that the law is carried out correctly and has extensive powers to ensure that it can do its job. It can make spot checks in the workplace, bring the police, examine anything on the premises and take things away to be examined.

If the HSE finds a health and safety problem that breaks health and safety law it might issue an **improvement notice** giving the employer a set amount of time to correct the problem. For serious health and safety risks where there is a risk of immediate major injury, it can issue a **prohibition notice** which will stop all work on site until the health and safety issues are rectified. It may take an employer, employee, self-employed person (subcontractor) or anyone else

Approved Code of Practice

ACoP gives practical advice for those in the construction industry in relation to using machinery

INDUSTRY TIP

There are many other trade organisations, eg the Timber Research and Development Association (TRADA), which also offer advice on safe practices.

ACTIVITY

You have been asked to give a tool box talk because of several minor injuries involving tripping on site. What topics would you include in this talk?

INDUSTRY TIP

To find out more information on the sources in the table, enter their names into a search engine on the internet.

Improvement notice

Issued by an HSE or local authority inspector to formally notify a company that improvements are needed to the way it is working

Prohibition notice

Issued by an HSE or local authority inspector when there is an immediate risk of personal injury. They are not issued lightly and if you are on the receiving end of one, you are clearly breaking a health and safety regulation

involved with the building process to court for breaking health and safety legislation.

The HSE provides a lot of advice on safety and publishes numerous booklets and information sheets. One example of this is the Approved Code of Practice (ACoP) which applies to woodworking machinery. The ACoP has a special legal status and employers and employees are expected to work within its guidelines.

The duties of the HSE are to:

■ give advice

■ issue improvement and prohibition notices

■ caution

■ prosecute

■ investigate.

The Approved Code of Practice booklet is available free online

CONTROL OF SUBSTANCES HAZARDOUS TO HEALTH (COSHH) REGULATIONS 2002

The Control of Substances Hazardous to Health (COSHH) Regulations 2002 control the use of dangerous substances, eg preservatives, fuels, solvents, adhesives, cement and oil based paint. These have to be moved, stored and used safely without polluting the environment. It also covers hazardous substances produced while working, eg wood dust produced when sanding or drilling.

Hazardous substances may be discovered during the building process, eg lead-based paint or asbestos. These are covered by separate regulations.

When considering substances and materials that may be hazardous to health an employer should do the following to comply with COSHH:

■ Read and check the COSHH safety data sheet that comes with the product. It will outline any hazards associated with the product and the safety measures to be taken.

■ Check with the supplier if there are any known risks to health.

■ Use the trade press to find out if there is any information about this substance or material.

■ Use the HSE website, or other websites, to check any known issues with the substance or material.

When assessing the risk of a potentially dangerous substance or material it is important to consider how operatives could be exposed to it. For example:

Example of COSHH data sheet

- by breathing in gas or mist
- by swallowing it
- by getting it into their eyes
- through their skin, either by contact or through cuts.

Safety data sheets

Products you use may be 'dangerous for supply'. If so, they will have a label that has one or more hazard symbols. Some examples are given here.

These products include common substances in everyday use such as paint, bleach, solvent or fillers. When a product is 'dangerous for supply', by law, the supplier must provide you with a safety data sheet. Note: medicines, pesticides and cosmetic products have different legislation and don't have a safety data sheet. Ask the supplier how the product can be used safely.

Safety data sheets can be hard to understand, with little information on measures for control. However, to find out about health risks and emergency situations, concentrate on:

- Sections 2 and 16 of the sheet, which tell you what the dangers are;
- Sections 4-8, which tell you about emergencies, storage and handling.

Since 2009, new international symbols have been gradually replacing the European symbols. Some of them are similar to the European symbols, but there is no single word describing the hazard. Read the hazard statement on the packaging and the safety data sheet from the supplier.

European symbols

Toxic Very toxic Harmful Irritant

Highly flammable Extremely flammable Explosive Dangerous to the environment

Oxidising Corrosive

New International symbols

Hazard checklist

- ☐ Does any product you use have a danger label?
- ☐ Does your process produce gas, fume, dust, mist or vapour?
- ☐ Is the substance harmful to breathe in?
- ☐ Can the substance harm your skin?
- ☐ Is it likely that harm could arise because of the way you use or produce it?
- ☐ What are you going to do about it?
  - Use something else?
  - Use it in another, safer way?
  - Control it to stop harm being caused?

CONTROL MEASURES

The control measures below are in order of importance.

1 Eliminate the use of the harmful substance and use a safer one. For instance, swap high **VOC** oil based paint for a lower VOC water-borne paint.

2 Use a safer form of the product. Is the product available ready mixed? Is there a lower strength option that will still do the job?

VOC

The measurement of volatile organic compounds shows how much pollution a product will emit into the air when in use

INDUSTRY TIP

Product data sheets are free and have to be produced by the supplier of the product.

3 Change the work method to emit less of the substance. For instance, applying paint with a brush releases fewer VOCs into the air than spraying paint. Wet grinding produces less dust than dry grinding.

4 Enclose the work area so that the substance does not escape. This can mean setting up a tented area or closing doors.

5 Use extraction or filtration (eg a dust bag) in the work area.

6 Keep operatives in the area to a minimum.

7 Employers must provide appropriate PPE.

Paint with high VOC content

European symbols

Toxic	Very toxic	Harmful	Irritant

Highly flammable	Extremely flammable	Explosive	Dangerous to the environment

Oxidising	Corrosive

New International symbols

Toxic	May explode when heated	Irritant

Causes fire	Explosive	Dangerous to the environment

Intensifies fire	Long-term health hazard	Corrosive

COSHH symbols. The international symbols will replace the European symbols in 2015

INDUSTRY TIP

For more detailed information on RIDDOR visit the HSE webpage at www.hse.gov.uk/riddor.

REPORTING OF INJURIES, DISEASES AND DANGEROUS OCCURRENCES REGULATIONS (RIDDOR) 2013

Despite all the efforts put into health and safety, incidents still happen. The Reporting of Injuries, Diseases and Dangerous Occurrences Regulations (RIDDOR) 2013 state that employers must report to the HSE all accidents that result in an employee needing more than seven days off work. Diseases and dangerous occurrences must also be reported. A serious occurrence that has not caused an injury (a near miss) should still be reported because next time it happens things might not work out as well.

Below are some examples of injuries, diseases and dangerous occurrences that would need to be reported:

- A joiner cuts off a finger while using a circular saw.

- A plumber takes a week off after a splinter in her hand becomes infected.

- A ground operative contracts **leptospirosis**.

- A labourer contracts dermatitis (a serious skin problem) after contact with an irritant substance.

- A scaffold suffers a collapse following severe weather, unauthorised alteration or overloading but no one is injured.

Leptospirosis

Also known as Weil's disease, this is a serious disease spread by rats and cattle

The purpose of RIDDOR is to enable the HSE to investigate serious incidents and collate statistical data. This information is used to help reduce the number of similar accidents happening in future and to make the workplace safer.

INDUSTRY TIP

Accidents do not just affect the person who has the accident. Work colleagues or members of the public might be affected and so will the employer. The consequences may include:
- a poor company image (this may put off potential customers)
- loss of production
- insurance costs increasing
- closure of the site
- having to pay sick pay
- other additional costs.

New HSE guidelines require employers to pay an hourly rate for time taken by the HSE to investigate an accident. This is potentially very costly.

	Health and Safety Executive

Health and Safety at Work etc Act 1974
The Reporting of Injuries, Diseases and Dangerous Occurrence Regulations 1995

F2508 - Report of an injury   Zoom 100   KS i ?

About you and your organisation

*Title	*Forename	*Family Name

*Job Title	*Your Phone No

*Organisation Name

Address Line 1   (eg building name)
Address Line 2   (eg street)
Address Line 3   (eg district)
*Town
County
*Post Code   Fax Number
*E-Mail

☐ Remember me   ?

*Did the incident happen at the above address?   ☐ Yes ☐ No

*Which authority is responsible for monitoring and inspecting health and safety where the incident happened?   ☐ HSE ☐ Local Authority   ?
Please refer to the help for guidance on the responsible authority

[Next] [Form Preview]
                          Page 1 of 5

An F2508 injury report form

Although minor accidents and injuries are not reported to HSE, records must be kept. Accidents must be recorded in the accident book. This provides a record of what happened and is useful for future reference. Trends may become apparent and the employer may take action to try to prevent that particular type of accident occurring again.

CONSTRUCTION, DESIGN AND MANAGEMENT (CDM) REGULATIONS 2007

The Construction, Design and Management (CDM) Regulations 2007 focus attention on the effective planning and management of construction projects, from the design concept through to maintenance and repair. The aim is for health and safety considerations to be integrated into a project's development, rather than be an inconvenient afterthought. The CDM Regulations reduce the risk of harm to those that have to work on or use the structure throughout its life, from construction through to **demolition**.

The CDM Regulations play a role in safety during demolition

Demolition

When something, often a building, is completely torn down and destroyed

CDM Regulations protect workers from the construction to demolition of large and complex structures

The CDM Regulations apply to all projects except for those arranged by private clients, ie work that isn't in furtherance of a business interest. Property developers need to follow the CDM Regulations.

Under the CDM Regulations, the HSE must be notified where the construction work will take:

- more than 30 working days or

- 500 working days in total, ie if 100 people work for 5 days (500 working days) the HSE will have to be notified.

DUTY HOLDERS

Under the CDM Regulations there are several duty holders, each with a specific role.

Duty holder	Role
Client	This is the person or organisation who wishes to have the work done. The client will check that: - all the team members are competent - the management is suitable - sufficient time is allowed for all stages of the project - welfare facilities are in place before construction starts. HSE notifiable projects require that the client appoints a CDM co-ordinator and principal contractor, and provides access to a health and safety file.
CDM co-ordinator	Appointed by the client, the co-ordinator advises and assists the client with CDM duties. The co-ordinator notifies the HSE before work starts. This role involves the co-ordination of the health and safety aspects of the design of the building and ensures good communication between the client, designers and contractors.
Designer	At the design stages the designer removes hazards and reduces risks. The designer provides information about the risks that cannot be eliminated. Notifiable projects require that the designer checks that the client is aware of their CDM duties and that a CDM co-ordinator has been appointed. The designer will also supply information for the health and safety file.
Principal contractor	The principal contractor will plan, manage and monitor the construction in liaison with any other involved contractors. This involves developing a written plan and site rules before the construction begins. The principal contractor ensures that the site is made secure and suitable welfare facilities are provided from the start and maintained throughout construction. The principal contractor will also make sure that all operatives have site inductions and any further training that might be required to make sure the workforce is competent.
Contractor	Subcontractors and self-employed operatives will plan, manage and monitor their own work and employees, co-operating with any main contractor in relation to site rules. Contractors will make sure that all operatives have any further training that might be required to make sure they are competent. A contractor also reports any incidents under RIDDOR to the principal contractor.
Operatives	Operatives need to check their own competence: Can you carry out the task you have been asked to do safely? Have you been trained to do this type of activity? Do you have the correct equipment to carry out this activity? You must follow all the site health and safety rules and procedures and fully co-operate with the rest of the team to ensure the health and safety of other operatives and others who may be affected by the work. Any health and safety issues must be reported.

What would you do if you spotted any of these hazards?

A client, a contractor and an operative looking over building plans ahead of construction

WELFARE FACILITIES REQUIRED ON SITE UNDER THE CDM REGULATIONS

The table below shows the welfare facilities that must be available on site.

Facility	Site requirement
Sanitary conveniences (toilets)	▪ Suitable and sufficient toilets should be provided or made available. ▪ Toilets should be adequately ventilated and lit and should be clean. ▪ Separate toilet facilities should be provided for men and women.
Washing facilities 	▪ Sufficient facilities must be available, and include showers if required by the nature of the work. ▪ They should be in the same place as the toilets and near any changing rooms. ▪ There must be a supply of clean hot (or warm) and cold running water, soap and towels. ▪ There must be separate washing facilities provided for men and women unless the area is for washing hands and the face only.

Facility	Site requirement
Clean drinking water 	■ This must be provided or made available. ■ It should be clearly marked by an appropriate sign. ■ Cups should be provided unless the supply of drinking water is from a water fountain.
Changing rooms and lockers 	■ Changing rooms must be provided or made available if operatives have to wear special clothing and if they cannot be expected to change elsewhere. ■ There must be separate rooms for, or separate use of rooms by, men and women where necessary. ■ The rooms must have seating and include, where necessary, facilities to enable operatives to dry their special clothing and their own clothing and personal effects. ■ Lockers should also be provided.
Rest rooms or rest areas 	■ Rest rooms should have enough tables and seating with backs for the number of operatives likely to use them at any one time. ■ Where necessary, rest rooms should include suitable facilities for pregnant women or nursing mothers to rest lying down. ■ Arrangements must be made to ensure that meals can be prepared, heated and eaten. It must also be possible to boil water.

PROVISION AND USE OF WORK EQUIPMENT REGULATIONS (PUWER) 1998

The Provision and Use of Work Equipment Regulations (PUWER) 1998 place duties on:

■ people and companies who own, operate or have control over work equipment

■ employers whose employees use work equipment.

Work equipment can be defined as any machinery, appliance, apparatus, tool or installation for use at work (whether exclusively or not). This includes equipment that employees provide for their own use at work. The scope of work equipment is therefore extremely wide. The use of work equipment is also very widely interpreted and, according to the HSE, means 'any activity involving work equipment and includes starting, stopping, programming, setting, transporting, repairing, modifying, maintaining, servicing and cleaning.' It includes equipment such as diggers, electric planers, stepladders, hammers or wheelbarrows.

Under PUWER, work equipment must be:

- suitable for the intended use
- safe to use
- well maintained
- inspected regularly.

Regular inspection is important as a tool that was safe when it was new may no longer be safe after considerable use.

Additionally, work equipment must only be used by people who have received adequate instruction and training. Information regarding the use of the equipment must be given to the operator and must only be used for what it was designed to do.

Protective devices, eg emergency stops, must be used. Brakes must be fitted where appropriate to slow down moving parts to bring the equipment to a safe condition when turned off or stopped. Equipment must have adequate means of isolation. Warnings, either by signs or other means such as sounds or lights, must be used as appropriate. Access to dangerous parts of the machinery must be controlled. Some work equipment is subject to additional health and safety legislation which must also be followed.

Employers who use work equipment must manage the risks. ACoPs (see page 9) have been developed in line with PUWER. The ACoPs have a special legal status, as outlined in the introduction to the PUWER ACoP:

> *Following the guidance is not compulsory and you are free to take other action. But if you do follow the guidance you will normally be doing enough to comply with the law. Health and safety inspectors seek to secure compliance with the law and may refer to this guidance as illustrating good practice.*

ACTIVITY

All the tools you use for your work are covered by PUWER. They must be well maintained and suitable for the task. A damaged head on a bolster chisel must be reshaped. A split shaft on a joiner's wood chisel must be repaired. Why would these tools be dangerous in a damaged condition? List the reasons.

MANUAL HANDLING OPERATIONS REGULATIONS 1992

Employers must try to avoid manual handling within reason if there is a possibility of injury. If manual handling cannot be avoided then they must reduce the risk of injury by means of a risk assessment.

An operative lifting heavy bricks

LIFTING AND HANDLING

Incorrect lifting and handling is a serious risk to your health. It is very easy to injure your back – just ask any experienced builder. An injured back can be very unpleasant, so it's best to look after it.

Here are a few things to consider when lifting:

- Assess the load. Is it too heavy? Do you need assistance or additional training? Is it an awkward shape?

- Can a lifting aid be used, such as any of the below?

Wheelbarrow

Gin lift

Scissor lift

Kerb lifter

- Does the lift involve twisting or reaching?

- Where is the load going to end up? Is there a clear path? Is the place it's going to be taken to cleared and ready?

How to lift and place an item correctly

If you cannot use a machine, it is important that you keep the correct posture when lifting any load. The correct technique to do this is known as **kinetic lifting**. Always lift with your back straight, elbows in, knees bent and your feet slightly apart.

Kinetic lifting

A method of lifting that ensures that the risk of injury is reduced

Safe kinetic lifting technique

When placing the item, again be sure to use your knees and beware of trapping your fingers. If stacking materials, be sure that they are on a sound level base and on bearers if required.

Heavy objects that cannot easily be lifted by mechanical methods can be lifted by several people. It is important that one person in the team is in charge, and that lifting is done in a co-operative way. It has been known for one person to fall down and the others to then drop the item!

CONTROL OF NOISE AT WORK REGULATIONS 2005

Under the Control of Noise at Work Regulations 2005, duties are placed on employers and employees to reduce the risk of hearing damage to the lowest reasonable level practicable. Hearing loss caused by work is preventable. Hearing damage is permanent and cannot be restored once lost.

EMPLOYER'S DUTIES UNDER THE REGULATIONS

An employer's duties are:

- to carry out a risk assessment and identify who is at risk

- to eliminate or control its employees' exposure to noise at the workplace and to reduce the noise as far as practicable

- to provide suitable hearing protection

- to provide health surveillance to those identified as at risk by the risk assessment

- to provide information and training about the risks to their employees as identified by the risk assessment.

EMPLOYEES' DUTIES UNDER THE REGULATIONS

Employees must:

- make full and proper use of personal hearing protectors provided to them by their employer

- report to their employer any defect in any personal hearing protectors or other control measures as soon as is practicable.

NOISE LEVELS

Under the Regulations, specific actions are triggered at specific noise levels. Noise is measured in decibels and shown as dB(a). The two main action levels are 80dB(a) and 85dB(a).

Requirements at 80dB(a) to 85dB(a):

- Assess the risk to operatives' health and provide them with information and training.

- Provide suitable ear protection free of charge to those who request ear protection.

Requirements above 85dB(a):

- Reduce noise exposure as far as practicable by means other than ear protection.

- Set up an ear protection zone using suitable signage and segregation.

- Provide suitable ear protection free of charge to those affected and ensure they are worn.

PERSONAL PROTECTIVE EQUIPMENT (PPE) AT WORK REGULATIONS 1992

Employees and subcontractors must work in a safe manner. Not only must they wear the PPE that their employers provide but they must also look after it and report any damage to it. Importantly, employees must not be charged for anything given to them or done for them by the employer in relation to safety.

Ear defenders

Ear plugs

INDUSTRY TIP

The typical noise level for a hammer drill and a concrete mixer is 90 to 100dB (a).

ACTIVITY

Think about your place of work or training. What PPE do you think you should use when working with cement or using a powered planer?

The hearing and respiratory PPE provided for most work situations is not covered by these Regulations because other regulations apply to it. However, these items need to be compatible with any other PPE provided.

The main requirement of the Regulations is that PPE must be supplied and used at work wherever there are risks to health and safety that cannot be adequately controlled in other ways.

The Regulations also require that PPE is:

- included in the method statement

- properly assessed before use to ensure it is suitable

- maintained and stored properly

- provided to employees with instructions on how they can use it safely

- used correctly by employees.

An employer cannot ask for money from an employee for PPE, whether it is returnable or not. This includes agency workers if they are legally regarded as employees. If employment has been terminated and the employee keeps the PPE without the employer's permission, then, as long as it has been made clear in the contract of employment, the employer may be able to deduct the cost of the replacement from any wages owed.

Using PPE is a very important part of staying safe. For it to do its job properly it must be kept in good condition and used correctly. If any damage does occur to an article of PPE it is important that this is reported and it is replaced. It must also be remembered that PPE is a last line of defence and should not be used in place of a good safety policy!

A site safety sign showing the PPE required to work there

The following table shows the type of PPE used in the workplace and explains why it is important to store, maintain and use PPE correctly. It also shows why it is important to check and report damage to PPE.

PPE	Correct use
Hard hat/safety helmet 	Hard hats must be worn when there is danger of hitting your head or danger of falling objects. They often prevent a wide variety of head injuries. Most sites insist on hard hats being worn. They must be adjusted to fit your head correctly and must not be worn back to front! Check the date of manufacture as plastic can become brittle over time. Solvents, pens and paints can damage the plastic too.
Toe-cap boots or shoes  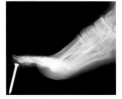 Safety boots A nail in a construction worker's foot	Toe-cap boots or shoes are worn on most sites as a matter of course and protect the feet from heavy falling objects. Some safety footwear has additional insole protection to help prevent nails going up through the foot. Toe caps can be made of steel or lighter plastic.
Ear defenders and plugs   Ear defenders Ear plugs	Your ears can be very easily damaged by loud noise. Ear protection will help prevent hearing loss while using loud tools or if there is a lot of noise going on around you. When using earplugs always ensure your hands are clean before handling the plugs as this reduces the risk of infection. If your ear defenders are damaged or fail to make a good seal around your ears have them replaced.
High-visibility (hi-viz) jacket 	This makes it much easier for other people to see you. This is especially important when there is plant or vehicles moving in the vicinity.
Goggles and safety glasses   Safety goggles Safety glasses	These protect the eyes from dust and flying debris while you are working. It has been known for casualties to be taken to hospital after dust has blown up from a dry mud road. You only get one pair of eyes: look after them!

PPE	Correct use
Dust masks and respirators  Dust mask Respirator	Dust is produced during most construction work and it can be hazardous to your lungs. It can cause all sorts of ailments from asthma through to cancer. Wear a dust mask to filter this dust out. You must ensure it is well fitted. Another hazard is dangerous gases such as solvents. A respirator will filter out hazardous gases but a dust mask will not! Respirators are rated P1, P2 and P3, with P3 giving the highest protection.
Gloves Latex glove Nitrile glove 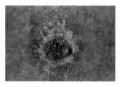 Gauntlet gloves Leather gloves	Gloves protect your hands. Hazards include cuts, abrasions, dermatitis, chemical burns or splinters. Latex and nitrile gloves are good for fine work, although some people are allergic to latex. Gauntlets provide protection from strong chemicals. Other types of gloves provide good grip and protect the fingers. 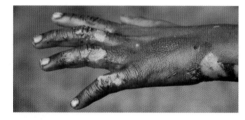 **A chemical burn as a result of not wearing safety gloves**
Sunscreen Suncream Melanoma	Another risk, especially in the summer months, is sunburn. Although a good tan is sometimes considered desirable, over-exposure to the sun can cause skin cancer such as melanoma. When out in the sun, cover up and use sunscreen (ie suncream) on exposed areas of your body to prevent burning.
Preventing HAVS 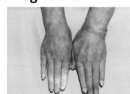	Hand–arm vibration syndrome (HAVS), also known as vibration white finger (VWF), is an industrial injury is caused by using vibrating power tools (such as a hammer drill, vibrating poker and vibrating plate) for a long time. This injury is controlled by limiting the time such power tools are used. For more information see page 31.

ACTIVITY

You are working on a site and a brick falls on your head. Luckily, you are doing as you have been instructed and you are wearing a helmet. You notice that the helmet has a small crack in it. What do you do?

1 Carry on using it as your employer will charge you for a new one; after all it is only a small crack.
2 Take it to your supervisor as it will no longer offer you full protection and it will need replacing.
3 Buy a new helmet because the old one no longer looks very nice.

INDUSTRY TIP

The most important pieces of PPE when using a disc cutter are dust masks, glasses and ear protection.

WORK AT HEIGHT REGULATIONS 2005 (AS AMENDED)

The Work at Height Regulations 2005 (as amended by the Work at Height (Amendment) Regulations 2007) put several duties upon employers:

- Working at height should be avoided if possible.
- If working at height cannot be avoided, the work must be properly organised with risk assessments carried out.
- Risk assessments should be regularly updated.
- Those working at height must be trained and competent.
- A method statement must be provided.

Workers wearing safety harnesses on an aerial access platform

Several points should be considered when working at height:

- How long is the job expected to take?
- What type of work will it be? It could be anything from fitting a single light bulb, through to removing a chimney or installing a roof.
  - □ How is the access platform going to be reached? By how many people?
  - □ Will people be able to get on and off the structure safely? Could there be overcrowding?
- What are the risks to passers-by? Could debris or dust blow off and injure anyone on the road below?
- What are the conditions like? Extreme weather, unstable buildings and poor ground conditions need to be taken into account.

A cherry picker can assist you when working at height

ACCESS EQUIPMENT AND SAFE METHODS OF USE

The means of access should only be chosen after a risk assessment has been carried out. There are various types of access.

Ladders

Ladders are normally used for access onto an access platform. They are not designed for working from except for light, short-duration work. A ladder should lean at an angle of 75°, ie one unit out for every four units up.

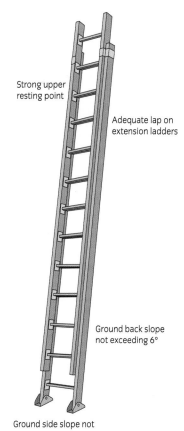

Strong upper resting point

Adequate lap on extension ladders

Ground back slope not exceeding 6°

Ground side slope not exceeding 16°, clean and free of slippery algae and moss

Using a ladder correctly

Roof ladder

Resting ladders on plastic guttering can cause it to bend and break

The following images show how to use a ladder or stepladder safely.

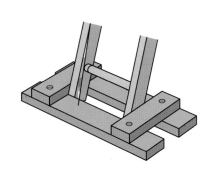

A ladder secured at the base.

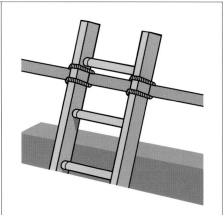

A ladder secured at the top of a platform for working from.

Access ladders should extend 1m above the landing point to provide a strong handhold.

Certain stepladders are unsafe to work from the top three rungs.

Don't overreach, and stay on the same rung.

Grip the ladder when climbing and remember to keep three points of contact.

INDUSTRY TIP

Always complete ladder pre-checks. Check the stiles (the two uprights) and rungs for damage such as splits or cracks. Do not use painted ladders because the paint could be hiding damage! Check all of the equipment including any stays and feet.

Stepladders

Stepladders are designed for light, short-term work.

Working from the side can make stepladders unstable. Do not overreach

Don't stand on the top three steps

Stepladder is fully open

Locked open firm and level on the ground

Using a stepladder correctly

Trestles

This is a working platform used for work of a slightly longer duration.

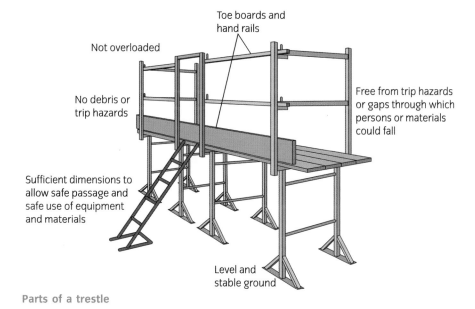

Not overloaded

Toe boards and hand rails

No debris or trip hazards

Free from trip hazards or gaps through which persons or materials could fall

Sufficient dimensions to allow safe passage and safe use of equipment and materials

Level and stable ground

Parts of a trestle

Tower scaffold

These are usually proprietary (manufactured) and are made from galvanised steel or lightweight aluminium alloy. They must be erected by someone competent in the erection and dismantling of mobile scaffolds.

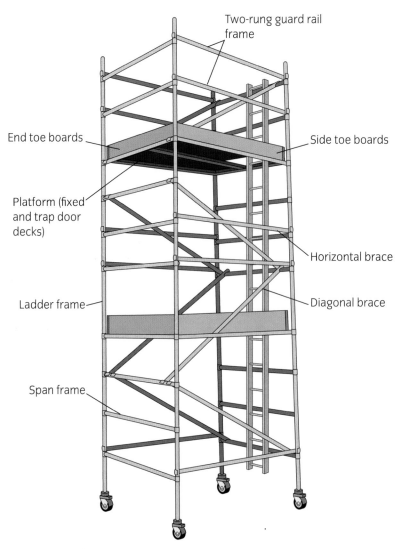

Two-rung guard rail frame

End toe boards

Side toe boards

Platform (fixed and trap door decks)

Horizontal brace

Ladder frame

Diagonal brace

Span frame

Parts of a tower scaffold

To use a tower scaffold safely:

- Always read and follow the manufacturer's instruction manual.

- Only use the equipment for what it is designed for.

- The wheels or feet of the tower must be in contact with a firm surface.

- Outriggers should be used to increase stability. The maximum height given in the manufacturer's instructions must not be exceeded.

- The platform must not be overloaded.

- The platform should be unloaded (and reduced in height if required) before it is moved.

- Never move a platform, even a small distance, if it is occupied.

INDUSTRY TIP

Remember, even a mobile access tower should have toe boards and guard rails fitted at all times when in use.

Tubular scaffold

This comes in two types:

- independent scaffold has two sets of standards or uprights
- putlog scaffold is built into the brickwork.

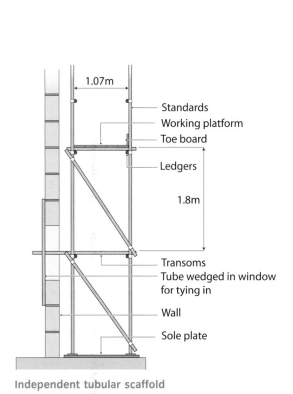

Independent tubular scaffold

Labels: Standards, Working platform, Toe board, Ledgers, 1.07m, 1.8m, Transoms, Tube wedged in window for tying in, Wall, Sole plate

Putlog tubular scaffold

Labels: Standards, Working platform, Toe board, Putlogs, At least 75mm, Ledgers, Putlogs, 1.8m, Horizontal tie, Tube wedged in window for tying in, Wall, Sole plate

Tubular scaffold is erected by specialist scaffolding companies and often requires structural calculations. Only trained and competent scaffold erectors should alter scaffolding. Access to a scaffold is usually via a tied ladder with three rungs projecting above the step off at platform level.

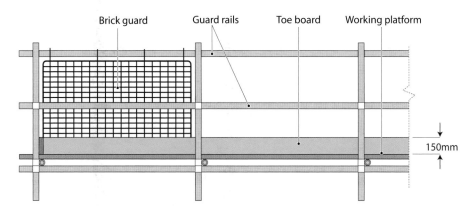

Labels: Brick guard, Guard rails, Toe board, Working platform, 150mm

A safe working platform on a tubular scaffold

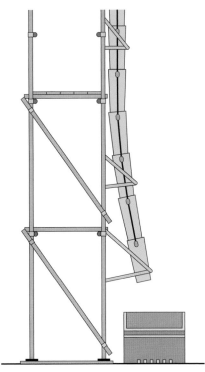

A debris chute for scaffolding

All scaffolding must:

- not have any gaps in the handrail or toe boards

- have a safe system for lifting any materials up to the working height

- have a safe system of debris removal.

Fall protection devices include:

- harnesses and lanyards

- safety netting

- air bags.

A harness and lanyard or safety netting will stop a person falling too far, leaving them suspended in the air. Air bags (commonly known as 'bouncy castles') are set up on the ground and inflated. If a person falls, they will have a soft landing. Air bags have fallen out of favour somewhat as some operatives use them as an easy way to get off the working platform – not the purpose they were intended for!

Using a scissor lift at height

LIFTING OPERATIONS AND LIFTING EQUIPMENT REGULATIONS (LOLER) 1998

The Lifting Operations and Lifting Equipment Regulations (LOLER) 1998 put responsibility upon employers to ensure that the lifting equipment provided for use at work is:

- strong and stable enough for the particular use and marked to indicate safe working loads

- positioned and installed to minimise any risks

- used safely, ie the work is planned, organised and performed by competent people

- subject to on-going thorough examination and, where appropriate, inspection by competent people.

THE CONTROL OF VIBRATION AT WORK REGULATIONS 2005

Vibration white finger or hand–arm vibration syndrome (HAVS) (see page 23) is caused by using vibrating tools such as hammer drills, vibrating pokers or hand-held breakers over a long period of time. The most efficient and effective way of controlling exposure to hand–arm vibration is to look for new or alternative work methods that remove or reduce exposure to vibration.

Follow these steps to reduce the effects of HAVS:

- Always use the right tool for each job.

- Check tools before using them to make sure they have been properly maintained and repaired to avoid increased vibration caused by faults or general wear.

- Make sure cutting tools are kept sharp so that they remain efficient.

- Reduce the amount of time you use a tool in one go, by doing other jobs in between.

- Avoid gripping or forcing a tool or work piece more than you have to.

- Encourage good blood circulation by:

  □ keeping warm and dry (when necessary, wear gloves, a hat, waterproofs and use heating pads if available)
  □ giving up or cutting down on smoking because smoking reduces blood flow
  □ massaging and exercising your fingers during work breaks.

Damage from HAVS can include the inability to do fine work and cold can trigger painful finger blanching attacks (when the ends of your fingers go white).

An operative taking a rest from using a power tool

Don't use power tools for longer than you need to

CONSTRUCTION SITE HAZARDS

DANGERS ON CONSTRUCTION SITES

Study the drawing of a building site. There is some demolition taking place, as well as construction. How many hazards can you find? Discuss your answers.

Dangers	Discussion points
Head protection	The operatives are not wearing safety helmets, which would prevent them from hitting their head or from falling objects.
Poor housekeeping	The site is very untidy. This can result in slips, trips and falls and can pollute the environment. An untidy site gives a poor company image. Offcuts and debris should be regularly removed and disposed of according to site policy and recycled if possible.
Fire	There is a fire near a building; this is hazardous. Fires can easily become uncontrollable and spread. There is a risk to the structure and, more importantly, a risk of operatives being burned. Fires can also pollute the environment.

Dangers	Discussion points
Trip hazards	Notice the tools and debris on the floor. The scaffold has been poorly constructed. There is a trip hazard where the scaffold boards overlap.
Chemical spills	There is a drum leaking onto the ground. This should be stored properly – upright and in a lockable metal shed or cupboard. The leak poses a risk of pollution and of chemical burns to operatives.
Falls from height	The scaffold has handrails missing. The trestle working platform has not been fitted with guard rails. None of the operatives is wearing a hard hat for protection either.
Noise	An operative is using noisy machinery with other people nearby. The operative should be wearing ear PPE, as should those working nearby. Better still, they should be working elsewhere if at all possible, isolating themselves from the noise.
Electrical	Some of the wiring is 240V as there is no transformer, it's in poor repair and it's also dragging through liquid. This not only increases the risk of electrocution but is also a trip hazard.
Asbestos or other hazardous substances	Some old buildings contain **asbestos** roofing which can become a hazard when being demolished or removed. Other potential hazards include lead paint or mould spores. If a potentially hazardous material is discovered a supervisor must be notified immediately and work must stop until the hazard is dealt with appropriately.

Asbestos

A naturally occurring mineral that was commonly used for a variety of purposes including: **insulation**, fire protection, roofing and guttering. It is extremely hazardous and can cause a serious lung disease known as asbestosis

Insulation

A material that reduces or prevents the transmission of heat

Cables can be a trip hazard on site

Boiler suit

Hand cleaner

PERSONAL HYGIENE

Working in the construction industry can be very physical, and it's likely to be quite dirty at times. Therefore you should take good care with your personal hygiene. This involves washing well after work. If contaminants are present, then wearing a protective suit, such as a boiler suit, that you can take off before you go home will prevent contaminants being taken home with you.

You should also wash your hands after going to the toilet and before eating. This makes it safer to eat and more pleasant for others around you. The following steps show a safe and hygienic way to wash your hands.

STEP 1 Apply soap to hands from the dispenser.

STEP 2 Rub the soap into a lather and cover your hands with it, including between your fingers.

STEP 3 Rinse hands under a running tap removing all of the soap from your hands.

STEP 4 Dry your hands using disposable towels. Put the towels in the bin once your hands are dry.

WORKING WITH ELECTRICITY

Electricity is a very useful energy resource but it can be very dangerous. Electricity must be handled with care! Only trained, competent people can work with electrical equipment.

THE DANGERS OF USING ELECTRICAL EQUIPMENT

The main dangers of electricity are:

- shock and burns (a 230V shock can kill)

- electrical faults which could cause a fire

- an explosion where an electrical spark has ignited a flammable gas.

VOLTAGES

Generally speaking, the lower the voltage the safer it is. However, a low voltage is not necessarily suitable for some machines, so higher voltages can be found. On site, 110V (volts) is recommended and this is the voltage rating most commonly used in the building industry. This is converted from 230V by use of a transformer.

110V 1 phase – yellow

230V (commonly called 240V) domestic voltage is used on site as battery chargers usually require this voltage. Although 230V is often used in workshops, 110V is recommended.

230V 1 phase – blue

400V (otherwise known as 3 phase) is used for large machinery, such as joinery shop equipment.

Voltages are nominal, ie they can vary slightly.

BATTERY POWER

Battery power is much safer than mains power. Many power tools are now available in battery-powered versions. They are available in a wide variety of voltages from 3.6V for a small screwdriver all the way up to 36V for large masonry drills.

400V 3 phase – red

The images on the next page are all examples of battery-powered tools you may come across in your workplace or place of training.

Battery drill   Battery-powered planer   Battery-powered jigsaw

WIRING

The wires inside a cable are made from copper, which conducts electricity. The copper is surrounded by a plastic coating that is colour coded. The three wires in a cable are the live (brown), which works with the neutral (blue) to conduct electricity, making the appliance work. The earth (green and yellow stripes) prevents electrocution if the appliance is faulty or damaged.

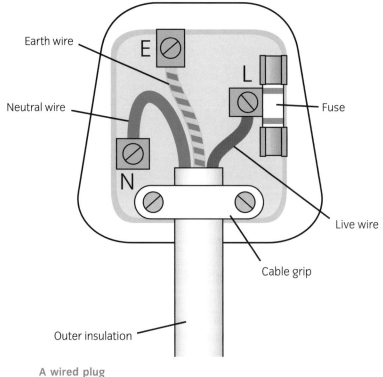

A wired plug

POWER TOOLS AND CHECKS

Power tools should always be checked before use. Always inform your supervisor if you find a fault. The tool will need to be repaired, and the tool needs to be kept out of use until then. The tool might be taken away, put in the site office and clearly labelled 'Do not use'.

Power tool checks include:

- *Look for the portable appliance testing (PAT) label*: PAT is a regular test carried out by a competent person (eg a qualified electrician) to ensure the tool is in a safe electrical condition. A sticker is placed on the tool after it has been tested. Tools that do not pass the PAT are taken out of use.

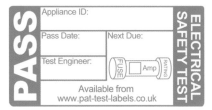

PAT testing labels

- *Cable*: Is it damaged? Is there a repair? Insulation tape may be hiding a damaged cable. Damaged cables must be replaced.

Cable protection

- *Casing*: Is the casing cracked? Plastic casings ensure the tool is double-insulated. This means the live parts inside are safely shielded from the user. A cracked casing will reduce the protection to the user and will require repair.

- *Guards and tooling*: Are guards in place? Is the tooling sharp?

- *Electricity supply leads*: Are they damaged? Are they creating a trip hazard? You need to place them in such a way that they do not make a trip hazard. Are they protected from damage? If they are lying on the floor with heavy traffic crossing them, they must be covered.

- *Use appropriate equipment for the size of the job*: For example, too many splitters can result in a web of cables.

- *Storage*: After use, power tools and equipment should be stored correctly. Tools must be returned to the boxes, including all the guards and parts. Cables need to be wound onto reels or neatly coiled as they can become tangled very easily.

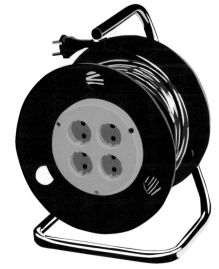

Cable reel

INDUSTRY TIP

Remember, always fully unroll an extension lead before use because it could overheat and cause a fire.

FIRE

Fire needs three things to start; if just one of them is missing there will be no fire. If all are present then a fire is unavoidable:

1 *Oxygen*: A naturally occurring gas in the air that combines with flammable substances under certain circumstances.

2 *Heat*: A source of fire, such as a hot spark from a grinder or naked flame.

3 *Fuel*: Things that will burn such as acetone, timber, cardboard or paper.

The fire triangle

If you have heat, fuel and oxygen you will have a fire. Remove any of these and the fire will go out.

PREVENTING THE SPREAD OF FIRE

Being tidy will help prevent fires starting and spreading. For instance:

- Wood offcuts should not be left in big piles or standing up against a wall. Instead, useable offcuts should be stored in racks.

- Put waste into the allocated disposal bins or skips.

- Always replace the cap on unused fuel containers when you put them away. Otherwise they are a potential source of danger.

- Flammable liquids (not limited to fuel-flammable liquids) such as oil based paint, thinners and oil must be stored in a locked metal cupboard or shed.

- Smoking around flammable substances should be avoided.

- Dust can be explosive, so when doing work that produces wood dust it is important to use some form of extraction and have good ventilation.

FIRE EXTINGUISHERS AND THEIR USES

You need to know where the fire extinguishers and blankets are located and which fire extinguishers can be used on different fires. The table below shows the different classes of fire and which extinguisher to use in each case.

Class of fire	Materials	Type of extinguisher
A	Wood, paper, hair, textiles	Water, foam, dry powder, wet chemical
B	Flammable liquids	Foam, dry powder, CO_2
C	Flammable gases	Dry powder, CO_2
D	Flammable metals	Specially formulated dry powder
E	Electrical fires	CO_2, dry powder
F	Cooking oils	Wet chemical, fire blanket

Fire blanket

INDUSTRY TIP

Remember, although all fire extinguishers are red, they each have a different coloured label to identify their contents.

CO$_2$ extinguisher

Dry powder extinguisher

Water extinguisher

Foam extinguisher

It is important to use the correct extinguisher for the type of fire as using the wrong one could make the danger much worse, eg using water on an electrical fire could lead to the user being electrocuted!

EMERGENCY PROCEDURES

In an emergency, people tend to panic. If an emergency were to occur, such as fire, discovering a bomb or some other security problem, would you know what to do? It is vital to be prepared in case of an emergency.

It is your responsibility to know the emergency procedures on your work site:

- If you discover a fire or other emergency you will need to raise the alarm:

  ☐ You will need to tell a nominated person. Who is this?
  ☐ If you are first on the scene you will have to ring the emergency services on 999.

- Be aware of the alarm signal. Is it a bell, a voice or a siren?

- Where is the assembly point? You will have to proceed to this point in an orderly way. Leave all your belongings behind; they may slow you or others down.

- At the assembly point, there will be someone who will ensure everyone is out safely and will do so by taking a count. Do you know who this person is? If during a fire you are not accounted for, a firefighter may risk their life to go into the building to look for you.

- How do you know it's safe to re-enter the building? You will be told by the appointed person. It's very important that you do not re-enter the building until you are told to do so.

Emergency procedure sign

ACTIVITY

What is the fire evacuation procedure at your workplace or place of training?

SIGNS AND SAFETY NOTICES

The law sets out the types of safety signs needed on a construction site. Some signs that warn us about danger and others tell us what to do to stay safe.

The following table describes five basic types of sign.

Type of sign	Description
Prohibition 	These signs are red and white. They are round. They signify something that must *not* be done.
Mandatory 	These signs are blue. They are round. They signify something that *must* be done.

Type of sign	Description
Caution 	These signs are yellow and black. They are triangular. These give warning of hazards.
Safe condition 	These signs are green. They are usually square or rectangular. They tell you the safe way to go, or what to do in an emergency.
Supplementary 	These white signs are square or rectangular and give additional important information. They usually accompany the signs above.

Case Study: Graham and Anton

An old barn had planning passed in order for it to be converted into a dwelling.

Keith, the contractor, was appointed and the small building company turned up first thing Monday morning.

Graham, the foreman, took a short ladder off the van to access the building's asbestos and slate roof to inspect its condition. The ladder just reached fascia level. As Graham stepped off onto the roof the ladder fell away, leaving him stranded. Luckily for him, Anton the apprentice, who was sitting in the van at the time noticed what had happened and rushed over to put the ladder back up.

While inspecting the whole roof Graham found that the asbestos roof covering was rather old and had become brittle over time, especially the clear plastic roof light sections. It was also clear upon close inspection that the ridge had holes in it and was leaking water. On the slated area of the roof it was noted that many slates were loose and some of them had fallen away leaving the battens and rafters exposed which was leading to severe decay of the timbers.

It was decided that the whole roof needed to be replaced.

- Was the survey carried out safely?

- What accidents could have happened during the survey?

- What could have been done to make the whole operation safer?

- What is the builder's general view of safety?

- How would you carry out the roof work in a safe fashion?

Work through the following questions to check your learning.

1   Which one of the following **must** be filled out prior to carrying out a site task?

   a   Invoice.

   b   Bill of quantities.

   c   Risk assessment.

   d   Schedule.

2   Which one of the following signs shows you something you **must** do?

   a   Green circle.

   b   Yellow triangle.

   c   White square.

   d   Blue circle.

3   Two parts of the fire triangle are heat and fuel. What is the third?

   a   Nitrogen.

   b   Oxygen.

   c   Carbon dioxide.

   d   Hydrogen sulphite.

4   Which of the following types of fire extinguisher would **best** put out an electrical fire?

   a CO_2.

   b   Powder.

   c   Water.

   d   Foam.

5   Which piece of health and safety legislation is designed to protect an operative from ill health and injury when using solvents and adhesives?

   a   Manual Handling Operations Regulations 1992.

   b   Control of Substances Hazardous to Health (COSHH) Regulations 2002.

   c   Health and Safety (First Aid) Regulations 1981.

   d   Lifting Operations and Lifting Equipment Regulations (LOLER) 1998.

6   What is the correct angle at which to lean a ladder against a wall?

   a   70°.

   b   80°.

   c   75°.

   d   85°.

7   Which are the **most** important pieces of PPE to use when using a disc cutter?

   a   Overalls, gloves and boots.

   b   Boots, head protection and overalls.

   c   Glasses, hearing protection and dust mask.

   d   Gloves, head protection and boots.

8   Which one of the following is **not** a lifting aid?

   a   Wheelbarrow.

   b   Kerb lifter.

   c   Gin lift.

   d   Respirator.

9   Which one of the following is a 3 phase voltage?

   a   400V.

   b   230V.

   c   240V.

   d   110V.

10   Above what noise level **must** you wear ear protection?

   a   75dB(a).

   b   80dB(a).

   c   85dB(a).

   d   90dB(a).

Chapter 2
Unit 101: Principles of building construction, information and communication

Working in the building industry involves more than just the physical construction of buildings such as laying blocks, screwing timber together or soldering pipes. Building is an expensive business and for the work to progress smoothly (and on budget) the work needs to be well organised.

This involves interpreting information such as drawings, specifications and schedules. It also involves calculating quantities and dimensions and knowing how to communicate well with others.

By reading this chapter you will know about:

1 Identifying information used in the workplace.
2 Environmental considerations in relation to construction.
3 Construction of foundations.
4 Construction of internal and external walls.
5 Construction of floors.
6 Construction of roofs.
7 Communicating in the workplace.

TECHNICAL INFORMATION

This section will discuss the three main sources of technical information that are used when constructing buildings:

- working drawings and **specifications**
- schedules
- **bill of quantities**.

These are all essential information and form the contract documents (those that govern the construction of a building). All documentation needs to be correctly interpreted and correctly used. The contract documents need to be looked after and stored (filed) correctly and safely. If documents are left lying around they will become difficult to read and pages may be lost, leading to errors. The contract documents will need to be **archived** at the end of the contract, so they can be referred back to in case of any query or dispute over the work carried out or the materials used.

DRAWING SCALES

It is impossible to fit a full-sized drawing of a building onto a sheet of paper, so it is necessary to **scale** (shrink) the size of the building to enable it to fit. The building has to be shrunk in proportion; this makes it possible to convert measurements on the drawing into real measurements that can be used. Scale rules are made specifically for this purpose.

Triangular scale rule

How do scale rules work? Let's say we are using a scale of 1:5. That means that what we draw – using the sizes on the scale rule – will be five times smaller on the drawing than the object's actual size. So, a line 30mm long will represent an object 150mm long (30 × 5 = 150).

Specification

A contract document that gives information about the quality of materials and standards of workmanship required

Bill of quantities

A document containing quantities, descriptions and cost of works and resources

Archived

Kept in storage

Scale

The ratio of the size on a drawing to the size of the real thing that it represents

INDUSTRY TIP

Do not scale from photocopies because these can easily become distorted in the process of photocopying.

INDUSTRY TIP

If a drawing has **dimensions**, use these instead of using a scale rule to take a measurement.

Dimension

A measurement

The British Standards Institute's BS 1192 (Drawing office practice) gives a range of standard scales that are used for various drawing types and scale rules are manufactured to meet this purpose.

British Standards Institute

The British Standards Institute (BSI) is the UK authority that develops and publishes standards in the UK

SCALES IN COMMON USE

Scale	Use
1:1	Full size (used for rods)
1:2 **1:5** **1:10**	Building details
1:20 **1:50** **1:100** **1:200**	Plans, elevations and sections
1:200 **1:500** **1:1250**	Site plans
1:1250 **1:2500**	Location plans

The documents these scales are used for are described on pages 49–51.

DATUM POINTS

Heights of buildings and the relative heights of components within the building are calculated from a common **datum point**. Datum points are determined by transferring a known fixed height from a bench mark. There are two types of datum point:

- A permanent Ordnance bench mark (OBM) is a given height on an Ordnance Survey map. This fixed height is described as a value, eg so many metres above sea level (as calculated from the average sea height at Newlyn, Cornwall).

- A temporary bench mark (TBM) is set up on site.

Datum point

A fixed point or height from which reference levels can be taken. The datum point is used to transfer levels across a building site. It represents the finished floor level (FFL) on a dwelling

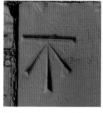 

Ordnance and temporary bench marks

ACTIVITY

Find your local OBM or your site TBM.

BASIC DRAWING SYMBOLS (HATCHINGS)

Standard symbols, also known as hatching symbols, are used on drawings as a means of passing on information simply. If all the parts of a building were labelled in writing, the drawing would soon become very crowded. Additionally, it is important to use standard symbols so that everyone can read them and they mean the same to everyone. The following images are just some of the standard symbols used.

Sink	Sinktop	Wash basin	Bath	Shower tray
WC	Window	Door	Radiator	Lamp
Switch	Socket	North symbol	Sawn timber (unwrot)	Concrete
Insulation	Brickwork	Blockwork	Stonework	Earth (subsoil)
Cement screed	Damp proof course/ membrane	Hardcore	Hinging position of windows	Stairs up and down
Timber – softwood. Machined all round (wrot)	Timber – hardwood. Machined all round (wrot)			

INFORMATION SOURCES

Type of drawing	Description
Location drawings	Usually prepared by an **architect** or **architectural technician**. Show the location of the building plot, position of the building and areas within the building. The term location drawings covers all of the drawings in this table.
Block plans 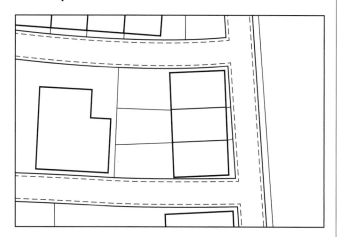	Show the proposed development in relation to its surrounding properties. The scales used are 1:1250 or 1:2500. Very little detail is available from this type of plan. The direction North is usually shown.
Site plans 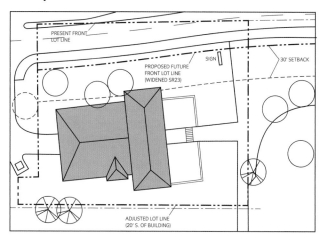	Show the plot in more detail, with drain runs, road layouts and the size and position of the existing building (and any extensions proposed) in relation to the property boundary. A scale of 1:500 or 1:200 is used. The Planning Portal sometimes refers to site plans as block plans, but the two types of plan have been distinguished in this book.

Architect

A trained professional who designs a structure and represents the client who wants the structure built. They are responsible for the production of the working drawings. They supervise the construction of buildings or other large structures

Architectural technician

A draftsperson who works in an architectural practice

Type of drawing	Description
Floor plans 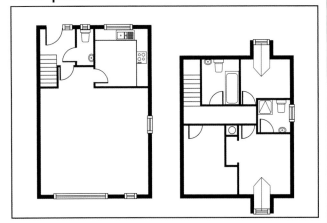	Show the positioning of walls, size of rooms along with the positioning of elements within the building such as units.
Elevations 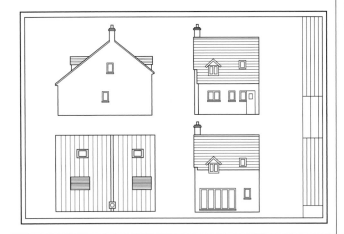	Show a building from a particular side and show the positioning of features such as doors and windows.
Sections 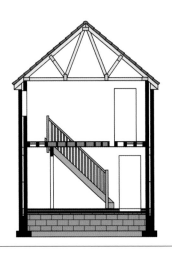	Show in greater detail what the section of a component looks like and how it might fit in relation to another component. A typical example would be a cross-section of a window showing the size of the features and how they fit together. Using these drawings it is possible to determine the positions of rooms, windows, doors, kitchen units and so on. Elevations are shown. These drawings are more detailed, and are often scaled to provide construction measurements. Some of the scales used are 1:200, 1:100, 1:50, 1:10, 1:5 and 1:1. A scale of 1:1 is full size.

Type of drawing	Description
Construction drawings (Detail drawings) Detail showing typical exterior corner detail External walls — Exterior cladding — Breather membrane paper Exterior cladding Wall plate stud Breather membrane paper Vapour control membrane on the inside of the timber frame	Show details of construction, normally as a cross-section.

SPECIFICATIONS

A specification accompanies the working drawings. It gives further information that cannot be shown on the drawings, because the drawings need to be clear and not covered in notes. A specification would include information such as:

- the colour of paint required

- a specific timber species

- the brick type required

- the plaster finish required.

It is prepared by construction professionals such as architects and building services engineers. They can be produced from previous project specifications, in-house documents or master specifications such as the National Building Specification (NBS). The NBS is owned by the Royal Institute of British Architects (RIBA).

Example of a specification

COMPONENT RANGE DRAWINGS

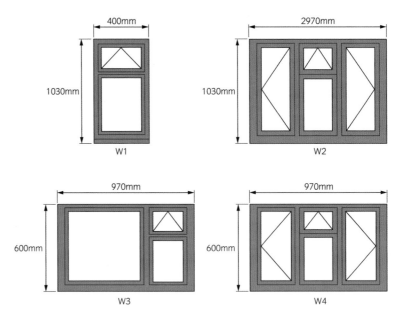

Component range drawing of windows

A component range drawing shows the range of components available from a manufacturer. It includes:

- sizes available

- coding for ordering purposes

- availability (whether it can be bought off-the-shelf or whether pre-ordering is required).

Availability is particularly important when planning delivery dates. Schedules reference this type of drawing.

SCHEDULES

A schedule is used to record repeated design information that applies to a range of components or fittings, such as:

- windows

- doors

- kitchen units

- joinery fittings.

A schedule is mainly used on bigger sites where there are multiples of several designs of houses, with each type having different components and fittings. It avoids a house being given the wrong component or fitting.

A schedule is usually used in conjunction with a component range drawing and a floor plan.

In a typical plan, the doors and windows are labelled D1, D2, W1, W2 etc. These components would be included in the schedule, which would provide additional information on them. For example see the following schedule.

Master Internal Door Schedule							
Ref:	Door size	S.O. width	S.O. height	Lintel type	FD30	Self closing	Floor level
D1	838 × 1981	900	2040	BOX	Yes	Yes	GROUND FLOOR
D2	838 × 1981	900	2040	BOX	Yes	Yes	GROUND FLOOR
D3	762 × 1981	824	2040	BOX	No	No	GROUND FLOOR
D4	838 × 1981	900	2040	N/A	Yes	No	GROUND FLOOR
D5	838 × 1981	900	2040	BOX	Yes	Yes	GROUND FLOOR
D6	762 × 1981	824	2040	BOX	Yes	Yes	FIRST FLOOR
D7	762 × 1981	824	2040	BOX	Yes	Yes	FIRST FLOOR
D8	762 × 1981	824	2040	N/A	Yes	No	FIRST FLOOR
D9	762 × 1981	824	2040	BOX	Yes	Yes	FIRST FLOOR
D10	762 × 1981	824	2040	N/A	No	No	FIRST FLOOR
D11	686 × 1981	748	2040	N/A	Yes	No	SECOND FLOOR
D12	762 × 1981	824	2040	BOX	Yes	Yes	SECOND FLOOR
D13	762 × 1981	824	2040	100 HD BOX	Yes	Yes	SECOND FLOOR
D14	686 × 1981	748	2040	N/A	No	No	SECOND FLOOR

Example of a schedule

BILLS OF QUANTITIES

A bill of quantities is produced by the quantity surveyor and describes everything that is required for the job based on the drawings, specification and schedules. A bill of quantities contains the following information:

- *Preliminaries*: General information including the names of the client and architect, details of the work and descriptions of the site.

- *Preambles*: Like the specification, this outlines the quality and description of materials and workmanship, etc.

- *Measured quantities*: A description of how each task and material is to be measured, with measurements in metres (linear and square), hours, litres, kilogrammes and the number of components required.

The completed document is sent out to contractors who will then price the work and enter the costs into the blank spaces. The bill of quantities ensures that all the contractors are pricing for the job using the same information.

BILL OF QUANTITIES

(Assuming Civil Engineering Standard Method of Measurement (CESSM3) is used.)

Number	Item description	Unit	Quantity	Rate	Amount £	p
	CLASS A: GENERAL ITEMS					
	Specified Requirements					
	Testing of Materials					
A250	Testing of recycled and secondary aggregates	sum				
	Information to be provided by the Contractor					
A290	Production of Materials Management Plan	sum				
	Method Related Charges					
	Recycling Plant / Equipment					
A339.01	Mobilise; Fixed	sum				
A339.02	Operate; Time-Related	sum				
A339.03	De-mobilise; Fixed	sum				
	CLASS D: DEMOLITION AND SITE CLEARANCE					
	Other Structures					
D522.01	Other structures; Concrete;	sum				
D522.02	Grading / processing of demolition material to produce recycled and secondary aggregates	m³	70			
D522.03	Disposal of demolition material offsite	m³	30			
	CLASS E: EARTHWORKS					
	Excavation Ancillaries					

Bill of quantities

WORK SCHEDULES

It is very important indeed that the progress of work is planned out. A work schedule or programme of work is an easy way of showing what work is to be carried out and when. This is usually shown in the form of a bar chart called a Gantt chart. The chart lists the tasks that need to be done on the left-hand side and shows a timeline across the top. The site manager or trade supervisors can quickly tell from looking at this chart:

- if work is keeping to schedule

- what materials, equipment and labour are required

- when they are required.

Materials very often have a **lead-in time** and so cannot be delivered immediately. These need to be ordered and delivered at the correct time. Labour planning is also required as the trades may be working elsewhere when needed.

Task	Time (days)						
	1	2	3	4	5	6	7
Prepare the ground	▓	▓					
Spread foundations			▓	▓			
Lay cables for services				▓	▓		
Build walls up to DPC						▓	▓
Proposed time in green							

Gantt chart

INDUSTRY TIP

Use of a planning document such as a Gantt chart will reduce waste and ensure effective use of labour.

Lead-in time

The time taken between ordering an item and it being delivered

CALCULATING QUANTITIES FOR MATERIALS

Calculations are required throughout the building process. It is important that these calculations are accurate, as mistakes can be very expensive. A company can lose a lot of money if it underestimates:

- the amount of materials required

- how much they cost

- how long it will take to complete a job.

It could also lead to the company gaining a bad reputation for not being able to complete a job on time and in budget.

Materials are usually better priced if bought in bulk, whereas a buy-as-you go approach can cost more.

Consider these points when buying materials:

- Is there sufficient storage room for delivered materials?

- Is there a risk of the materials being damaged if there is nowhere suitable to store them or if they are delivered too early?

- Will it be a problem to obtain the same style, colour or quality of product if they are not all ordered at the same time?

- Will over-ordering cause lots of wastage?

These and many other considerations will help determine when and in what quantity materials are ordered.

Some wastage is unavoidable. Allowances must be made for wastage, eg cut bricks that cannot be re-used, short ends of timber, partly full paint cans. Up to 5% waste is allowed for bricks and blocks and 10% for timber and paint.

It may be that all the materials are ordered by the office or supervisory staff, but you still need to know how to recognise and calculate material requirements. Deliveries have to be checked before the delivery note is signed and the driver leaves. Any discrepancies in the type or quantity of materials, or any materials that have arrived damaged, must be recorded on the delivery note and reported to the supervisor. Any discrepancies will need to be followed up and new delivery times arranged.

You must be able to identify basic materials and carry out basic calculations. You will often have to collect sufficient materials to carry out a particular operation. Being able to measure accurately will mean you can make the most economic use of materials and therefore reduce waste.

Deliveries must be checked before signing the delivery note

UNITS OF MEASUREMENT

The construction industry uses metric units as standard; however, you may come across some older measures called imperial units.

Units for measuring	Metric units	Imperial units
Length	millimetre (mm) metre (m) kilometre (km)	inch (in) or " eg 6" (6 inches) foot (ft) or ' eg 8' (8 ft)
Liquid	millilitre (ml) litre (l)	pint (pt)
Weight	gramme (g) kilogramme (kg) tonne (t)	pound (lb)

ACTIVITY

Look online to find out:
- What other imperial units are still commonly used?
- How many millimetres are there in an inch?
- How many litres are there in a gallon?

Units for measuring	Quantities	Example
Length	There are 1,000mm in 1m There are 1,000m in 1km	1mm × 1,000 = 1m 1m × 1,000 = 1km 6,250mm can be shown as 6.250m 6,250m can be shown as 6.250km
Liquid	There are 1,000ml in 1l	1ml × 1,000 = 1l
Weight	There are 1,000g in 1kg There are 1,000kg in 1t	1g × 1,000 = 1kg 1kg × 1,000 = 1t

CALCULATIONS

Four basic mathematical operations are used in construction calculations.

ADDITION

The addition of two or more numbers is shown with a plus sign (**+**).

Example

A stack of bricks is 3 bricks long and 2 bricks high. It contains 6 bricks.

$$3 + 3 = \mathbf{6}$$

More examples:

$$5 + 2 = \mathbf{7}$$
$$19 + 12 = \mathbf{31}$$
$$234 + 105 = \mathbf{339}$$

Pallet of bricks

SUBTRACTION

The reduction of one number by another number is shown with a minus sign (**–**).

Example

A pallet containing 100 bricks is delivered on site, but you only need 88 bricks. How many are left over?

$$100 - 88 = \mathbf{12}$$

More examples:

$$5 - 2 = \mathbf{3}$$
$$19 - 12 = \mathbf{7}$$
$$234 - 105 = \mathbf{129}$$

MULTIPLICATION

The scaling of one number by another number is shown with a multiplication sign (×).

Example

A stack of bricks is 3 bricks long and 2 bricks high. It contains 6 bricks.

$$3 \times 2 = \mathbf{6}$$

More examples:

$$19 \times 12 = \mathbf{228}$$

$$234 \times 10 = \mathbf{2,340}$$

$$234 \times 105 = \mathbf{24,570}$$

In the two last examples, the comma (,) is used to show we are in the thousands. In words we would say, twenty-four thousand, five hundred and seventy.

DIVISION

Sharing one number by another number in equal parts (how many times it goes into the number) is shown with a division sign (÷).

Example

$$5 \div 2 = \mathbf{2.5}$$

$$36 \div 12 = \mathbf{3}$$

$$600 \div 4 = \mathbf{150}$$

LINEAR LENGTH

Linear means how long a number of items would measure from end to end if laid in a straight line. Examples of things that are calculated in linear measurements are:

- skirting board

- lengths of timber

- rope

- building line

- wallpaper.

We use this form of measurement when working out how much of one of the materials listed above we need, eg to find out how much

Skirting boards are calculated using linear measurements

A joiner measuring a room

Perimeter

The distance around an object or room

skirting board is required for a room. First, we need to measure the **perimeter** (sides) of a room. To find the linear length we add the length of all four sides together. This can be done in two ways: adding or multiplying.

Example 1

A site carpenter has been asked how many metres of skirting are required for the rooms below.

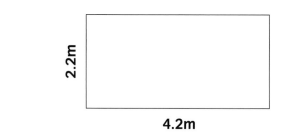

They can add all the sides together:
$$2.2 + 4.2 + 2.2 + 4.2 = 12.8m$$

Or, they can multiply each side by 2, and add them together:
$$(2.2 \times 2) + (4.2 \times 2) = 12.8m$$

Either way, **12.8m** is the correct answer.

Example 2

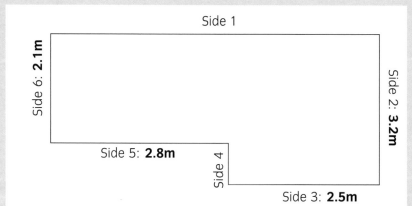

To work out the perimeter of this room we need to add all the sides together. In this example each side has been given a reference number, so all we need to do is add all the sides together, like this:

side 1 (side 3 + side 5) + side 2 + side 3 + side 4 (side 2 – side 6) + side 5 + side 6

Now, let's show the working out: (2.8 + 2.5) + 3.2 + 2.5 + (3.2 – 2.1) + 2.8 + 2.1 = 17m

The amount of skirting board required is **17m**.

Now let's put some door openings in. This symbol 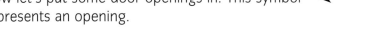 represents an opening.

Example 3

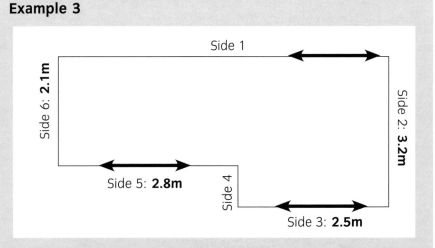

On side 1 there is an opening 0.9m wide, on side 3 there is an opening 1.5m wide and on side 5 there is an opening 2.1m wide.

We know from Example 2 that the perimeter of the room is 17m. We now need to remove the openings. Skirting board will not be needed for the openings.

Step 1

Add together the lengths of the three combined openings:

0.9 + 1.5 + 2.1 = 4.5m

Step 2

Deduct this from 17m:

17 − 4.5 = 12.5m

The linear length of skirting board required is 12.5m.

Step 3

However, this calculation does not take into account any waste. We would normally add 10% extra to allow for waste:

12.5 + 10% = 12.5 + 1.25 = 13.75m

The total amount of skirting board required is **13.75m**.

PERCENTAGES

An easy way to find a percentage (%) of a number is to divide the number by 100 and then multiply it by the percentage you require.

> **Example**
>
> Increase 19m by 12%
>
> $19 \div 100 = 0.19$
>
> $0.19 \times 12 = 2.28$
>
> $19 + 2.28 = 21.28m$
>
> Total required **21.28m**.

AREA

Floors

The structured layers of a building, eg ground floor, first floor, second floor

To find out how much material is required to cover a surface such as a **floor** or wall you need to calculate its area. Area is the measurements of a two-dimensional surface, eg the surface of floors, walls, glass or a roof.

To find the area of a surface you need to multiply its length by its width (L × W) or one side by the other. This will give you an answer which is expressed in square units (^{2}). For example, mm², m² or km².

> **Example 1**
>
> A bricklayer has been asked to work out the area of the floors below. 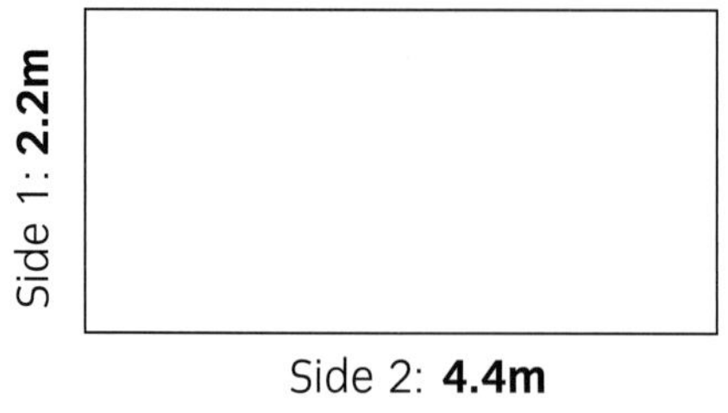
>
>
> Side 1: **2.2m**
>
> Side 2: **4.4m**
>
> side 1 × side 2 = floor area
>
> $2.2 \times 4.4 = 9.68m^2$
>
> The total floor area is **9.68m²**.

Irregularly shaped areas can be calculated by breaking up the area into sections that can be worked out easily, and then adding them together.

Example 2

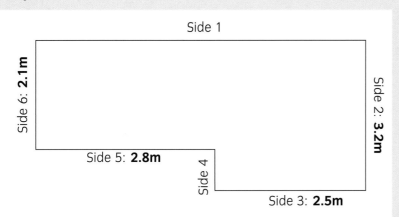

Irregularly shaped rooms can be split into sections to calculate the area

Step 1

Divide the area into two parts, and then calculate the area of each part. The easiest way to do this is to divide it into two smaller sections:

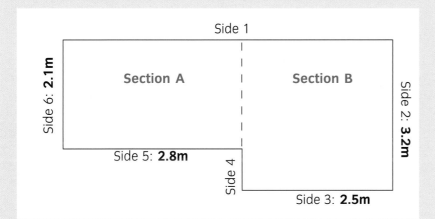

Step 2

Work out the areas of section A and section B:

section A: $2.1 \times 2.8 = 5.88m^2$

section B: $2.5 \times 3.2 = 8m^2$

Step 3

Add the areas of section A and section B together:

section A + section B = total floor area

$5.88 + 8 = 13.88m^2$

The total floor area is **13.88m²**.

A tiler tiling a floor

ACTIVITY

Find the area of the following measurements:

1 2.1m × 2.4m
2 0.9m × 2.7m
3 250mm × 3.4m

Answers: 1) 5.04m², 2) 2.43m², 3) 0.85m²

Now let's say the floor requires tiling. The tiler needs to calculate the number of floor tiles required.

Example 3

The size of each floor tile is 305mm × 305mm. We can also show this as 0.305m × 0.305m.

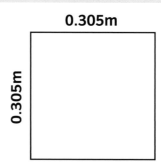

How many floor tiles are required for the floor area in Example 2? The total floor area is 13.88m².

Step 1

Calculate the area of one tile. As the floor area is given in m², we need to calculate the size of the tile in the same unit, ie m².

0.305 × 0.305 = 0.093m²

Step 2

Now you need to divide the total floor area by the area of one tile to find out the total number of tiles required.

total floor area ÷ area of one tile = total number of tiles

13.88 ÷ 0.093 = 149.247 tiles

This number is rounded up to the next full tile, so a total of 150 floor tiles are required.

Step 3

However, this total does not allow for any waste.

Add 5% to allow for waste:

150 + 5% = 158 tiles (to the next full tile)

Let's look at the working out:

150 ÷ 100 = 1.5 tiles (this is 1%)

1.5 × 5 = 7.5 tiles (this is 5%)

5% of 150 tiles, rounded up to the next full tile, is 8 tiles.

Therefore **158 tiles** are required.

AREA OF A TRIANGLE

Sometimes you will be required to work out an area that includes a triangle.

A decorator measuring a room

Example 1

A painter has been asked to work out how much paint will be needed to paint the front of this house.

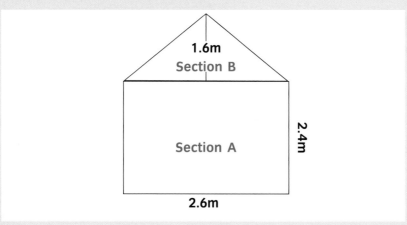

Section B — 1.6m

Section A

2.4m

2.6m

Step 1

Divide the area up into a rectangular section (section A) and a triangular section (section B).

Step 2

Find the area of section A:

2.4 × 2.6 = 6.24m²

The area of section A is 6.24m².

Step 3

Find the area of section B

The area of a triangle can be found by multiplying the base by the height, then dividing by 2.

(base × height) ÷ 2 = area

2.6 × 1.6 = 4.16

4.16 ÷ 2 = 2.08m²

The area of section B is 2.08m².

Step 4

area of section A + area of section B = total wall area

6.24 + 2.08 = 8.32m²

The total wall area is **8.32m²**.

ACTIVITY

Look at the diagram. Work out the area of the wall in order to arrange the delivery of sufficient paint.

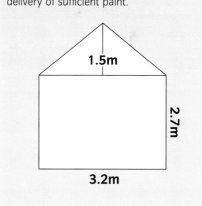

1.5m

2.7m

3.2m

Answer: 11.04m²

RIGHT-ANGLED TRIANGLE

Now let's look at the right-angled triangle below. It has three sides, A, B and C. Pythagorean theorem tells us that in a right-angled triangle the **hypotenuse** is equal to the sum of the square of the lengths of the two other sides, in other words $a^2 + b^2 = c^2$. In this example the hypotenuse is side C.

Using the Pythagorean theorem we can work out the length of any side.

Hypotenuse

The longest side of a right-angled triangle. It is always opposite the right angle

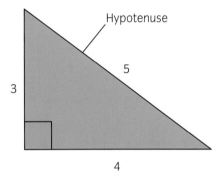

The hypotenuse

INDUSTRY TIP

If a triangle has a small square in the corner, this shows you the corner is a right angle.

Example 1

If side A is 3m long and side B is 4m long, what is the length of side C?

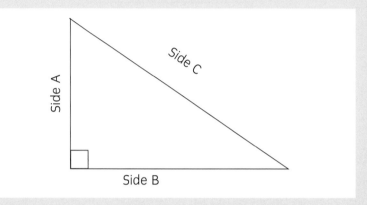

$3 \times 3 = 9$

$4 \times 4 = 16$

$9 + 16 = 25$

$\sqrt{25} = 5$

($\sqrt{}$ means square root. A square root of a number is the number that is multiplied by itself to make that number, in this case $5 \times 5 = 25$)

Side C is **5m** long.

Example 2

A joiner has been asked to work out the length of a roof (side C).

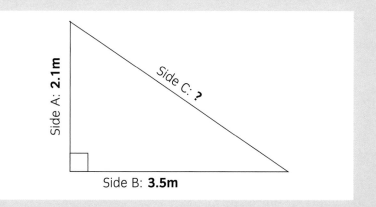

2.1×2.1 (side A) = 4.41

3.5×3.5 (side B) = 12.25

$4.41 + 12.25 = 16.66$

$\sqrt{16.66} = 4.08\text{m}$

The length of side C is **4.08m**.

Example 3

A bricklayer needs to find the rise of a roof (side A).

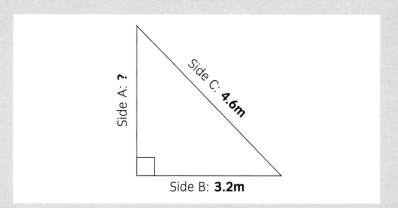

3.2×3.2 (side B) = 10.24

4.6×4.6 (side C) = 21.16

$21.16 - 10.24 = 10.92$

$\sqrt{10.92} = 3.30\text{m}$

The length of side A is **3.3m**.

PERIMETERS AND AREAS OF CIRCLES

Circumference

The distance around the edge of a circle

Diameter

The length of a straight line going through the centre of a circle connecting two points on its circumference

Sometimes you are required to find the perimeter or **circumference** of a circle.

circumference of a circle = π × **diameter**

$$C = \pi d$$

π (or 'pi') is the number of times that the diameter of a circle will divide into the circumference.

π = 3.142

This is equal to the number of diameters in one revolution of a circle. It is the same for any sized circle.

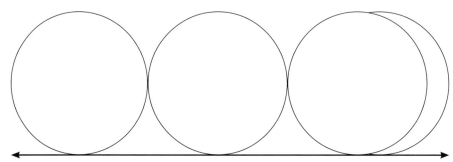

There are 3.142 diameters in one complete revolution

Example 1

A joiner is making a circular window that has a diameter of 600mm. Its circumference is:

0.600 × 3.142 = **1.885m**

The diameter of a circle from a given circumference is:

diameter = circumference ÷ π

Example 2

A window has a circumference of 2.250m. Its diameter is:

2.250 ÷ 3.142 = **0.716m** (or 716mm)

Radius

The length of a line from the centre to a point on the circumference of a circle. It is exactly half the length of the diameter

The area of a circle is found by:

area of a circle = π × **radius**² (radius is equal to half the diameter)

Example 3

A painter needs to paint a circle that is 1.2m in diameter and is required to find the area of the circle to enable them to order the correct quantity of paint.

1.2 ÷ 2 = **0.6m** (the radius)

3.142 × 0.6m² = **1.13m²**

VOLUME

The volume of an object is the total space it takes up, eg a tin of paint, a foundation for a wall or the capacity of a concrete mixer, and is shown as m³ (cubic metres). To find the volume of an object you must multiply length by width by height.

$$\text{volume} = \text{length} \times \text{width} \times \text{height}$$

Example 1

Each side of this cube is 1m. The total space it takes up is 1m³.

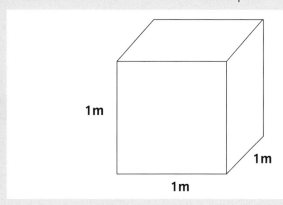

1m × 1m × 1m = **1m³**

Example 2

A bricklayer has been asked to work out how many m³ of **concrete** is required for a strip foundation. The size of the foundation is 3.2m long, 0.600m wide and 0.900m deep.

length × width × height = volume

3.2 × 0.600 × 0.900 = 1.728m³

The volume of concrete needed for the strip foundation is **1.728m³**.

A bricklayer taking levels

Concrete

Composed of cement, sand and stone, of varying size and in varying proportions

To work out the volume of a cylinder:

$$\text{volume} = \pi r^2 h \; (\pi \times r^2 \times h)$$

Example 3

A joiner has a tin of preservative and needs to know its volume. The tin has a diameter of 250mm and a height of 700mm.

$\pi r^2 h \; (\pi \times r^2 \times h) = \text{volume}$

The radius (r) is half the diameter:

$250 \div 2 = 125\text{mm}$

$3.142 \times 0.125^2 \times 0.700 = 0.034\text{m}^3$

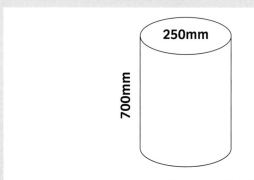

The volume of the tin of paint is **0.034m³**.

COMMUNICATION

Good communication is vital to the smooth running of any building project.

Communication involves sharing thoughts, information and ideas between people. For communication to be effective, information must be:

- given in a clear way
- received without misunderstanding.

It has been said that to be a good communicator it is just as important to be a good listener as it is to be a good speaker! Good communication leads to a safer and more efficient workplace, not to mention helping to maintain a pleasant working environment.

Most sites will have policies and procedures in place that govern the chain of command and communication between supervisory staff and workers.

WRITTEN COMMUNICATION

There are many methods of communication within the building industry. In this chapter we have discussed drawings, schedules and specifications etc. The architect uses these methods to communicate details about the building to the team who will **tender** for and erect the building.

Communication is usually electronic via email (with or without attachments) or through intranet sites. Drawings are very commonly distributed in electronic formats which are printed on to paper when required. Messages are often given via text.

Sometimes communication will be via a memorandum (memo), a written form of communication with a message.

Site rules, risk assessments and method statements (see Chapter 1) communicate safety information.

Tender

To supply a client with a fixed quotation for work

INDUSTRY TIP

Messages that are passed on by word of mouth are open to interpretation, so written messages can often be clearer.

SITE PAPERWORK

Communication on site is aided by the use of paperwork and without it no building site could operate. It is an important method of communication between operatives and supervisory staff, builders, architects and clients.

Type of paperwork	Description
Timesheet **Timesheet** Employer: CPF Building Co. | Employee Name: Louise Miranda | Week starting: 17/6/14 Date: 21/6/13 <table><tr><th>Day</th><th>Job/Job Number</th><th>Start Time</th><th>Finish Time</th><th>Total Hours</th><th>Overtime</th></tr><tr><td>Monday</td><td>Penburthy, Falmouth 0897</td><td>9am</td><td>6pm</td><td>8</td><td></td></tr><tr><td>Tuesday</td><td>Penburthy, Falmouth 0897</td><td>9am</td><td>6pm</td><td>8</td><td></td></tr><tr><td>Wednesday</td><td>Penburthy, Falmouth 0897</td><td>8.30am</td><td>5.30pm</td><td>8</td><td></td></tr><tr><td>Thursday</td><td>Trelawney, Truro 0901</td><td>11am</td><td>8pm</td><td>8</td><td>2</td></tr><tr><td>Friday</td><td>Trelawney, Truro 0901</td><td>11am</td><td>7pm</td><td>7</td><td>1</td></tr><tr><td>Saturday</td><td>Trelawney, Truro 0901</td><td>9am</td><td>1pm</td><td>4</td><td></td></tr><tr><td>Totals</td><td></td><td></td><td></td><td>43</td><td>3</td></tr></table> Employee's signature:_____ Supervisor's signature: _____	Used to record the hours completed each day, and is usually the basis on which pay is calculated. Timesheets also help to work out how much the job has cost in working hours, and can give information for future estimating work when working up a tender.

Type of paperwork	Description
Job sheet **CPF Building Co** **Job sheet** **Customer name:** Henry Collins **Date:** 9/12/14 **Address:** 57 Green St Kirkham London **Work to be carried out** Finishing joint work to outer walls **Instructions** Use weather struck and half round	Gives details of a job to be carried out, sometimes with material requirements and hours given to complete the task.
Variation order **Confirmation notice** **Architect's instruction** **CPF Building Co** **Variation order** **Project Name:** Penburthy House, Falmouth, Cornwall **Reference Number:** 80475 **Date:** 14/11/14 **From: :** _____ **To:** _____ **Reason for change:** **Tick** Customer requirements ☑ Engineer requirements ☐ Revised design ☐ **Instruction:** Entrance door to be made from Utile hardwood with brushed chrome finished ironmongery (changed from previous detail, softwood with brass ironmongery). Signature _____	Sometimes alterations are made to the contract which changes the work to be completed, eg a client may wish to move a door position or request a different brick finish. This usually involves a variation to the cost. This work should not be carried out until a variation order and a confirmation notice have been issued. Architect's instructions are instructions given by an architect, first verbally and then in writing to a site agent as work progresses and questions inevitably arise over details and specifications.

Type of paperwork	Description
Requisition order	Filled out to order materials from a supplier or central store. These usually have to be authorised by a supervisor before they can be used.

CPF Building Co
Requisition order

Supplier Information: Construction Supplies Ltd   **Date:** 9/12/14

Contract Address/Delivery Address: Penburthy House, Falmouth, Cornwall

Tel number: 0207294333

Order Number: 26213263CPF

Item number	Description	Quantity	Unit/Unit Price	Total
X22433	75mm 4mm gauge countersunk brass screws slotted	100	30p	£30
YK7334	Brass cups to suit	100	5p	£5
V23879	Sadikkens water based clear varnish	1 litre	£20.00	£20.00
Total:				£55.00

Authorised by: Denzil Penburthy

Delivery note	Accompanies a delivery. Goods have to be checked for quantity and quality before the note is signed. Any discrepancies are recorded on the delivery note. Goods that are not suitable (because they are not as ordered or because they are of poor quality) can be refused and returned to the supplier.

Construction Supplies Ltd
Delivery note

Customer name and address: CPF Building Co Penburthy House Falmouth Cornwall	**Delivery Date:** 16/12/14 **Delivery time:** 9am **Order number:** 26213263CPF

Item number	Quantity	Description	Unit Price	Total
X22433	100	75mm 4mm gauge countersunk brass screws slotted	30p	£30
YK7334	100	Brass cups to suit	5p	£5
V23879	1 litre	Sadikkens water based clear varnish	£20	£20

Subtotal	£55.00
VAT	20%
Total	£66.00

Discrepancies: ....

Customer Signature: ....

Print name: ....

Date: ....

Type of paperwork	Description
Delivery record	Every month a supplier will issue a delivery record that lists all the materials or hire used for that month.

Davids & Co
Monthly delivery record

Customer name and address:	Customer order date:
CPF Building Co Penburthy House Falmouth Cornwall	28th May 2014

Item number	Quantity	Description	Unit Price	Date Delivered
BS3647	2	1 tonne bag of building sand	£60	3/6/14
CM4324	12	25kg bags of cement	£224	17/6/14

Customer Signature: ....

Print name: ....

Date: ....

Invoices	Sent by a supplier. It lists the services or materials supplied along with the price the contractor is requested to pay. There will be a time limit within which to pay. Sometimes there will be a discount for quick payment or penalties for late payment.

Davids & Co
Invoice

Invoice number: 75856 **Date:** 2nd January 2014
PO number: 4700095685

Company name and address:	Customer name and address:
Davids & Co 228 West Retail Park Ivybridge Plymouth	CPF Building Co Penburthy House Falmouth Cornwall

VAT registration number: 663694542

For:

Item number	Quantity	Description	Unit Price
BS3647	2	1 tonne bag of building sand	£30
CM4324	12	25kg bags of cement	£224

Subtotal	£2748.00
VAT	20%
Total	£3297.60

Please make cheques payable to Davids & Co

Payment due in 30 days

Site diary	This will be filled out daily. It records anything of note that happens on site such as deliveries, absences or occurrences, eg delay due to the weather.

VERBAL COMMUNICATION

Often, managers, supervisors, work colleagues and trades communicate verbally. This can be face to face or over a telephone. Although this is the most common form of communication, it is also the most unreliable.

Mistakes are often made while communicating verbally. The person giving the information might make an error. The person receiving the information might misunderstand something because the information is unclear or it is noisy in the background, or because they later forget the details of the conversation.

Confusion can be minimised by recording conversations or by using a form of written communication. If there is a record it can be used for future reference and help to clear up any misunderstandings.

TAKING A TELEPHONE MESSAGE

It is a good idea to take down details of telephone calls and many companies provide documentation for this purpose. When taking a message it is important to record the following details:

- *Content*: This is the most important part of the message – the actual information being relayed. Take and write down as many details as possible.

- *Date and time*: Messages are often time sensitive, and may require an urgent response.

- *Who the message is for*: Ensure the person gets the message by giving it to them or leaving it in a place where they will find it.

- *Contact name and details*: Write down the name of the person leaving the message, and how to get back to them with a response.

UNACCEPTABLE COMMUNICATION

When communicating, it is very important to stay calm. Think about what you are going to say. An angry word will often encourage an angry response. However, keeping calm and composed will often diffuse a stressful situation. A shouting match rarely ends with a good or productive result.

There are several types of communication that are unacceptable and could result in unemployment. Unacceptable communication includes:

- aggressive communication such as swearing or using inappropriate hand gestures

An operative taking notes during a phone call

- racist or sexist comments or gestures

- showing prejudice against people with disabilities.

This type of behaviour shows a lack of respect for others and does not create a safe or pleasant working environment. It will also give your company a poor image if customers see or hear this behaviour. Acting in this way is likely to result in trouble for you and your employer and could even result in a **tribunal** and loss of employment.

Tribunal

A judgement made in court

KNOWLEDGE OF THE CONSTRUCTION INDUSTRY AND BUILT ENVIRONMENT

Buildings come in a wide variety of types in relation to appearance and methods of construction. Despite the variety of buildings, they all have design features in common. In this section we will discuss various parts of buildings and their purpose.

We will also discuss sustainable construction – how buildings can be designed to sit better within the environment, with lower pollution levels and energy requirements both during the building process and when in use.

A house with solar panels

FOUNDATIONS

Foundations serve as a good base on which to put the building. They need to be capable of carrying the weight of the building and any further load that may be put upon it. These are known as **dead loads** and **imposed loads**.

Foundations must be designed to resist any potential movement in the ground on which the building will sit. Ground conditions can vary widely. Soil samples are taken to help decide on the type of foundation to use. This usually takes the form of bore holes dug or drilled around the site. These samples are sent away for testing in a laboratory. The results will identify:

- the soil condition (clay or sandy)

- the depth of the soil

- the depth of the water table

- if any contaminations are present.

The soil condition is important: clay soil drains poorly and can move if it gets waterlogged or dries out completely. Sandy soils drain very well, but can become unstable. A foundation that is suitable for the ground type and load of the building will be designed.

Foundation

Used to spread the load of a building to the subsoil

Dead load

The weight of all the materials used to construct the building

Imposed load

Additional loads that may be placed on the structure, eg people, furniture, wind and snow

INDUSTRY TIP

The type of foundation to be used will usually be decided by the architect and a structural engineer and will be the result of tests.

TYPES OF FOUNDATION

Different types of structures, such as detached houses, high-rise and low-rise buildings, will all require different types of foundation.

Low-rise building

High-rise building

Detached house

STRIP FOUNDATIONS

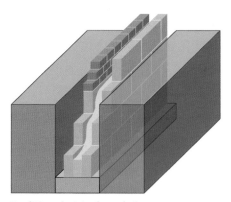

Traditional strip foundation

A strip foundation is the traditional type of foundation used for residential developments (ordinary houses). It is formed by digging a trench to the required width and depth as determined by the soil conditions and the weight of the structure. It is either filled with concrete or a layer of concrete is poured into the bottom. This layer must be a minimum of 150mm thick and is commonly 225mm thick.

Footings are brought up to the level of the **damp proof course** (DPC) using concrete blocks or bricks. These are set out from the centre of the strip of concrete in order to spread the weight evenly. A variety of specialist bricks and blocks are used for this purpose. They need to be able to resist water penetration and therefore frost damage.

It can be economical to fill the trench up to the top with concrete rather than build a substructure – this is known as trench fill. Sometimes it is necessary to build on the edge of the concrete – this is known as an eccentric foundation.

Footings

The substructure below ground level. These are projecting courses at the base of a wall

Damp proof course (DPC)

A layer of plastic that prevents damp rising up through a wall needs to be positioned at least 150mm above ground level

Engineering brick

Trench block

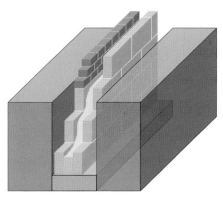

Eccentric foundation

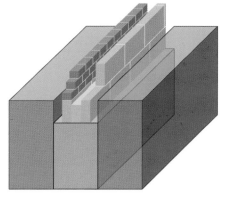

Trench fill foundation

WIDE STRIP FOUNDATIONS

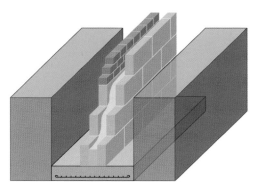

Wide strip foundation

A wide strip foundation is very similar to a strip foundation in most of its aspects. The main difference between the two is that a wide strip foundation has steel reinforcements placed within the concrete. The steel gives considerably more strength to the foundation and enables greater loads to be placed on it. Without the steel reinforcements the foundation would need to be much deeper and would need vast amounts of concrete.

PAD FOUNDATIONS

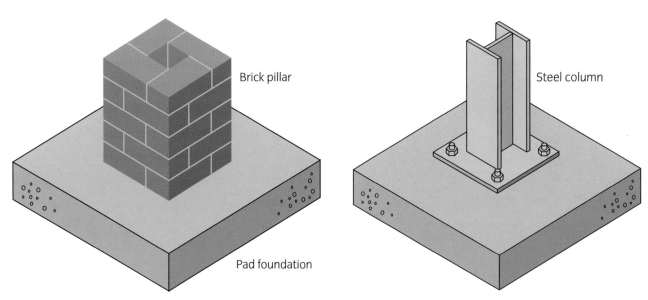

Brick pillar

Pad foundation

Steel column

Pad foundation

Pad foundation with bolts

A pad foundation is used to support a point load such as a column in a steel-framed building. This type of foundation often has bolts set into the top ready for fixing the steel.

PILE FOUNDATIONS

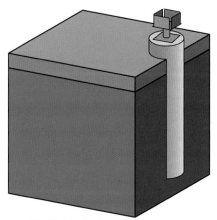

A cylindrical pile foundation

INDUSTRY TIP

Foundations are made from concrete. Concrete is made from fine and coarse aggregate (crushed stone) and cement mixed with water. Water reacts with the cement causing it to harden and lock the aggregates together. Concrete is very strong under compression (when weight is put upon it) but is weak when it is pulled (put under tension); therefore steel rods are cast into it to make it stronger.

Friction

Resistance between the surface of the concrete foundation and the soil around it

Deep piles are used to transfer the load through unsuitable soil layers into the harder layers of ground below, even down to rock if required (known as end bearing). Some piles use **friction** to provide support. This is known as skin friction. Tall buildings (and especially narrow buildings such as chimneys or towers) have large lateral forces due to side winds and pile foundations resist these forces well.

RAFT FOUNDATIONS

A raft foundation is often laid over an area of softer soil that would be unsuitable for a strip foundation. A raft foundation is a slab of concrete covering the entire base of the building; it spreads the weight of the building over a wider area but still maintains a deeper base around the load-bearing walls.

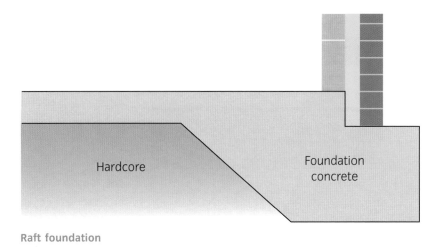

Raft foundation

FLOORS

Floors can be divided into two main categories:

- ground floors

- upper floors.

Floors are required to be load-bearing, and there is a wide variety of construction methods depending on the type of building and potential load that will be imposed upon the floor. Floors also may need to prevent:

- heat loss

- transfer of sound

- moisture penetration.

GROUND FLOORS

These may be either solid ground floors or suspended floors.

SOLID FLOORS

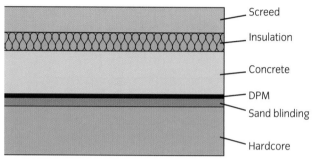

Screed
Insulation
Concrete
DPM
Sand blinding
Hardcore

Concrete floor

Hardcore

A mixture of crushed stone and sand laid and compacted to give a good base for the concrete

Damp proof membrane (DPM)

An impermeable layer that prevents damp coming up through the floor. A layer of sand known as blinding is placed below the DPM to prevent any sharp stones below piercing the membrane when the concrete is poured

Insulation

Materials used to retain heat and improve the thermal value of a building; may also be used for managing sound transfer

Solid concrete floors are laid upon **hardcore** and have a **damp proof membrane** (DPM) built into them to prevent damp coming up through the floor. **Insulation** is also laid into the floor to reduce heat loss. It is important that the insulation is not affected by the high water content of the wet concrete when being poured.

Steel reinforcement can also be used within the concrete to increase strength and reduce cracks.

HOLLOW AND SUSPENDED FLOORS

Upper floors, and some ground floors, are suspended or hollow meaning that instead of resting on the ground beneath, the load is transferred via beams to the walls. Two types of beam used are Posi-Joist and I-beam. Timber joists are usually covered with either chip board or solid timber floor boards.

Concrete with steel reinforcement

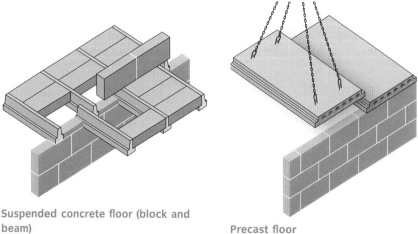

Suspended concrete floor (block and beam)

Precast floor

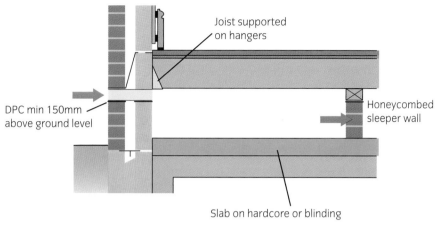

DPC min 150mm above ground level

Joist supported on hangers

Honeycombed sleeper wall

Slab on hardcore or blinding

Suspended wood floor

Posi-Joist

I-beam

UPPER FLOORS

In most domestic dwellings timber floor joists are used following the same principle as timber ground floors, while in large commercial and industrial buildings solid concrete floors are used.

WALLS

Walling for a building can usually be divided in two categories:

- external

- internal.

Walling can be load or non-load-bearing. Load-bearing walls carry the weight of the floors and roof and transfer this weight down to the foundations. A non-load-bearing wall carries no weight.

Lintel

A horizontal member for spanning an opening to support the structure above

Bond

The arrangement or pattern of laying bricks and blocks to spread the load through the wall, also for strength and appearance

Solid wall

Walls of a thickness of one brick and greater

Cavity wall

Walling built in two separate skins (usually of different materials) with a void held together by wall ties

Walls often have openings in them, eg doors and windows, which will weaken them if they are not constructed correctly. Openings require support (via a **lintel** or arch) across the top to give the wall support and **bond** it together.

EXTERNAL WALLING

External walls need to:

- keep the elements (wind and rain) out of the building
- look good
- fit into the surrounding landscape.

Several methods of construction are used for external walling. Common construction methods are:

- **solid wall**
- **cavity wall**
- timber framing.

SOLID WALLS

Solid wall

INDUSTRY TIP

Remember, cement will give chemical burns so use the correct PPE while using and mixing it.

ACTIVITY

What are the walls in the building you are sitting in made from? Why do you think these materials were chosen? What are the advantages or disadvantages of these materials?

Many older traditional buildings have solid walls made from brick, block or stone: see the following table. Solid walls have the disadvantage of being more easily penetrated by damp. Older solid walls are often upgraded by having insulating and waterproofing layers applied to the outside of the wall.

Material used	Description
Bricks 	A very traditional building material made from fired clay, calcium silicate or concrete. A standard sized brick is 215mm × 102.5mm × 65mm.
Blocks 	These are made of either concrete (crushed stone and cement) or a light-weight cement mixture. They are much bigger than a brick, and are available in various sizes. The most commonly used size is 440mm × 215mm × 100mm. Wider blocks are used for walls where a higher strength or improved sound insulation is required.
Stone 	A natural building material, which varies widely in use and appearance from area to area. Stone may be cut to a uniform size before use or used in its quarried state.
Mortar 	This is used between bricks, blocks and stones to bind them together and increase the strength of the wall. It is a mixture of soft sand and cement mixed with water and other additives if required, eg **plasticiser**, colouring or **lime**. It is important that the strength of the mortar is correct for the type of material that is being used to construct the wall. If the mortar has too much cement in the mix it will be so strong that it will not allow movement in the walling due to settlement, and the bricks could crack resulting in the wall needing to be rebuilt. Mortars are mixed to a ratio of materials, eg 1:6. The first number is the proportion of cement with the second being the proportion of sand. A typical mix ratio for masonry walling is 1:5.

Plasticiser	Lime
An additive that is used to make the mortar more pliable and easier to work with	A fine powdered material traditionally used in mortar

CAVITY WALLS

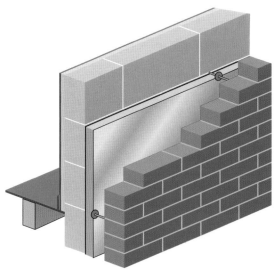

Cavity wall

Leaves

The two walls or skins that make up a cavity wall to comply with current building regulations

Building regulations

A series of documents that set out legal requirements for the standards of building work

The most common type of external walling used today is cavity wall construction.

Cavity walls are two masonry walls built side by side to form an inner and outer leaf (sometimes called skins). The **leaves** are held together with wall ties. These ties are made from rust- and rot-proof material and are built in as the walls are being constructed. The cavity is partially filled with insulation (typically fibreglass batts or polystyrene boards) as required by the **building regulations**. This reduces heat loss and saves energy.

The inner leaf usually carries any loads from the roof and floors down to the foundations and has a decorative finish on the inside, typically plaster which is either painted or papered. The outer leaf resists the elements and protects the inside of the building.

TIMBER FRAMING

Stainless steel wall tie

Structural timber frame

Plasterboard

Vapour control layer

Sheathing board

Thick insulating quilt–CFC free

Waterproof breather membrane

Ventilated cavity

Masonry outer cladding

Timber frame wall

Timber framing is both a traditional and modern method of building. Traditional buildings using timber framing were made mostly from oak with various in-fills such as brick or plaster to form the walls. Modern timber frame homes are generally built from softwood and have an outer skin of masonry or are clad with timber or plaster to waterproof the structure. Oak framing, as a traditional building method, is becoming increasingly popular again.

Elizabethan oak frame

PREFABRICATED WALLS

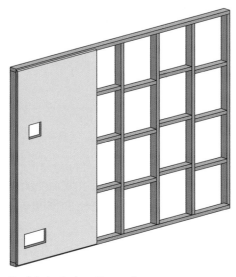

Prefabricated wall panel

There are a variety of prefabricated products available, generally made in a factory and then transported to site to be erected. These products enable quick and easy building. Often the **services** are pre-installed.

Services

Those provided by the utility companies, eg gas, electric and water

INTERNAL WALLING

Internal walling can be load or non-load bearing. Internal partitions divide large internal spaces into smaller rooms.

Internal partitions can be made from studwork or masonry. Studwork partitions consist of studs (which can be made from timber or metal) covered with a sheet material (usually plasterboard).

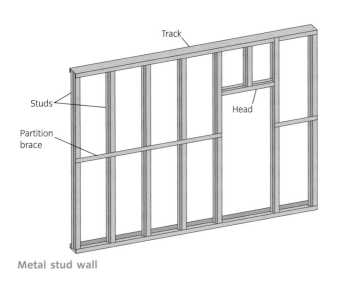

Metal stud wall

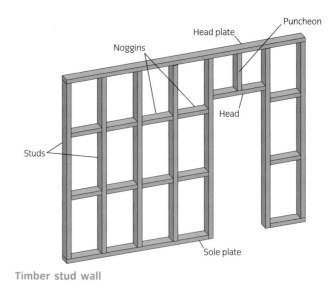

Timber stud wall

WALL FINISHES

External walls made from brick usually have no further finishes added while walls made from blocks are rendered. This is a covering of sand and cement mortar which is then finished with masonry paint.

Internal walls are most often plastered with a thin layer of gypsum plaster over plasterboard; this gives a very smooth hardwearing finish which is then usually finished with emulsion paint or papered coverings.

It is important to **size** new plaster to give a good base before applying further coverings of paint or paper coverings. This first coat of paint or paste is usually thinned down by 10% with clean water.

INDUSTRY TIP

At least two coats of emulsion are usually required for new plaster.

Size

To apply a watered-down or mist-coat of paint or paste to new plaster

ROOFS

Roofs are designed to protect the structure below by keeping the weather out. As heat rises, the roof must be well insulated to prevent heat loss and improve the energy efficiency of the building.

TYPES OF ROOFS

Roofs come in a wide variety of designs as the following pictures show.

Pitched roof

Flat roof

ROOF COMPONENTS

Roofs are commonly covered with slates or tiles. Slates are a natural product. Slate is a type of mineral that can be split into thin sheets. Artificial cement fibre slates are also available. Tiles can be made from clay or concrete.

Slate

Cement fibre slate

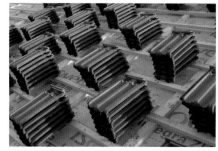

Roof tiles

A felt is laid below the roofing material to provide additional protection in case some water gets through the tiles.

Flashings are commonly made from lead and are used to provide waterproofing at joints where roofing materials meet walls and around chimneys.

Flashing providing waterproofing

Flashing around a chimney

SERVICES

Buildings contain services such as:

- water

- electricity

- gas supplies.

Additionally, waste such as sewage and water run-off have to be considered.

WATER

Water is brought into a building using pipes. Supply pipes used are usually made of plastic, with internal domestic plumbing being made from plastic or copper. Plumbing is installed using a variety of fittings including tees, elbows and reducers. Bathrooms, kitchens and most heating systems require plumbing.

Copper pipe

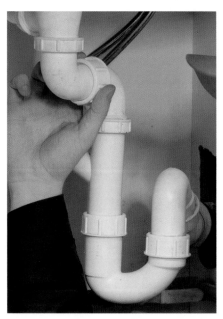

Plastic waste water pipe

Pipe fittings: Tee (left), elbow (middle) and reducer (right)

Not only is water carried into a building, it is also taken away. Rainwater run-off is collected into gutters and taken away via downpipes and drains and returned to the ground or stored for later use.

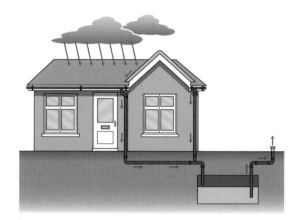

Rainwater gutter flowing down pipes and into drain

SEWAGE

Sewage is taken away from the building via drains and is disposed of either into a sewer or into a septic tank/sewage treatment plant.

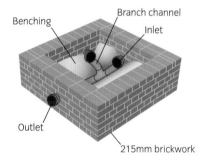

Benched drain

Septic tank

Sewage treatment plant

ELECTRICITY

Electricity is an important service provided to buildings. It powers lighting and heating. It is brought into a building through cables.

Electricity cables, switches and socket

Pipework to boiler

GAS

Gas is brought into a building using pipes. Gas powers heating systems and provides fuel for cooking.

OTHER SERVICES

Other services that are installed include telephone systems and other data cables for broadband and entertainment systems.

SUSTAINABILITY

Our planet is a fixed size. Fossil fuels, eg oil and coal, that we take from the ground are not infinite, ie they will run out one day. However, the wind, the sun and the tides will always be there. These are sustainable sources of energy.

Building materials can be sustainable if they are chosen carefully. For example, the process of manufacturing concrete uses a lot of fuel and produces a lot of carbon dioxide (a gas that some say is damaging the climate).

On the other hand, trees absorb carbon dioxide as they grow, look nice and the timber they produce is an excellent building material. However, some timber is harvested from rainforests without thought for the surrounding environment or are harvested to such an extent that certain species are close to extinction. Managed forests where trees are replanted after harvesting provide a sustainable source of timber.

Here are some questions to consider regarding sustainability in construction.

MATERIALS

- How far have the materials been brought? Locally sourced materials do not have to be transported far, thus reducing fuel use.

- Are the materials sustainably sourced? Has the timber come from a managed forest or has it come from a rainforest with no regard to the environment?

- Have the materials been manufactured with the minimum of energy and waste?

DESIGN

Is there an alternative design that can be used that uses more sustainable materials? For example, a timber frame instead of concrete block or brick.

The table below shows some sustainable materials.

Material	Image
Straw bales	
Cob (soil)	
Timber	 Redwood　Spruce　Oak
Bamboo	

ENERGY EFFICIENCY

Energy is expensive and is only going to get more expensive. As the population increases more and more energy will be required. This needs to come from somewhere and its production can be damaging to the environment. The less power a building uses the better and if it can produce its own that is a bonus. Energy-saving measures can save a lot of power consumption.

INSULATION

Light, air-filled materials tend to have better thermal insulation properties than heavy, dense materials. This means that heat cannot easily pass from one side to another and so if these materials are used in a building it will require less heating during the winter and will remain cooler during the summer.

The following drawing shows how much heat a typical home loses through different parts of the property. Better insulation will reduce the amount of heat lost.

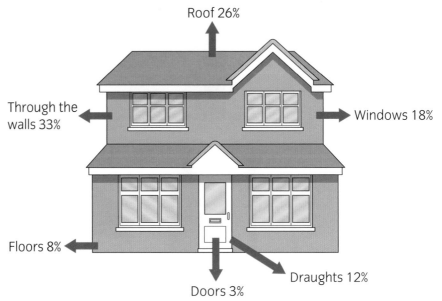

Sources of heat loss from a house

The table below shows some examples of insulation.

Type of insulation	Description
Blue jean and lambswool	Lambswool is a natural insulator. Blue jean insulation comes from recycled denim.
Fibreglass/Rockwool™	This is made from glass, often from old recycled bottles or mineral wool. It holds a lot of air within it and therefore is an excellent insulator. It is also cheap to produce. It does however use up a fair bit of room as it takes a good thickness to comply with building regulations. Similar products include plastic fibre insulation made from plastic bottles and lambswool.
PIR (polyisocyanurate)	This is a solid insulation with foil layers on the faces. It is lightweight, rigid and easy to cut and fit. It has excellent insulation properties. Polystyrene is similar to PIR. Although polystyrene is cheaper, its thermal properties are not as good.
Multifoil	A modern type of insulation made up of many layers of foil and thin insulation layers. These work by reflecting heat back into the building. Usually used in conjunction with other types of insulation.
Double glazing and draughtproofing measures	The elimination of draughts and air flows reduces heat loss and improves efficiency.

MAKING BETTER USE OF EXISTING AND FREE ENERGY

SOLAR POWER

The sun always shines and during the day its light reaches the ground (even on cloudy days). This energy can be used. A simple use of this is to allow sunlight to enter a building. With a little thought in design, light can reach deep into a building via roof lights and light tunnels. This means that internal artificial lighting requirements are reduced, therefore saving energy.

Solar panels can generate hot water or electricity, and once the cost of installation has been covered the energy they produce is totally free.

Solar panel

A panel that absorbs sun rays to generate electricity or hot water

Solar panels

HEAT SOURCE AND RECOVERY

Humans give off a fair bit of energy as they go through a normal day (eg body heat, heat given off by hairdryers, cookers, refrigerators and other activities) and this can be conserved. Modern air-conditioning systems take the heat from stale air and put it into the fresh air coming in.

Heat can be taken from the ground and even the air outside.

WIND POWER

Wind power is becoming more widespread. However some people feel that wind turbines are damaging the visual environment as they spoil the appearance of the countryside. Individuals will have their own opinion on whether wind power is a good thing or not as there are many considerations to be taken into account.

Wind turbine

WATER POWER

Water is another source of power, whether that be hydro-electric (water from dams turning turbines) or wave power, which is currently under development.

BIOMASS HEATING

Biomass heating (using wood and other non-fossil fuels) is also becoming more popular as these systems can heat water efficiently as well as heat rooms, and of course a well-insulated building does not require a lot of heating.

ENERGY-EFFICIENT GOODS AND APPLIANCES

Energy-efficient electrical goods (eg low-energy light bulbs) and appliances (eg dishwashers, fridges and washing machines) which use a reduced amount of power and less water are available.

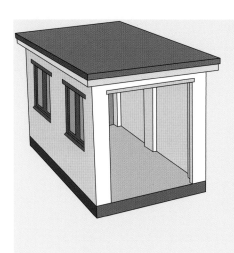

Case Study: Kayleigh

Kayleigh is to build a small single garage at the rear of a house. It must be big enough to accommodate an estate car and give enough room to allow the user to get out and walk around the car. The garage has two windows, an up-and-over door at the front and a flat roof. She has been asked to provide a plan of this garage for the client.

Draw this garage to a scale that will fit onto an A4 piece of paper. Include the window openings, the door, the thickness of the walls (which will be single block) and the piers.

Work through the following questions to check your learning.

1 What is the perimeter of this room?

Side 1: **2.5m**

Side 2: **5m**

a 5m.

b 7m.

c 15m.

d 17m.

2 A message that is passed on by word of mouth rather than in writing is

a open to interpretation

b very accurate

c easy to understand if shouted

d easily remembered.

3 What is a component drawing?

a A plan of the whole building, floor by floor.

b A section through a part of the structure.

c An elevation of the walls.

d A detail in a room.

4 What is the foundation type shown?

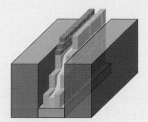

a Strip.

b Pile.

c Raft.

d Pad.

5 What is the foundation type shown?

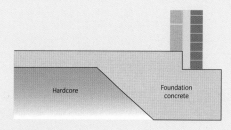

Hardcore

Foundation concrete

a Strip.

b Pile.

c Raft.

d Pad.

6 What is the component shown?

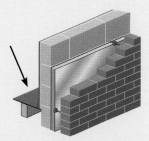

a Damp proof membrane.

b Strip foundation.

c Damp proof course.

d Raft foundation.

7 Which one of the following materials has the **best** thermal insulation properties?

a Brick.

b Concrete.

c Glass.

d Polystyrene.

8 Concrete sets because it contains

a aggregate

b sand

c hardcore

d cement.

9 A flat roof has a pitch of less than

    a 8°

    b 10°

    c 12°

    d 15°.

10 Load-bearing walls transmit weight down to the

    a foundations

    b floors

    c roof

    d windows.

Chapter 3
Unit 116: Erecting and dismantling access equipment and working platforms

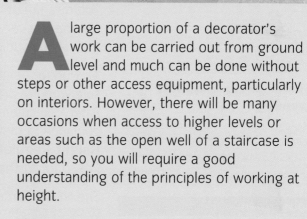

A large proportion of a decorator's work can be carried out from ground level and much can be done without steps or other access equipment, particularly on interiors. However, there will be many occasions when access to higher levels or areas such as the open well of a staircase is needed, so you will require a good understanding of the principles of working at height.

There are various types of equipment you can use for working at height. At Level 1 you will consider the use of ladders, stepladders, leaning/standing ladders, platform steps, trestle platforms, podiums/hop-ups, scaffolding and mobile tower scaffolds. This unit covers the knowledge and skills required to erect and dismantle access equipment and working platforms.

By reading this chapter you will know how to:

1 Prepare to use access equipment and working platforms.

2 Check access equipment and working platforms.

3 Erect access equipment and working platforms.

4 Dismantle and store access equipment and working platforms.

WORKING AT HEIGHT

Access equipment is equipment that will enable you to gain access to work at a higher level than you can reach from the floor. Using **access equipment** and working platforms involves working at height, which means there is a risk of injury or fatality as a result of a fall. By taking the correct precautions this risk can be minimised.

In 2011 and 2012 falls from height were the most common cause of fatalities in the construction industry, accounting for just more than half (51%) of fatal injuries to operatives.

Many of these incidents could have been avoided by using common sense and taking precautions.

Effective training in health and safety at the start of your career will embed good practice and awareness of risks. This will go a long way towards improving safety across the industry.

Too often people think that accidents will not happen to them. These may be the very people who do have accidents, though, because they give insufficient thought to ensuring safe working practice.

All work at height must be properly planned and organised to ensure safe working practice. To help you achieve this, the Health and Safety Executive (HSE) has provided a wealth of knowledge and guidance to make sure that the work complies with the **Work at Height Regulations 2005 (as amended)** (see Chapter 1, pages 24–30 for further information).

The HSE enforces the regulations where necessary in relation to the Work at Height Regulations 2005 (as amended) and helps businesses to keep people safe at work by providing guidance and information. It carries out research into accidents, safety procedures and other health, safety and welfare topics.

Throughout this chapter extensive reference is made to the HSE website, and it is highly recommended that you become familiar with this resource – the information provided is concise and easy to follow. Many of the activities in this chapter will require you to access and download information from this site.

The workforce should be properly trained in the precautions needed. Risk assessments and method statements are widely used in the construction industry to help manage the work and communicate what is required to all those involved.

Key considerations for all work at height are:

- risk assessment
- precautions required
- method statements.

ACTIVITY

Familiarise yourself with the HSE website (www.hse.gov.uk/construction) and create a favourites folder in which to store any useful HSE information.

Work at Height Regulations 2005 (as amended)

These regulations aim to prevent deaths and injuries caused each year by falls at work. They apply to all work at height where it is likely that someone will be injured if they fall

INDUSTRY TIP

Working at height is the biggest single cause of fatal and serious injuries in the construction industry, particularly on smaller projects. Over half of all deaths during work at height involve falls from ladders, scaffolds, working platforms or roof edges, or through fragile roofs or roof lights. Don't become another statistic – ensure that you properly assess risks and take a safe approach.

ACTIVITY

Look at the graph and pie chart on page 2 in Chapter 1.

1 Which year was the worst for recorded fatalities?
2 Which year shows the fewest fatalities?
3 According to this information, is the industry improving its performance in relation to fatalities?

PREPARE TO USE ACCESS EQUIPMENT AND WORKING PLATFORMS

The most important safety precaution when using access equipment and working platforms is to prepare correctly. Plan to ensure that the correct equipment is selected, the correct personal protective equipment (PPE) (see Chapter 1, pages 20–23) is being worn and that adequate consideration has been given to factors such as ground conditions, weather conditions and the height, type and duration of work.

TYPES OF ACCESS EQUIPMENT AND WORKING PLATFORMS

This section will look at the various types of access equipment available for carrying out work at height. The following equipment will be covered in detail in this section:

- ladders
- stepladders
- trestles
- podium steps
- scaffold boards
- lightweight staging
- folding work platforms or hop-ups
- tower scaffolds.

LADDERS

There are four types of ladders in common use on construction sites, usually for external activities. Occasionally an extension ladder may be used for interior work such as staircases. Remember that leaning ladders are only intended for short-term work.

Pole ladders
A pole ladder is a single-section ladder. Traditionally the stiles (the vertical parts) are made from a single tree cut vertically down the middle. Timber ladders have now often been replaced by aluminium ones. Pole ladders are typically used as access ladders to tubular scaffolding.

A pole ladder (not in use)

A standing ladder

INDUSTRY TIP

Timber ladders must not be painted, as this may hide defects. You can use a clear varnish to provide protection if required. Aluminium ladders must not be used near overhead electrical power lines.

A typical roof ladder

Standing ladders

A standing ladder is a fixed single-section ladder manufactured to length as required up to a maximum of 4m, again commonly used to access scaffold platforms. It has limited flexibility of use due to being a fixed length, as opposed to a double or triple extension ladder.

Double and treble extending ladders

These consist of two or three sections of ladder connected together by brackets and guides. Many longer extending ladders, in particular triple extending ladders, will be rope operated to enable them to be more easily raised to the operating height required.

An extending ladder

Roof ladders

Roof ladders or crawling boards should be used for access to sloping and fragile roofs. The hook should be used to provide a secure attachment to the roof ridge and the ladder should span across at least three roof supports.

Working on roofs of any type will present an additional challenge to the decorator, as it is quite common to have to carry out maintenance on items such as wooden skylights or decorate whole sections of corrugated iron roof cladding.

Roof ladders or crawling boards will be essential for gaining access over fragile roof surfaces to reach other items that require decoration. They should be long enough to span the supports (at least three rafters) and be securely placed.

Roof ladder anchorages should bear on the opposite roof and not rely on the ridge tiles for support, as these can easily break away. It is advisable to attach a safety harness and lanyard (see pages 128–129) to the ladder when working from a roof. You should also protect the edges of the roof area where you are working. For more information about the correct PPE see Chapter 1, pages 22–23.

INDUSTRY TIP

Do not use a gutter to support any ladder. It is better to use a ladder stand-off accessory to keep the ladder off the gutter when working.

A stand-off accessory

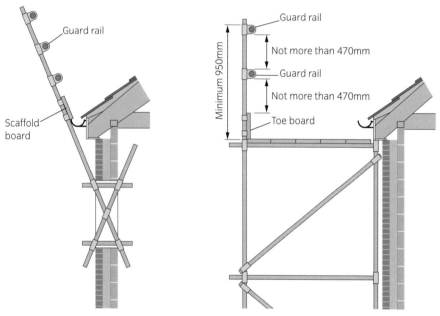

Types of edge protection for work on roofs

Ladder classification

Ladders can be made from wood, aluminium, steel or fibreglass. There are three classes of ladder stated in BS 1129 and BS 2037 for use with working platforms:

1 industrial (heavy duty)

2 light trades

3 domestic.

Many accidents happen as a result of the wrong class of ladder being used in working situations. It is best to aim to use Class 1 equipment where possible to ensure you are adequately covered for insurance purposes.

Check that the ladder you are using conforms to relevant standards. For example:

- Aluminium ladders must conform to BS 2037:1994.
- Wooden ladders must conform to BS 1129:1990.
- Aluminium and wooden ladders must conform to BS EN 131 (or EN 131).

It is recommended that you use one of the following:

- Class 1 (industrial) maximum static load: 175kg (27.5 stone)
- BS EN 131 (or EN 131) maximum static load: 150kg (23.5 stone).

INDUSTRY TIP

When you see a product with the Kitemark this means the British Standards Insititute (BSI) has independently tested it and confirmed that the product conforms to the relevant British Standard. The Kitemark symbol therefore assures consumers that the product should be safe and reliable.

Ladder classification

A ladder with Kitemark labels

The ladder should be marked with the class number, maximum weight and instructions on how to use the ladder safely – follow these instructions at all times. Using ladders without the BSI Kitemark could lead you into using equipment that has not been properly assessed against the correct standards. Equipment without the Kitemark might have insufficient strength or be an incorrect design.

Leaning ladders should be used for:

- short-duration work (maximum 30 minutes)
- light work (up to 10kg).

Safety precautions for using a leaning ladder include:

- Maintain a ladder angle of 75° – remember the 1 in 4 rule (1 unit out for every 4 units up).
- Do not work from the top three rungs – these provide a handhold.
- Always grip the ladder when climbing.
- Do not over-reach – make sure your belt buckle (navel) stays within the stiles and keep both feet on the same rung or step throughout the task.

STEPLADDERS

Stepladders are typically used for interior work, or external work where there is a level and solid base. The most common use is for domestic decoration where the work carried out is not excessively high. There are two main types of stepladder:

- platform steps
- swingback steps.

These can be made from timber, aluminium or fibreglass. Fibreglass steps may be chosen for work near electrical installations – there will be no risk of electric shock, as they contain no metal parts.

Platform steps are particularly useful because they provide a platform to keep materials and tools in easy reach while working at a safe height from the steps.

The swingback steps (shown on the opposite page) are rated Class 1 and are Kitemarked to show that they meet the appropriate standard. Timber steps are made from straight-grained softwood and usually have grooved non-slip treads. Metal tie rods are fitted under some of the treads to add stability and to stop the stiles springing apart.

Fibreglass platform stepladder

Stepladders should be used for:

- short-duration work (maximum 30 minutes)
- light work (up to 10kg).

Safety precautions for using a stepladder include:

- Do not work from the top two steps (or the top three steps for swingback/double-sided stepladders) unless you have a safe handhold on the steps.

- Avoid side-on working.

- Do not over-reach – make sure your belt buckle (navel) stays within the stiles and keep both feet on the same rung or step throughout the task.

TRESTLES

Trestles are made from timber, aluminium and fibreglass. They are made wide enough to support two scaffold boards or a lightweight staging, and make an A-frame shape when in use. They are usually tapered towards the top and should be wide enough to take two 230mm scaffold boards or one lightweight 450mm-wide staging.

Swingback steps

Timber trestle

Each side of the trestle should have at least two tie bars. The trestle is designed so that it does not collapse when it is opened, thanks to a special lipped hinge. When the hinge is fully opened the stiles lock against one another.

When using a trestle with a working platform, your risk assessment will determine whether you need to use guard rails and a toe board. You should access the platform by an additional ladder. Never use trestles as steps – the space between supports is designed to allow variation in platform height and is too wide for stepping.

Guard rails and toe boards attached to trestle platform

Adjustable-height steel trestles

Adjustable-height steel trestles

Adjustable-height steel trestles are commonly used by bricklayers and plasterers together with scaffold boards to provide low-level platforms. They can also be useful for low-level ceiling work by painters. They are best used with a handrail attachment to reduce the risk of falling. They are sometimes referred to as bandstands.

Adjustable-height steel trestles are designed to be used with four standard 225mm-wide scaffold boards or two 450mm-wide lightweight stagings. The trestles feature an adjustment pin that is permanently secured, therefore reducing the cost of replacing lost pins and wires.

It is often best to use a purpose-made handrail system to fully comply with the Work at Height Regulations 2005 (as amended), but this depends on your risk assessment for the particular task at hand.

Some manufacturers have designed purpose-made handrail and toe-board systems that can be attached either to the steel trestles themselves or to the working platform.

Handrails and toe boards are used to comply with the Work at Height Regulations 2005 (as amended)

PODIUM STEPS

Podium steps, or podiums, provide low-level height access and offer a firm platform with adjustable height, as well as a guard rail. The steps may be tubular, self-erecting or folded prior to erection, to enable them to pass through standard doors and corridors.

Podium steps

A key message from the HSE is to put tools and materials onto the podium at ground level where possible and always to close and lock the gate before starting work.

SCAFFOLD BOARDS

Scaffold boards (planks) are used to provide a working platform on trestles and tubular scaffolds. If you are using scaffold boards as a working platform you should always consider whether a safer mode of scaffolding could be used instead. Painters in particular use two boards, and this is only suitable in certain situations such as working from low-level platforms using hop-ups. For some short-term jobs such as papering ceilings it may be better to use this type of working platform, as long as there is sufficient support over the length. This will mean supports every 1.2m. Where possible a lightweight staging should be used instead.

There are four points of safety you should look for when inspecting scaffold boards prior to use. They must be:

- straight grained
- free from knots and shakes
- free from splits
- free from any decay (usually at the ends).

Scaffold boards in use on a tubular scaffold

LIGHTWEIGHT STAGING

Lightweight staging is a specially constructed timber and aluminium platform designed to span greater widths than scaffold boards. Stagings can be used without intermediate supports when used on trestles and placed directly on roof trusses.

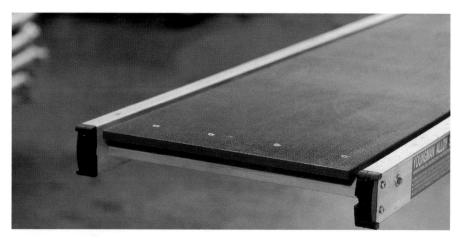

Lightweight staging

Sizes of stagings vary, and start at 450mm wide, with lengths of 1.8m to 7.3m. Stiles are reinforced with high tensile steel wire. Cross supports are every 380mm or 450mm along the length of the staging and can be reinforced with steel ties.

FOLDING WORK PLATFORM OR HOP-UP

Folding work platforms, also known as hop-ups, generally have a 600 × 600mm square platform – this is now the preferred choice of health and safety officials and is often the only size allowed on sites. Typically they are built of aluminium alloy and will withstand loads of 175kg. The fold-flat models are easily folded for moving and transporting.

Hop-up or folding work platform

This type of equipment can be used safely with lightweight platforms or scaffold boards to form a low-level working platform ideal for decorating or papering ceilings. It does not take up too much space and can be easily transported when moving to new contracts.

TOWER SCAFFOLDS

An aluminium alloy tower scaffold is often chosen by decorators, in many interior and exterior work situations. It may be static or mobile, and this aspect will be determined by the work height, type of activity and the duration of the work.

OTHER ACCESSORIES FOR USE WITH ACCESS EQUIPMENT

Sometimes it may be necessary to use another accessory or device with the piece of access equipment.

A sturdy aluminium stand-off fits directly onto your ladder, and creates a 300mm gap between the ladder and wall at the top. It reduces the risk of the ladder twisting or slipping and prevents damage to guttering. It is essential that ladders are not rested on guttering – apart from causing damage they are more likely to slip.

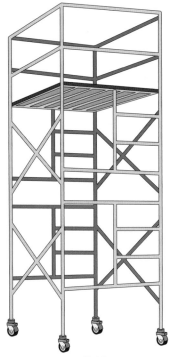

A mobile tower scaffold

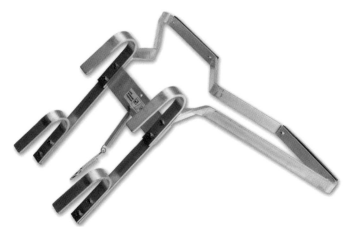

A stand-off accessory

A proprietary ladder stabiliser is used at the base of a ladder to effectively widen the base, making it less likely to slip.

Proprietary ladder stabiliser

KEEPING EQUIPMENT ON SITE

Whether equipment is hired or owned, there are a number of key points to incorporate into your planning. Ensure that you have only the required amount of equipment delivered and kept on site during operations, as this can affect costs and impact greatly on the original estimate. Unused equipment may be stolen or damaged, and must also be stored. Ladders present particular additional risks as they can be taken and used for burglary, so whenever possible equipment should either be stored in locked compounds or chained together with padlocks. The cost of insuring equipment will increase with the amount of time on site – it will need to be adequately covered for loss or damage. Finally, equipment can add greatly to the overall cost if it is no longer required but still on hire.

INDUSTRY TIP

It is always best to combine accessory devices with securing the ladder at the top for added safety.

Make sure equipment kept on site is safe and secure

GUIDANCE INFORMATION

When preparing access equipment and working platforms for use it is essential to follow all the guidance information available, and this includes manufacturers' instructions, the Work at Height Regulations 2005 (as amended) and the Provision and Use of Work Equipment Regulations 1998 (PUWER).

ACTIVITY

Look online for an example of a manufacturer's instructions for equipment for working at height. What items help to prevent falls from the items of equipment shown in the manufacturer's leaflet?

You may need to study the Work at Height Regulations 2005 (as amended) for clear guidance on the requirements for guard rails, toe boards, barriers and similar collective means of protection as defined in Schedule 2.

INDUSTRY TIP

Any height above ground level is deemed to be working at height.

Competent

Properly trained or having the sufficient skills and knowledge to carry out a task properly

MANUFACTURERS' INSTRUCTIONS

It is extremely important to obtain guidance from either the manufacturer or the hire company to enable you to comply with their recommendations. It should be possible to obtain this type of detailed information for any type of equipment you use.

WORK AT HEIGHT REGULATIONS 2005 (AS AMENDED)

The Work at Height Regulations 2005 (as amended) apply to all work at height where there is a risk of a fall which could cause personal injury.

The regulations set out three simple rules for work at height:

1 Avoid working at height if you can – if you don't need to go up there, don't.

2 If working at height cannot be avoided, prevent falls by selecting and using the right access equipment.

3 Minimise the impact of any fall. Where you cannot eliminate the risk of a fall, use equipment or other means to minimise the distance and consequences of a fall, should one occur.

Each point should be considered in the order shown.

If you are going to work at height you should be trained and **competent**, and should be able to complete the task safely and operate the selected access equipment.

The law requires employers and self-employed contractors to assess the risk of working at height and go on to organise and plan the work so it is carried out safely.

Avoid working at height if you can. Otherwise, you must try to prevent or arrest a fall if working at height is necessary.

PROVISION AND USE OF WORK EQUIPMENT REGULATIONS (PUWER) 1998

Your employer must ensure that the work equipment you are provided with meets the requirements of PUWER. They should ensure that it is:

■ suitable for use, and for the purpose and conditions in which it is to be used

- maintained in a safe condition for use so that people's health and safety are not at risk

- inspected in certain circumstances, to ensure that it is safe for use.

Any inspection should be carried out by a competent person (this could be an employee if they have the necessary skills, knowledge and experience to perform the task) and a record kept until the next inspection.

The employer should also ensure that risks created by using the equipment are eliminated or controlled as far as possible by taking appropriate measures – for example by providing suitable guards, protection devices, markings and warning devices, system control devices (such as emergency stop buttons), and personal protective equipment (PPE). There should also be measures in place such as following safe systems of work (ensuring maintenance is only performed when equipment is shut down, etc), and provision of adequate information, instruction and training about the equipment used.

A combination of these measures may be necessary depending on the requirements of the work, your assessment of the risks involved, and how practical the measures are.

This regulation will relate to the items of access equipment in use as well as the safe systems of work outlined in the method statements and risk assessments, and will be especially relevant to the use of mobile elevating work platforms (MEWPs).

ACTIVITY

What does the Health and Safety at Work Act 1974 say about an employer's responsibilities with regard to welfare? You can find this information within this chapter or by visiting hse.org.uk.

FACTORS TO CONSIDER WHEN USING ACCESS EQUIPMENT AND WORKING PLATFORMS

A range of factors must be taken into account before the final selection of access equipment. Remember, the second rule when working at height is to *prevent falls* by selecting the right equipment, and the third rule is to *minimise the impact* of a fall. You will need to consider these aspects in your risk assessment.

Consider the following in a little more detail.

GROUND CONDITIONS

Internal
Make sure internal areas are clear from any potential trip hazard or obstruction. If working on sloping areas or stairs, make sure that the equipment chosen is fit for purpose.

External

Soft, rough or uneven ground and unstable ground conditions will all need to be considered. You should also ensure that the site area is clear and tidy and that any likely obstructions or restrictions of full use are noted.

Whether the work is to be carried out inside or outside, the ground should ideally be level, firm and preferably clean and dry. Adequate steps and additional accessories may be necessary to achieve some of these key points particularly when working externally. Whatever steps are taken to achieve these conditions, the method must be safe.

For example, when levelling a ladder on a slope ensure that the wedges or blocks used cannot slip when in use. The ladder should also be secured, preferably at the top, in case anything happens that will further affect stability. Ensure that any form of ground support under any of the selected equipment will not sink into soft ground.

Ensure also that stability is not compromised when working on rough ground. This will be particularly important if using tower scaffolds – you will need to check that the structure is level after every move, and re-level it if needed.

> **INDUSTRY TIP**
>
> Always check that the surface on which your access equipment will stand is level, firm, stable, clean and dry.

HEIGHT, TYPE AND DURATION OF WORK, AND WEATHER CONDITIONS

An assessment relative to the height of the project needs to be carried out whatever the height. Remember that any height from which a person may fall is deemed to be working at height. The decision about access equipment selection should also take into account the type and duration of the work.

Further aspects to consider involve being able to access equipment freely, without obstructions. Ensure that due regard is given to the general public when working from access equipment. You may need to erect safety barriers to keep the public from being too close to the activity.

Weather conditions are also a factor. Work at height must not go ahead in unsuitable weather conditions such as rain, wind or ice.

You must ensure that if the user is not deemed competent in the use of the equipment, adequate training is carried out. All risk assessments will make the assumption that the user is competent and trained.

Consider the height, type and duration of the work and ensure you use the ladder safely

RISK ASSESSMENTS

As discussed in Chapter 1, risk assessments are an essential part of preparation.

A hazard is anything that can cause harm. Risk is the chance, high or low, that somebody will be harmed by the hazard. In order to carry out work and use equipment and materials required for a job in the safest manner, it is necessary to first undertake a risk assessment.

This is simple, but necessary. Look at what, in the planned work, could cause harm to people – you can then decide whether you have taken enough precautions, or whether more should be done to prevent harm. The aim of the risk assessment is to reduce minor, major and fatal injuries.

There are five steps to risk assessment:

1 Identify the hazards.

2 Decide who might be harmed and how.

3 **Evaluate** the risks and decide on whether the existing precautions are adequate or whether more should be done.

4 Record your findings and implement them.

5 Review your assessment and update if necessary.

Risk assessments must always address the following:

- task description and location

- expected duration

- hazards identified

- population exposed

- risks arising

- control measures.

Formalised risk assessments should always be phrased and structured in a manner that is understandable to supervisors and operatives, and is subject to ongoing review. Each control or requirement should be explained to operatives before any safety-critical task, operation or process is started.

It is your employer's responsibility to provide a risk assessment for many tasks that you may be involved in, and working at height is one of them.

A risk assessment

Evaluate

Consider something in order to make a judgement about it

ACTIVITY

Undertake Step 1 of the risk assessment process by listing all the hazardous activities and materials involved in using an extension ladder, working at a height of 3m. How can we minimise the risks associated with working from a ladder?

ACTIVITY

Download or look at the following document referring to risk assessments on the HSE website: http://www.hse.gov.uk/risk/fivesteps.htm.

Make sure you are familiar with the content – it may be a useful document to access in future.

ENVIRONMENTAL AND HEALTH AND SAFETY REGULATIONS

Producing a risk assessment not only helps to identify risks and hazards, but is also a legal requirement. You have seen how guidance information should be followed when preparing to use access equipment and working platforms, but there are also a number of additional regulations.

In addition to the Work at Height Regulations 2005 (as amended), and the Provision and Use of Work Equipment Regulations 1998 (PUWER), the construction industry must conform to a range of regulations including the Health and Safety at Work Act 1974 (HASAWA), the Management of Health and Safety at Work Regulations 1999, the Manual Handling Operations Regulations 1992, the Construction, Design and Management (CDM) Regulations 2007 and the Environmental Protection Act 1990. More detailed information about some of these regulations can be found in Chapter 1.

Two important environmental legislations you need to know are the Management of Health and Safety at Work Regulations 1999 and the Environmental Protection Act 1990. The Management of Health and Safety at Work Regulations 1999 generally makes more explicit what employers are required to do to manage health and safety under the Health and Safety at Work Act. Like the Act, they apply to every work activity. The main requirement for employers is to carry out a risk assessment. Employers with five for more employees need to record the significant findings of the risk assessment.

The Environmental Protection Act 1990 deals with issues relating to waste on land, defining all aspects of waste management. Local authorities have a responsibility to collect and segregate waste and construction companies have a responsibility to devise waste management plans that enable waste to be segregated and disposed of correctly. Equally as individuals, we also have a duty to ensure waste and particularly hazardous waste is dispose of correctly.

CHECK ACCESS EQUIPMENT AND WORKING PLATFORMS

It is very important that the access equipment is inspected to ensure that it is free of defects and other potential hazards. The end user must be satisfied with the good working order and condition of the equipment before it is used. Components of access equipment and working platforms must be checked regularly, and the person checking should know how to report any hazards presented by faulty equipment.

INSPECTION TIME PERIODS

Access equipment and working platforms must be inspected at the following times:

- pre-erection
- post-erection
- handover
- during **inclement** weather conditions
- during major alterations
- every seven days
- post-accident and -incident.

At all these stages there may be alterations to the condition of the equipment. At this level you will focus on pre-erection inspections.

The following are typical inspection documents that can be used to carry out safety checks to the access equipment to be used and identify any potential hazards. During your training you should be overseen by a competent person who can give you guidance in completing these simple documents.

It is important to check equipment before use

Inclement

Severe or harsh, ie cold, wet and stormy weather

INDUSTRY TIP

Inspections should be carried out by someone who is trained and competent.

Basic pre-use checklist

Employers and employees and all users of ladders should be able to answer 'Yes' to each of the questions, or to the alternative given, before a job is started.

Type of ladders: _____ Ref./Identification number: _____

Description of where used: _____

By whom: _____

Date: _____

(a)	Is a ladder, stepladder, etc the right equipment for the work?	YES [ ] NO [ ]
(b)	If so, is the equipment in good condition and free from slippery substances?	YES [ ] NO [ ]
(c)	Can the leaning ladder be secured at the top?	YES [ ] NO [ ]
(d)	If not, can it be secured at the bottom?	YES [ ] NO [ ]
(e)	If the ladder cannot be secured, will a second person stationed at the base provide sufficient safety?	YES [ ] NO [ ]
(f)	Is the top rung level with the platform?	YES [ ] NO [ ]
(g)	Is there an adequate handhold at the place of landing?	YES [ ] NO [ ]
(h)	Are there platforms at 9m maximum intervals?	YES [ ] NO [ ]
(i)	Is the ladder angle correct?	YES [ ] NO [ ]
(j)	Is the support for the ladder adequate at both the upper point of rest and the foot?	YES [ ] NO [ ]
(k)	Is the ladder properly positioned?	YES [ ] NO [ ]
(l)	If it is necessary to carry tools and equipment, has provision been made for carrying them so the user can keep their hands free for climbing?	YES [ ] NO [ ]
(m)	If an extension ladder is used, is there sufficient overlap between sections?	YES [ ] NO [ ]
(n)	On the stepladder, are the stays, chains or cords in good condition?	YES [ ] NO [ ]
(o)	Can the stepladder be placed sufficiently near the work on a firm level surface?	YES [ ] NO [ ]
(p)	Is the ladder clear of overhead electric cables?	YES [ ] NO [ ]

Condition checklist

Below is a simple checklist that could be used for checking the condition of ladders, steps and trestles.

LADDERS		
(6-MONTHLY INSPECTION)		
Department/Location: Ladder No:		TICK OK
Inspected by:		
NO: ITEM:	**Condition**	☑
STRAIGHT LADDER		
1.1 Loose rungs (move by hand)		
1.2 Loose nails, screws, bolts, etc		
1.3 Loose mounting brackets, etc		
1.4 Cracked, broken, split stays		
1.5 Splinters on stays or rungs		
1.6 Cracks in metal stays		
1.7 Bent metal stays or rungs		
1.8 Damaged/worn non-slip devices		
1.9 Wobbly		
STEPLADDER		
1.10 Wobbly		
1.11 Loose/bent hinge spreaders		
1.12 Stop on spreaders broken		
1.13 Loose hinges		
EXTENSION LADDER		
1.14 Defective extension locks		
1.15 Defective rope pulley		
1.16 Deterioration of rope		
TRESTLE LADDER		
1.17 Wobbly		
1.18 Defective hinges		
1.19 Defective hinge-spreaders		
1.20 Stop on spreads defective		
1.21 Defective centre guide for extension		
1.22 Defective extension locks		
FIXED LADDER		
1.23 Ladder cage		
1.24 Deterioration in all metal parts		
GENERAL		
1.25 Painting of wooden ladders		
1.26 Identification		
1.27 Storage		

Before any form of access platform or equipment is used, the components should be checked for damage and wear and tear.

Any faults found should be labelled on the equipment, and it should be taken out of service and reported.

COMPONENTS OF ACCESS EQUIPMENT AND WORKING PLATFORMS

Knowing the component parts of the access equipment and working platforms that you use will help you to identify any hazards or defects with the equipment.

Typically, components to check will be as shown in the illustration below and in the table on the following page.

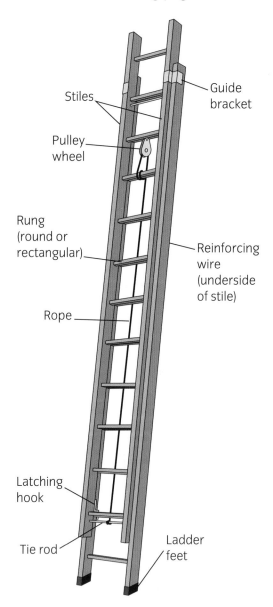

Stiles

Guide bracket

Pulley wheel

Rung (round or rectangular)

Reinforcing wire (underside of stile)

Rope

Latching hook

Tie rod

Ladder feet

Parts of a ladder

Component	Description
Stiles	The two long sides of the ladder in which the rungs are housed or fixed.
Rungs	The parts of the ladder that are stood on – usually round or a rectangular shape.
Tie rods	These are made from steel. They hold the stiles rigid and keep them from spreading and the joints becoming loose. They can be fitted under every rung but are typically set at eight-rung spacings. On timber ladders these may need to be tightened if the ladder has been allowed to become over-dry.
Scaffold boards	Used to provide a working platform, a minimum of two boards or 430mm wide. Maximum overhang is four times the thickness of the board but not less than 50mm. Scaffold boards should normally be supported at least every 1.2m.
Platform staging	Lightweight staging is a specially constructed timber and aluminium platform for spanning greater widths than scaffold boards. Stagings can be used without intermediate supports when used on trestles and placed directly on roof trusses.
Ropes	Hemp or synthetic material rope cord that is used for raising and lowering extension ladders.
Swingbacks	This is the name given to the rear frame of a pair of swingback steps. A framed back support is hinged to the back of the steps to provide support and enable the steps to be set at the correct angle.
Locking bars	These are used instead of ropes at the bottom of aluminium trestles. When fully extended and locked in position they ensure that cross members are level.
Non-slip inserts	These are typically rubber inserts inserted into the bottom of the stiles of aluminium ladders or steps to prevent them slipping.
Clip-on platforms	Purpose-made handrail and toe board systems that can be clipped onto either the steel trestles themselves or to the working platform.
Cross rails	**Cross member** parts of a trestle, usually spaced 500mm apart but staggered on each frame to enable a 250mm rise for greater flexibility of platform height. They are housed or fixed to stiles. Lightweight staging will rest on these bearers.

CHECKING LADDERS, STEPS AND TRESTLES

The following maintenance checklist can be used to ensure that access equipment is safe to use. The same checklist can be used after use and before storage.

- Check that the stiles (uprights) are not bent, bowed, twisted, dented, cracked, corroded or rotten.

  - ☐ **Do not use the ladder** if they are bent, damaged or split – the ladder could buckle or collapse.

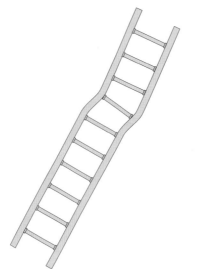

Stiles bent out of shape

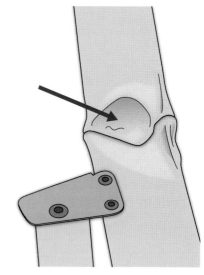

Damaged stile

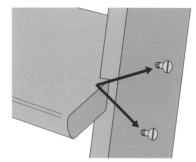

Loose fittings on a step

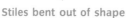

A damaged rung

- Check that the stiles around the fixing points for other components are in good condition.
- Check that the fixings (usually rivets, screws or bolts) are not missing, loose or corroded.
  - ☐ **Do not use the stepladder** if the fixings are loose – it could collapse.
- Check that rungs are not missing, loose, excessively worn, corroded or damaged.
  - ☐ **Do not use the ladder** if rungs are bent, missing or loose – the ladder could become unstable.
- Check that rung hooks are not missing, damaged, loose or corroded, and that they engage properly on the rungs.
- Check that the guide brackets are not missing, damaged, loose or corroded and that they engage properly on mating stiles.
- Check that feet are not missing, loose, excessively worn, corroded or damaged.
  - ☐ **Do not use the ladder** if they are missing, worn or damaged – the ladder could slip.

Safety feet on a ladder missing

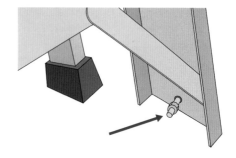

Safety foot missing from steps

THE CITY & GUILDS TEXTBOOK

- Check that the entire ladder is free from contaminants (eg dirt, mud, paint, oil or grease).

- Check that locking catches (if fitted) are not damaged or corroded and that they function correctly.

  ☐ **Do not use the stepladder** if they are bent or the fixings are worn or damaged – the ladder could collapse.

- Check that the stepladder platform is not damaged.

  ☐ **Do not use the stepladder** if it is split or buckled – the ladder could become unstable or collapse.

- Check that the steps or treads are safe to use.

  ☐ **Do not use the stepladder** if the treads are contaminated – they could be slippery.

Important: If the ladder or stepladder fails any of the above checks, you should not use it.

All timber parts can become dry and prone to splitting, and joints may become loose.

Ropes can become frayed or worn, hinges can become stiff in use, and the screws and bolts that hold them in place may become loose.

Loose fittings

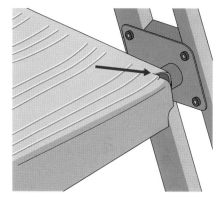

Damaged platform on steps

HAZARD IDENTIFICATION

It is important that you are not only aware of the hazards associated with access equipment and working platforms, but that you also know the correct methods of reporting these hazards. Hazard identification is an important aspect of risk assessment.

The following points may be considered when identifying hazards:

- falls from height (people/materials)

- slips

- trips

- cuts and abrasions

- faulty equipment

- altered/removed parts.

In the following table there have been a number of additional hazards identified that are specific to the task in hand. This information will help to identify some of the typical hazards and risks associated with working at height and show what control measures can be put in place.

Task	Hazard	Risk	Control
Using ladders as a means of access from one level to another	■ Falling from the ladder. ■ Displacement of the ladder. ■ Failure of the ladder.	■ Major or lost-time injury to head, legs, arms or internal organs.	■ Inspect the ladder for visible defects before use. ■ Ensure that the ladder is secured to the landing point and if necessary at the base. ■ Use both hands when climbing up or coming down the ladder.
Working at or adjacent to a leading edge	■ A person or persons falling from one level to another. ■ Materials falling from height.	■ Fatal, major or lost-time injury. ■ Fatal, major or lost-time injury due to being struck by falling material(s).	■ Check the work location prior to commencement. ■ Confirm the positioning, integrity and suitability of the barrier. ■ If considered unsuitable, stop and have the assembly upgraded.
Working from bandstand scaffolds or hop-ups	■ A person or persons falling from the work platform. ■ Structural failure of the assembly.	■ Major or lost-time injury.	■ Authorisation for the use of bandstand scaffolds or hop-ups to be recorded in the method statement. ■ The platform height must not exceed 1.2m. ■ Overloading must be prohibited. ■ Safe ladder access point must be established.
Working from tubular steel or proprietary system scaffolds	■ Structural failure or displacement of the scaffold. ■ Failure of scaffold boards. ■ Personnel falling from the scaffold. ■ Materials falling from the scaffold.	■ Fatal, major or lost-time injury. ■ Fatal, major or lost-time injury due to being struck by falling material(s).	■ Scaffold or section of the scaffold to be inspected by an authorised person to confirm suitability and structural integrity prior to use. ■ Inspection sequence and method to be in accordance with company health and safety procedures. ■ Work from incomplete or suspect scaffolding prohibited.

Task	Hazard	Risk	Control
Working from steps or ladders	■ Failure of the steps/ladder. ■ Falling from the steps/ladder. ■ Over-reaching from the steps/ladder.	■ Fatal, major or lost-time injury.	■ Task to be subject to a specific risk assessment. ■ If authorised, for short-duration, light-duty tasks only. ■ Ladder to be footed and secured. ■ Lone working prohibited.
Working from steps in the vicinity of energised electrical apparatus or apparatus capable of being energised	■ Making contact with or causing an arc from the apparatus to the steps.	■ Electric shock or flashover – fatal or major injury. ■ Damage to equipment.	■ Steps made from non-conductive material only may be used in such locations.
Working from or resting ladders/steps against cable trays or *in-situ* pipework	■ Failure of the tray suspension system. ■ Failure of or damage to *in-situ* pipework.	■ Fall from height – fatal or major injury. ■ Uncontrolled release of liquid, gas or other substance being piped – major injury and/or damage.	■ Working from suspended cable trays prohibited. ■ Resting ladders/steps against *in-situ* services prohibited unless authorised by the service owner.
Issuing or using safety harnesses for the purpose of arresting the fall of a person	■ Use of untrained personnel. ■ Failure to inspect the system before issue/use. ■ Attaching the system to an unapproved fixing point.	■ Fatal, major or lost-time injury in the event of a malfunction of the system or the anchorage point.	■ Safety harnesses to be issued to and used by trained personnel only. ■ The task and location shall be subject to a specific risk assessment. ■ The system shall be subject to a record-keeping regime as prescribed by the manufacturer.

REPORTING HAZARDS

If any hazards are identified, it is important to report the issue to the supervisor or manager, who can then arrange to have this remedied. This applies particularly to trip or slip hazards, faulty equipment or other aspects that will require immediate action to avert an accident. Using hazard checklists for recording hazard information will make it possible to check that remedies have been carried out.

INDUSTRY TIP

Remember that faulty or altered equipment should be taken out of use until it has been repaired or passed as safe for use.

ACTIVITY

You will be using a scaffold platform to apply paper to a ceiling in an empty room 3.5m long by 2.4m wide. List the equipment you plan to use, and complete a hazard identification record.

HAZARD IDENTIFICATION RECORD
Mobile access scaffold tower inspection

The Work at Height Regulations 2005 (as amended) require that mobile access scaffold towers are inspected after assembly and before use by a competent person. The regulations also require that a written report of that inspection is completed before the person goes off duty, and that a copy of the report is given to the person for whom the report was completed within 24 hours. The following section deals with the items that should be included when inspecting towers. It will be important to know what to look out for to ensure that you are going to be safe.

Scaffold tower inspection book

Inspection tags

The Provision and Use of Work Equipment Regulations (PUWER) 1998 and the Work at Height Regulations 2005 (as amended) make it a legal requirement to ensure that all commercial scaffold towers are safe to use. The photo above shows such a system in use. In order to comply with the regulations the scaffold is inspected on a regular and systematic basis.

Mobile access towers must be inspected by a competent person to ensure that they are not incorrectly erected or damaged. This should be someone with the experience, knowledge and appropriate qualifications to enable them to identify any risks and decide on the measures required to control the risks. The requirement for inspection is different for small towers under 2m, and for towers of 2m and above.

If the working platform is less than 2m in height, the tower must be inspected:

- after assembly in any position

- after any event liable to have affected its stability

- at suitable intervals, depending on frequency and conditions of use.

If the working platform is 2m or more in height, it must be inspected:

- after assembly in any position

- after any event liable to have affected its stability

- at intervals not exceeding seven days.

A new inspection and report are not required every time a mobile access tower is moved to a new location on the same site. However, if guard rails or other components have to be removed to enable the tower to be moved past an obstruction, then a pre-use check should be undertaken by a trained and competent user to make sure the tower has been reinstated correctly.

Here is a safety checklist to use with mobile tower scaffolds:

- Ensure that all brace claws operate and lock correctly prior to erection.

- Inspect components prior to erection.

- Inspect the tower prior to use.

- Ensure that the tower is upright and level.

- Ensure that **castors** are locked and legs correctly adjusted.

- Fit diagonal braces.

- Fit stabilisers/outriggers as specified.

- Locate platforms and ensure that windlocks are on.

- Locate toe boards.

- Check that guard rails are fitted correctly.

All towers must be inspected following assembly and then at suitable regular intervals by a competent person. In addition, if the tower is used for construction work and a person could fall 2m or more from the working platform, it must be inspected following assembly and then every seven days. Stop work if the inspection shows it is not safe to continue, and put right any faults.

ACTIVITY

Answer the following questions with the help of books, your own notes and Internet research:

1   State the purpose of a hazard identification record.
2   List the duties of an employer and an employee under the Work at Height Regulations 2005 (as amended).
3   State four essential safety checks to be made for any access equipment.

Mobile tower scaffold

Castors

The swivelling wheels fixed to a scaffold frame

ERECT ACCESS EQUIPMENT AND WORKING PLATFORMS

Once you have satisfied the preparation requirements and equipment checks you will be in a position to erect the access equipment or working platform for use.

In addition to selecting the correct equipment and ensuring it is safe to use, you will need to select the correct personal protective equipment (PPE) before starting to erect the equipment. It will be extremely important that proper guidance and training are followed and this may need to be practised before carrying out tasks in the real environment.

PERSONAL PROTECTIVE EQUIPMENT (PPE)

You must ensure that you are wearing the required PPE when erecting access equipment and working platforms. As a minimum, this is a hard hat, high visibility (hi-viz) jacket, gloves and toe-cap boots (see Chapter 1, pages 22–23). For certain tasks you may also be required to wear a full body harness with attached lanyard. This section will cover the typical items of protective equipment used or required when working at height in addition to those listed in Chapter 1. Many are now a basic requirement on new building construction sites, where gloves and goggles are also required as well as helmet, hi-viz jacket and safety boots.

SAFETY HARNESS

This is a full harness made from nylon that is provided to enable a safety lanyard to be attached. It provides a means of fall protection when working on projects such as bridges or high roof structures.

Fall arrest harness

LANYARD OR SAFETY LINE AND CLIP

A lanyard is attached to a safety harness as well as to a secure anchor point and a safety rope. This safety rope can be of fixed length or may incorporate an **inertia-operated anchor device** that locks to prevent a fall when weight is applied to it. This equipment will typically be worn as part of a fall protection system.

Inertia-operated anchor device

A safety device attached to a safety line that operates in the same way as car seat belts

Fall arrest equipment with inertia system

FALL PROTECTION SYSTEM

If operatives will be exposed to fall hazards that you cannot eliminate, you will need to ensure that if operatives do fall, they are not injured. A fall protection system is designed to prevent or **arrest** such falls. Typically you will be required to wear a safety harness and an inertia-operated safety lanyard in this situation.

Arrest

In this situation, arrest means to safely stop a person who is already falling

Types of fall protection systems

There are six general fall protection system types, as shown in the table below.

Fall protection system	Use
Personal fall arrest system (PFAS)	Arrests a fall.

Fall protection system	Use
Personal fall restraint system 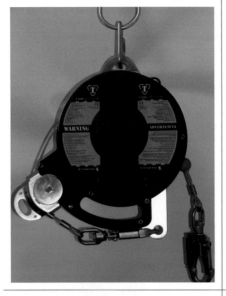	Prevents a fall.
Positioning device system 	Positions an operative and limits a fall to 60cm.
Guard-rail system 	Prevents a fall.
Safety-net system 	Arrests a fall.

Fall protection system	Use
Warning-line system for roofing work 	Warns an operative of a fall hazard.

MANUAL HANDLING

In addition to ensuring that you are wearing the correct PPE, it is essential to remember the Manual Handling Operations Regulations 1992, covered in Chapter 1, pages 17–19. Remember that you should not lift anything that you are not capable of lifting on your own, and make sure that you lift with a straight back and bent legs. Make sure too that the items of equipment you are lifting or carrying are well balanced and are moved or carried without twisting your body.

MECHANICAL HANDLING

As a decorator you are unlikely to be required to load access equipment with particularly heavy items. However, you may be required to work on scaffolding where loading is taking place ie using a forklift or telescopic handler. It will be the responsibility of the foreman or site agent to ensure that no overloading occurs. More detail on this topic can be found in Chapter 1.

A forklift

A telescopic handler

Mechanical hoist

Mechanical equipment may be used for transporting materials. Passenger hoists are also used for transporting operatives to work on high scaffolds.

None of these pieces of equipment should be misused and should only be operated by trained and competent personnel.

ERECTING ACCESS EQUIPMENT AND WORKING PLATFORMS

As mentioned on page 25 and discussed on page 115 a risk assessment must be carried out when erecting or using access equipment and working platforms. You should also always follow the manufacturer's instructions when erecting equipment.

Before using the equipment it is good practice to undertake an additional check, as detailed on pages 121–123.

You also need to adhere to current environmental and health and safety regulations, including the Health and Safety at Work Act 1974, the Management of Health and Safety at Work Regulations 1999, the Provision and Use of Work Equipment Regulations 1998 (PUWER) and the Work at Height Regulations 2005 (as amended).

LADDERS AND STEPLADDERS

Before erecting a ladder or stepladder, remember to check that it is safe to use. Look back at the checklist on pages 118–119.

The sequence for erecting and moving a ladder is as follows.

STEP 1 When setting up the ladder for use, push the base of the ladder into the bottom of the wall and start lifting as shown. Keep your back straight and bend from the knees.

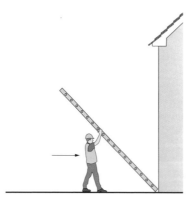

STEP 2 Continue to push the ladder into an upright position. Ensure that you only lift a weight that you are able to hold.

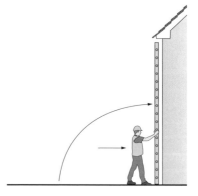

STEP 3 Continue lifting until the ladder is in a near-vertical position, then start to pull the bottom of the ladder out while the ladder rests on the wall.

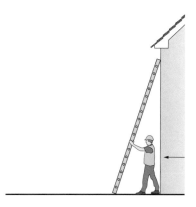

STEP 4 Once the ladder is in an inclined position it may be easier to move to the back of the ladder to set the correct angle.

STEP 5 Once you have finished using the ladder in one position, if you need to move the ladder a short distance to another position you can hold the ladder against your shoulder to get the right balance. Place your hands one above the other to enable lifting and to maintain balance. This method should only be used when moving short distances.

You should take the ladder down and carry it horizontally at your side. This will help you to keep your balance, and will make the ladder easier to handle. Lowering the ladder is the reverse of the method shown for putting it up.

If you have to move a ladder while it is up, be very careful and do it slowly. It is easy for an extended ladder to throw you off balance or knock something down. It is a good idea to have someone else give you a hand. Longer ladders and three-stage extension ladders in particular are likely to require more than one person to lift them into position.

The correct angle for a ladder is 75° or a ratio of 1:4 – in other words, for every four units up the ladder must be one unit out.

ACTIVITY

Make sure that the methods of erecting and moving ladders have been demonstrated to you. Practise them to ensure that you can carry out these activities out safely.

ACTIVITY

If a ladder is 4m long, how far should it be positioned from the wall at its base?

Answer: 1m

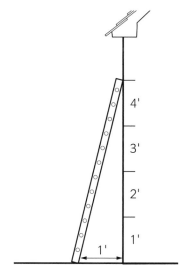

The correct angle for a ladder is 1:4

A ladder should not be used on a side slope of more than 16° or a back slope of more than 6°.

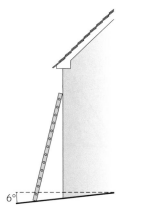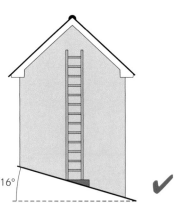

Ladder showing maximum angles at 6° on a back slope and 16° on a slide slope

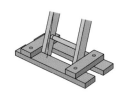

The top of a ladder secured by lashing

An anti-slip device

Ladders should always be secured when in use in one of the following ways:

- At the top, either lashed to a fixed item or to eyebolts fixed in the wall.

- At the bottom, preferably tied to stakes or secured/stabilised with a range of proprietary accessories.

- The least effective method is to have a person standing at the foot of the ladder to help stabilise it and prevent it slipping. This method is only appropriate for short-term use.

It is essential also to obtain a good grounding for the feet of a ladder. There are many devices available to assist with the stability of the ladder at ground level.

Anti-slip device with a 2000 pin base and a rubber grip

Anti-slip devices can be used on grass, oily concrete, tarmac, decking, paving slabs, gravel, snow and even ice. Some models come with a pin base which engages with the ground surface and a rubber shoulder to rest the ladder against (see the image in the margin).

They are primarily designed to prevent slip, but in some cases will also act as stabilisers or mini outriggers to effectively widen the base and increase the stability of the ladder in use. However, they do not replace the need to secure the ladder at the top or bottom.

Set-up for leaning ladders

- Do a daily pre-use check (include ladder feet).
- Secure the ladder.
- Ensure that the ground is firm and level.
  - ☐ The maximum safe ground side slope is 16° (level the rungs with a suitable device).
  - ☐ The maximum safe ground back slope is 6°.
- Have a strong upper resting point (not plastic guttering).
- Floors should be clean, not slippery.

Set-up for stepladders

- Do a daily pre-use check (include stepladder feet).

- Ensure there is space to fully open the stepladder.

- Use any available locking devices.

- Ensure that the ground is firm and level.

- Floors should be clean, not slippery.

Rules for using ladders and stepladders

- The ladder should be fit for purpose and free from defects.

- The ladder should be clear of excavations, and not causing a hazard or placed where it may be struck or dislodged. Place barriers around the foot of the ladder where necessary.

- The ladder should be secured at the top where possible, or at the base by lashing. If it is not lashed, someone at the base must stand with one foot on the bottom rung (footing the ladder) while holding the stiles with both hands. This is only permissible if the ladder is being used for short-term work.

- Do not secure ladders by the rungs. Lashing should be around the stiles

- The ladder should not rest against fragile surfaces. Use bracing boards for window openings.

- The ladder should be set at an angle of 75° (four units up to one unit out).

- Scaffold tubes should not interfere with the footing of the person on the ladder.

- There should be only one person on a ladder at any one time, except when an additional person is footing the ladder.

- Footwear should be suitable – either stout shoes or safety footwear, to enable the wearer to withstand being on the ladder rungs. Should anything be dropped on the feet the footwear will provide protection.

- Both hands should be free when climbing to enable three points of contact.

- Always face the ladder when climbing or descending.

- Remember: over-reaching leads to over-balancing.

- Do not attempt to reposition the ladder by 'jumping' it (while standing on the ladder). This is very dangerous and risks the ladder toppling over.

- Set stepladders at right angles to the work.

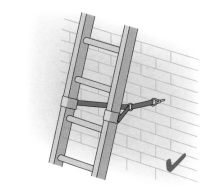

Secure ladders by lashing around the stiles, not the rungs

Safety boots

- Ladders should always be stored flat to avoid twisting (see pages 140–141 for more storage information).

- Tools that require the use of both hands should not be used when working from a ladder.

PODIUM STEPS

Rules for using podium steps

- Podium steps must be erected on a firm level base.

- Check that all components are free from damage to ensure correct function and use.

- Check for overhead hazards where work is to be carried out.

- The podium steps must be erected in accordance with the manufacturer's instructions. Once erected, check the podium steps to ensure that all components, hooks and locking mechanisms fit and operate correctly.

- Access must be via the steps and serrated rungs where provided. Climbing up the outside of the podium steps is not permitted.

- Podiums are provided with swivel castors. Each castor is fitted with a brake, and all brakes must be 'on' when the steps are in use. This means that people and materials should not be on the platform when the podium steps are moved.

Podium steps in use

- Move the podium steps by pushing horizontally near the base. Make sure the route is clear at ground level and up to the height of the steps before starting to push.

- Take extra care if outriggers are in use. Outriggers are only intended to provide extra stability for the podium steps. Raise outriggers by the minimum amount possible when moving the steps. If in doubt about stability, get help to steady the frame while you are moving the steps.

- Check the safe working load for the working platform. Do not overload the steps – they are intended to carry one person and hand tools. Do not store materials on the steps.

- Always work with the guard-rail gate fully closed and in the locked position. Never work with the gate open, as there is a high risk of falling from height.

Podium steps in use

- Ladders must not be leant against podium steps or stood on the platform to gain extra height. Never stand on the frame to gain extra height.

- When working on podium steps, pushing or pulling work actions such as pipe wrenching or cable pulling must be undertaken with thought given to position to avoid the risk of the podium steps overturning.

- Work end-on if possible, and *never* over-reach when working.

- Do not use another contractor's podium steps. They may not be correctly erected, or the equipment may be damaged or incomplete. Only use podium steps provided by your company and erected by a competent person.

- If in doubt about any application, refer to the supplier or manufacturer for advice.

TRESTLES

Trestles have splayed feet for stability and a telescopic adjustment mechanism that allows for height adjustment in approximately 100mm increments. Position steel trestles a maximum of 1.2m apart. This distance is between the top support bars, and not the base. Remove or retract both trestle pins, raise the trestle and re-insert both pins to the nearest location hole. Always fully insert each pin.

Trestle

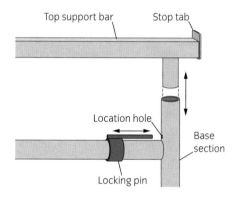

Steel trestle parts

With help, position each scaffold board on the trestles, then adjust the boards to bring them central to the trestle. The board must lie flat on the trestle without the possibility of rocking and with a minimum of four times the board's thickness overhanging at each end.

Ensure that you do not attempt to stand on the overhang areas, as the board may tip. A handrail system can help to prevent you from stepping into this area.

TOWER SCAFFOLDS

Tower scaffolds should ideally only be used on solid ground surfaces. If towers must be used on uneven or soft ground, suitable scaffold boards or similar should be used to ensure that the tower does not sink or topple over.

Tower scaffold

ACTIVITY

Visit the HSE site: http://www.hse.gov.uk/construction/safetytopics/scaffold.htm.

Download or refer to the guidance leaflet on tower scaffolds called 'Tower scaffolds CIS 10'.

List the recommendations given in this leaflet for the moving of a tower.

INDUSTRY TIP

Always lift with your back straight, elbows in, knees bent and your feet slightly apart.

Always climb up the inside of the tower, making use of the built-in ladders. Whenever tower scaffolds are moved, make sure that any material is not likely to fall off the platform and ensure that it is re-checked for level and adjusted where necessary.

The height of a mobile tower should not exceed three times the length of the shortest side, and a static freestanding tower should not exceed three-and-a-half times the shortest side when used internally.

DISMANTLE AND STORE ACCESS EQUIPMENT AND WORKING PLATFORMS

The earlier sections in this chapter have dealt with the preparation, inspection, erection and use of access equipment and working platforms. This final section deals with dismantling and storage procedures.

DISMANTLING ACCESS EQUIPMENT AND WORKING PLATFORMS

In nearly every case the dismantling of a piece of equipment will follow much the same as the erection procedure. Ladders, stepladders, trestles and podium steps will all need to be lowered safely to the ground while ensuring that they do not strike any obstacles. It is also important to ensure that no person is endangered during dismantling. It is best to try to maintain a clear workspace while the dismantling process is going on. This is especially important when dismantling tower scaffolds – this activity will require at least two people. Do make sure that adequate fall restraints (guard rails) remain in place as long as possible.

When erecting, dismantling or handling access equipment make sure that the correct manual handling techniques are employed to minimise injury.

The information in Chapter 1 (on pages 18–19) covers aspects related to lifting items from the floor and could apply to lifting ladders, frames or other access equipment from the floor. The correct technique for this is known as kinetic lifting.

This lifting technique can also be used when lifting materials onto the work platform, though decorators do not generally deposit any material of great weight when working at height. It is important to consider safe working load limits on the scaffold structure or working platform. For example, do not overload a tower scaffold with more people than it is designed for. This information will normally be included in the manufacturer's guidance leaflet.

Some items may be oddly shaped, making them difficult to carry. Make sure that difficult items are balanced correctly. Make an assessment as to whether you are strong enough to support, carry and handle the equipment. See the guidance below for techniques for carrying specific types of access equipment. Remember that it is important to be trained properly and to have had manual handling techniques demonstrated to you before putting them into practice.

The images show some points to remember.

When carrying scaffold boards over distance, depending on their length, it may be best to have two people, one at each end

As with scaffold boards, carrying ladders over any distance is best done in pairs

Try to take the weight onto your shoulder to carry platform steps

To carry tower scaffold frames, make sure they are properly balanced so that you are able to move without injury to yourself or others

Bear in mind that some parts of access equipment may be heavy, awkwardly shaped or particularly long, so do remember to call for assistance if the task becomes too difficult for one person.

STORING ACCESS EQUIPMENT AND WORKING PLATFORMS

In general terms, when storing access equipment it is important that the area is well ventilated, dry and protected from theft or damage. Properly designed racks are recommended to enable ladders, scaffold boards and stagings to be stored flat, so that they are adequately supported along their length to prevent bowing, warping and twisting.

Metal items may require hinges, joints and so on to be oiled regularly so they remain freely working.

Important considerations when storing a ladder include the following:

- Is the ladder stored away from areas where it could deteriorate more rapidly (where it is exposed to damp, excessive heat or the elements)?
- Is the ladder stored in a position that helps it to remain straight (eg supported by the stiles on proper ladder brackets or laid on a flat, clutter-free surface)?
- Is the ladder stored where it cannot be damaged by vehicles, heavy objects or contaminants?
- Is the ladder stored where it cannot cause a trip hazard or an obstruction?
- Is the ladder stored securely where it cannot be used for criminal purposes?
- If the ladder is permanently positioned (eg on scaffolding), is it secured against unauthorised climbing?

REPAIRS

You should not attempt to repair the ladder unless you are qualified to do so.

You should seek advice from the manufacturer about repair and replacement.

SAFETY WHEN NOT IN USE

When ladders are not in use, such as at night or at weekends, you need to prevent unauthorised people from climbing scaffolds. This is not just for security purposes but also for their safety. Scaffold boards chained vertically to cover the lower rungs of the ladder should prevent anyone gaining access.

If ladders are left 'open' during non-working periods and someone does have an accident on or around the scaffold, the company is liable for not making the site safe.

> **INDUSTRY TIP**
>
> Oiling equipment after use and before storage is a good maintenance tip, as well as checking for damage or decay.

OVERNIGHT SAFETY

Always store ladders in a covered, ventilated area, protected from the weather and away from too much damp or heat. Ladders can fall if stored vertically, so try to avoid this. If possible, secure the top, for instance with a bracket. Ladders should never be hung from a rung or in any place where a child might be tempted to climb them. For horizontal storage a rack or wall brackets are ideal. Timber ladders must be raised clear of the ground to avoid contact with damp.

Ladders stored horizontally on racks

Give careful thought to the storage of stepladders, platform steps, podiums, trestles and other access equipment. Many of these items are quite bulky, but in all cases they should be stored in a cool, well-ventilated dry atmosphere.

Consider how these items can remain accessible but secure. Everything should be stored tidily and preferably in separate bays with items of the same type so you don't need to move too much equipment to get to the item required.

Ladders in storage

Case Study: Eric

Stepladders are widely used for accessing out-of-reach areas and carrying out a range of working-at-height tasks. The range of access equipment available gives potential for falls from just above ground level to many metres high. Falls may be a result of incorrect ladder selection, incorrect positioning of the ladder, failure of the ladder due to poor maintenance, careless use (perhaps over-reaching), or a combination of these factors.

Eric is undertaking some decorating work at a height and has been provided with a stepladder by his employer. Before beginning the work he does a safety check on the steps and finds some defects. The general condition of the ladder is poor and one of the steps has failed. Eric discovers that the timber around the failed step has deteriorated significantly, probably due to poor storage conditions.

Eric reports the poor condition of the item to his employer and requests that a replacement is provided before undertaking the work. As a result of Eric's safety checks the stepladder is destroyed to prevent any other person from using it.

Ladder in poor condition

Deteriorating timber

ACTIVITY

The case study mentions storage conditions. Why do you think the storage conditions might have contributed to causing this accident? Are there any decorative coatings that could be applied to timber steps and ladders that might help protect them against drying out too much?

Work through the following questions to check your learning.

1   Which one of the following pieces of access equipment is **best** used to gain access to paint a window 2m off the ground?

a   Scaffold board.

b   Podium steps.

c   Lightweight staging.

d   Cherry picker.

2   What are support brackets on trestle scaffolds used for?

a   To help you stand on the platform.

b   To hold guard rails in place.

c   To fix the platform to the trestles.

d   To hold the trestles against the wall.

3   A risk assessment is normally provided for which one of the following reasons?

a   To work out how much material is needed.

b   To work out how much scaffold is required.

c   To determine safe working practices.

d   To show where equipment is stored.

4   Which one of the following weather conditions affects the use of external access equipment?

a   Bright sunlight.

b   Cloudy skies.

c   Windy weather.

d   No wind.

5   All access equipment should be inspected for damage. Who should carry out this task?

a   Someone trained and competent.

b   Any operative aged over 21.

c   The leading decorator.

d   A qualified decorator.

6   Stiles, treads, ropes and swingback are all terms related to which one of the following types of access equipment?

a   Wooden trestles.

b   Ladders.

c   Wooden steps.

d   Steel trestles.

7   Which one of the following is a common hazard of working at height?

a   Being struck by moving vehicles.

b   Falling from height.

c   Hazardous dust pollution.

d   Being trapped by collapse.

8   Which one of the following is the least effective method of securing a ladder in use?

a   Tying it to a ringbolt at the top.

b   Having it footed by another person.

c   Tying it to a stake at the bottom.

d   Tying it in the middle by a ringbolt.

9   Which type of accident kills most construction operatives?

a   Falling from height.

b   Contact with electricity.

c   Being run over by site transport.

d   Being hit by a falling object.

10 What are a lanyard and inertia-operated fall arrest used for?

a   Working from roof ladders.

b   Working below ground.

c   Driving a vehicle.

d   Working from hop-ups.

11 Which one of the following actions should be carried out on the discovery of a faulty ladder?

   a   Use it to complete the task in hand then take it out of use.

   b   Try to repair it prior to using the ladder.

   c   Use it only for a short period of time.

   d   Report it to your supervisor and take it out of use.

12 Which legislation covers the use of access equipment?

   a   Work at Height Regulations 2005 (as amended).

   b   Provision and Use of Work Equipment Regulations 1998 (PUWER).

   c   Management of Health and Safety at Work Regulations 1999.

   d   Health and Safety at Work Act 1974.

13 At what height are you considered to be working at height?

   a   1m above ground level.

   b   2m above ground level.

   c   3m above ground level.

   d   Any height above ground level.

14 What would be the benefit of using a lightweight platform over timber scaffold boards?

   a   It is heavier.

   b   It is lighter.

   c   It is less expensive.

   d   It is more expensive.

15 Which one of the following is the best storage option for access equipment?

   a   In the open air with no cover.

   b   In a closed shed with no air.

   c   On the ground outside.

   d   In a well-ventilated space, under cover.

16 What is the **maximum** base ratio for using mobile tower scaffolds internally?

   a   Length of shortest side × 2.5.

   b   Length of shortest side × 3.

   c   Length of shortest side × 3.5.

   d   Length of shortest side × 4.

17 Which one of the following types of access equipment features stiles, cross members, tie rods, check blocks and hinges?

   a   Steel trestles.

   b   Pole ladders.

   c   Extension ladders.

   d   Timber trestles.

18 Who is responsible for producing a written risk assessment for the use of access equipment?

   a   Chargehand.

   b   Employer.

   c   Foreman.

   d   Employee.

19 Which is the correct angle of use for ladders?

   a   25°.

   b   45°.

   c   75°.

   d   90°.

20 What is the correct pitch ratio to use for an extension ladder?

   a   1:2.

   b   1:3.

   c   1:4.

   d   1:5.

Chapter 4
Unit 117: Preparing surfaces for decoration

This chapter will give you an understanding of the tools, materials and equipment you will use for preparing a variety of surfaces before starting to paint or decorate them. It will help you to recognise tools and equipment so that you can select the right ones for the task.

Thorough preparation is one of the most important parts of a decorator's job – no matter how good you are, unless you have prepared, the finished product will never be of a high standard. This could mean that you don't get paid for the job or you may have to repeat the work at your own expense, costing you time and money. You could even lose your job or fail to get repeat work.

By reading this chapter you will know how to:

1 Carry out preparation of bare and previously painted and decorated surfaces.

2 Correct defects in surfaces and surface coatings.

3 Repair and make good surfaces.

PREPARATION OF BARE AND PREVIOUSLY PAINTED AND DECORATED SURFACES

Make sure you use the right PPE for the task

It is important to remember that working on a building site can be dangerous for you and others. Make sure you are using personal protective equipment (PPE), and follow all health and safety regulations. If you see a potential hazard or are unsure about an aspect of your safety always speak to the person responsible for the safe running of the site – usually your supervisor or employer.

You will be shown how to maintain and store your tools in good condition. Try to buy good-quality tools, as they will give you the best results and will last longer if looked after.

There are several reasons why a surface should need to be prepared before it can be painted or decorated:

- to provide a **key** (so that the material will **adhere** to the surface)
- to ensure that the surface is sound to receive coatings
- to give a good quality of finish.

This section covers different types of surfaces, preparation tools and equipment, and common defects and how to deal with them. You also need to consider health and safety and risk assessment associated with painting and decorating. This is covered in the following section about the preparation process.

Key

The condition of a surface to receive paint which will help adhesion of the coating. A 'key' can be provided by natural porosity, or by abrading the surface

Adhere

To stick to a substance or surface

SUBSTRATES

Substrate

Surface to be painted or decorated

The word **substrate** refers to the surface to be painted or decorated. Different substrates will require different preparation methods, so it is important to be able to identify the surface that you are preparing. These are the main types you will be working with:

- timber – softwood or hardwood
- sheet materials
- metal – **ferrous** or non-ferrous
- plaster
- plasterboard
- blockwork
- brickwork
- porous and non-porous.

Ferrous

Containing iron

TIMBER

Softwood timber

Softwoods, such as pine, are used for **first fix** and **second fix** joinery work, particularly skirting boards, **dado rails**, **architraves**, doors and window frames. They are used because they are relatively cheap and easy to work with, and are nearly always painted due to their knotty and resinous nature.

Hardwood timber

Hardwoods, such as oak, are more expensive to buy than softwoods and are used for exterior work, especially for doors and windows and where a more decorative finish is required. They need to be finished with lacquer, varnish or French polish to protect and enhance the grain, as painting masks the appearance of the wood.

First fix

The main elements of construction, eg roofing, flooring

Second fix

The final finish, eg windows and door frames

Dado rail

A rail secured to the wall that produces two individual areas in a room; the upper walls are normally much larger in area

Architraves

The moulded frames around doors or windows

Oak is used for external, decorative doors

Sheet material

This is timber in sheet form that can be cut to size for the job. Examples of sheet materials and their uses include:

- plywood – cladding, panelling, furniture, benches and tables

- chipboard – flooring and kitchen units

- sheathing ply – roofing and concrete work

- medium-density fibreboard (MDF) – flat-pack furniture, panelling

- fibreboard – wall coverings, notice boards.

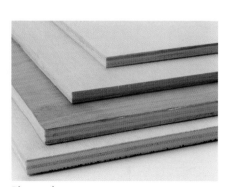

Plywood

FERROUS METALS

Ferrous metals are metal surfaces that are prone to rust, as they contain iron and will need to be cleared of all rust before painting. Some examples of ferrous metals include cast iron, wrought iron and mild steel. See the table below for a description and their uses.

Name	Description	Uses
Cast iron 	■ Non-toxic corroding metal.	■ Handrails ■ Bridges ■ Railings ■ Buildings ■ Stairs ■ Cast-iron columns ■ Radiators
Wrought iron 	■ Corroding metal available in bar form, sheets and hoops. ■ Can crack if heated, and brittle when cold. ■ Rough texture.	■ Ornamental ironwork ■ Pipework ■ Handrails ■ Roof trusses
Mild sheet steel 	■ High carbon content. ■ Likely to rust. ■ Strong, but bends easily.	■ Girders ■ Tubes ■ Screws ■ Nuts and bolts ■ Garage doors

NON-FERROUS METALS

Non-ferrous metals do not contain iron and are less likely to corrode. Some examples include galvanised steel, copper, aluminium and zinc. See the table below for their descriptions and uses.

Name	Description	Uses
Galvanised steel	■ Available in tubes, sheets and flat bars. ■ Highly resistant to corrosion – can withstand salt water, moisture, rain and snow. ■ Lightweight, fire resistant and maintenance free.	■ Girders ■ Frames ■ Roofing ■ Support beams ■ Piping
Copper	■ Available as tubes, sheets, wires, rods and flat bars. ■ Easy to bend but also easily damaged so must be stored carefully. ■ Tarnishes quickly.	■ Water pipes ■ Electrical wiring ■ Roofing
Aluminium	■ Lightweight and extremely resistant to corrosion.	■ Window frames
Lead	■ Very soft and heavy. ■ Highly resistant to corrosion. ■ Discolours to grey when exposed to the air. ■ Poisonous, so care must be taken when using.	■ Roofing

PLASTER

A material applied to internal surfaces such as ceiling and walls. It is usually applied over plasterboard to give a better, longer-lasting finish for both paint and wallpaper.

PLASTERBOARD

Plasterboard is plaster sandwiched between two boards of stiff lining paper and used for interior partition walls and ceilings.

BLOCKWORK

This is made up of concrete blocks that are heavy but produce strong finished work. They are used to support heavy structures such as floors and walls.

BRICKWORK

Bricks are smaller than blocks so more are needed per square metre. Like blockwork, brickwork is held together by mortar: a mixture of sand, cement and water.

POROUS AND NON-POROUS

The words **porous** and non-porous refer to the amount of liquid that is likely to be soaked up by a surface – some are more absorbent than others. See below for examples of porous and non-porous surfaces.

Plasterboarded wall

Porous

Having pores or passages along which fluids may travel

Porous	Non-porous
Plaster	Plastic
Plasterboard	Ferrous metalwork
Timber (softwood, hardwood)	Non-ferrous metalwork
Sheet materials	Glazed tiles
Brickwork, rendering, concrete, blockwork and stonework	Glass

ACTIVITY

Why do you think it is important for a decorator to know whether materials are porous or non-porous? Discuss this with your tutor.

DEFECTS

As stated in the introduction, preparation is the most important factor in achieving a high standard of finish – one that not only looks good, but will last.

All surfaces require preparation before work can start. Defects such as dust, loose paint, damp, flaking paint, rust, oil and protruding nails may stop the paint or wallpaper adhering to the surface.

COMMON DEFECTS

A defect is anything that makes a substrate less than perfect. A decorator will always try to make the surface as good as possible before painting to make sure that the finished job is to as high a standard as possible. How to repair and make good surfaces is covered in detail later in this chapter. Below are some of the defects that you will come across.

Knots

A knot is a place in the timber where a branch was formed during the growth of the tree and produces sap that can bleed through the paint work and stain the paint finish. It will need to be sealed with knotting solution. (For more information see the section on preparing bare and previously painted substrates on page 162.)

Knots need to be sealed with knotting solution

Splits and shrinkage cracks

Timber that has been treated or stored incorrectly can often split along the grain. Timber should always be stored in dry conditions to prevent it splitting. (If it gets wet and then dries out this can cause it to split.) To guard against splitting the timber will need to be lightly rubbed down using a fine abrasive – make sure to rub with the grain, not against it. It will then need to be primed and made good using stopper. These processes are explained later in the chapter.

Split timber should be made good before use

Open joints

Open joints occur when mortar between stones or bricks has eroded – a very common cause of water penetration. You can also get open joints on timbers that have been butted together during construction but have shrunk away from each other to leave a gap. The open joints of timber will need to be treated in the same way as splits and shrinkage cracks.

Open joints in brickwork must be treated before painting

Indentations

Surfaces, particularly in soft wood, may have been damaged by knocks, causing the surface to be dented. This should be filled to make the surface level. If the surface has been previously painted it will need rubbing down with a fine abrasive before filling.

Rust

Rust is the corrosion of iron and steel – it is caused by moisture and oxygen reacting with the surface and forming iron oxide. It is important to treat rust before decorating, because untreated rust will continue to spread and will eventually push the paint off. (See page 164 for rust removal methods.)

Stale paste

Paste past its sell-by date is less effective at sticking wallpaper. Old paste that has not been washed off properly after removing wallpaper can become infected by mould. If that happens the wall area should be washed down using an antifungal solution and allowed to dry before any work is done on the surface.

An example of a settlement crack

Protruding

Extending above or beyond the surrounding surface

Resin can stain the wood's surface

Exude

To ooze or give out liquid or gas

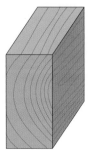
Seal end grain twice

Settlement cracks

These are usually found in new constructions where the moisture has dried out and materials have shrunk and cracked. Settlement cracks will need to be made good before decorating.

Protruding nail heads

Protruding nails usually occur where a carpenter has not hammered nails in properly when working on site. You will need to use a nail punch and hammer to knock them in so that they can be filled.

Nail holes

This is the opposite of protruding nails – where the nails have been hammered in below the surface and the holes will need filling.

Corrosion

When non-ferrous metals, such as iron or steel, corrodes, rust is formed. The corrosion of non-ferrous metals is caused by the wasting away of the metal through exposure to water, oxygen, acid, alkali or salt.

Resin exudation

This is where the natural oily resin in timber comes to the surface (**exudes**) and stains the wood.

End grain

This is the pattern seen when wood is cut across the grain. It is much more absorbent than the face of the wood because the cells that used to suck up moisture into the tree have been cut across. It is essential to seal the end grain twice with primer to stop liquids being absorbed into the timber before making good.

MATERIALS, TOOLS AND EQUIPMENT

When preparing surfaces it is important to use the correct equipment for the job. There are many specialist tools, equipment and materials that are essential to ensure that all surfaces are ready for decorating.

ABRASIVE PREPARATION MATERIALS

Abrasives are used to remove defects to make a smooth surface for decorating. The method for using abrasives to rectify defects is covered in more depth on page 174.

Types of abrasives used in preparation

Using an abrasive that is too coarse can damage the substrate and leave scratches that may show through when painted. On the other hand, using an abrasive that is too fine may be ineffective at removing or levelling rough surface imperfections. Badly prepared substrates will need making good before re-painting (see pages 173–175 for making good processes).

Abrading materials fall into two categories:

- dry

- wet and dry.

Examples of materials used for dry and wet and dry abrading are shown in the table.

Abrade

To scratch the surface with a coarse material to provide a 'key', which will help coatings adhere

Dry abrading materials	Wet and dry abrading materials
Glass paper	Emery cloth
Garnet paper	Emery paper
Emery cloth	Steel wool
Emery paper	Silicon carbide (wet and dry)
Steel wool	
Silicon carbide (wet and dry)	
Aluminium oxide	
Tungsten carbide	

All abrasive paper comes in different grades, ranging from P80 (coarse) to P1200 (fine), so the higher the number, the finer it is.

Wet and dry abrasives

A waterproof adhesive (glue) is used to fix abrasive particles to a backing sheet, which can be used in both wet and dry conditions. When used dry it tends to clog up, so it is more suited to wet use and is normally used with warm soapy water.

The table below outlines some of the advantages and disadvantages of this type of paper.

Wet and dry abrasive

Advantages of wet and dry abrasive paper	Disadvantages of wet and dry abrasive paper
■ Excellent for keeping dust at a low level. ■ Extremely good for high-quality work. ■ Helps to clean the surface as it abrades.	■ Unsuitable for bare surfaces. ■ The surface needs to dry before it can be decorated. ■ It will clog easily if used dry. ■ More expensive.

Dry abrasive paper

Dry abrasives

The materials traditionally used in this type of abrasive are glass and garnet, but it is more likely that your abrasive will be made from aluminium oxide grit. It is much harder wearing than wet and dry abrasive and there is less risk of clogging, as the gaps between the aggregate particles allow the waste to escape. The table below outlines some of the advantages and disadvantages of this type of paper.

Advantages of dry abrasive paper	Disadvantages of dry abrasive papers
■ Aluminium oxide paper is available in many grades ranging from P20 (very coarse) to P320 (very fine). ■ Available in sheets, rolls, belt and disc form. ■ More economical, as it can continue to be used for different surfaces as it wears.	■ Very high dust level. ■ Aluminium oxide paper is more expensive than glass paper (but it lasts longer so can be more economical). ■ Becomes unusable when wet or damp.

CHEMICAL SOLUTIONS

Some surfaces will need treating with a chemical solution before proceeding. The following are some of the most commonly used.

Shellac knotting/patent white knotting
This is a solution of **shellac** in methylated spirits, which is used to stop resin exuding from knots in timber.

Stabilising solution
Stabilising solution is designed to seal powdery or unstable surfaces. It binds the loose particles together to form a base for painting on. It may be clear or pigmented (coloured).

Mordant solution
This is also known as etching primer, and is used to corrode metal surfaces with acid to provide a key to help paint to stick. The metal surface should be de-greased (see page 170) before applying the mordant solution with a brush and allowing it to dry before painting.

Liquid paint remover
There are two types of liquid paint remover. One is water borne and the other is solvent borne. They both work in the same way to soften the paint so that it can be removed using a shavehook or scraper. Water-borne paint remover is most commonly used because it is quicker and easier to use.

Shellac

A natural resin found mainly in India, made of secretions from insects. When dissolved in spirit it forms the basis of French polish, knotting and sealers

Shellac sealer

FILLING MATERIALS

The following are some of the common filling materials you may come across.

Putty

This is a stiff dough-like material used for stopping holes and cracks in woodwork before painting. It can also be used for bedding glass. Good-quality putty is made from **whiting** ground in raw linseed oil.

Whiting

Chalk (calcium carbonate) prepared by drying and grinding, as used in whitewash and sometimes as an extender in paint

Stopping

A stiff paste used to fill up holes, cracks and similar defects in a surface.

Single-pack filler

This is used to achieve a perfectly smooth level surface on timber, plaster and plasterboard before applying finishing systems. Filler comes in powder form, and needs mixing with water. Once it is mixed it is usually workable for 30–40 minutes and sets hard within a couple of hours. When dry, it can be sanded back to make a smooth surface for decorating. It is also available ready mixed.

Two-pack filler

This term is used to describe filler that comes in two parts that need mixing before use. It dries to an extremely hard finish.

Tempered

Metal that has been hardened by heating

Nibs

Small particles of foreign matter, such as paint skin or grit, that have dried in the film of a coating and which cause it to feel rough

PREPARATION TOOLS

You will need to become familiar with the range of tools needed to prepare surfaces.

Tool	Use
Stripping knife	A good-quality knife will have a hardwood handle and the steel blade will be **tempered**. It is used to remove wallpaper, loose or flaking paint and other debris or **nibs** to ensure that the surface is ready for painting or decorating. Stripping knifes are also known as scrapers.
Filling knife	This is used to apply filler to open grain work on timber, holes, cracks or any defect to a surface. It looks very much like a stripping knife but the blade is more flexible as it is made of a thinner-gauge metal. It is very important not to damage the tip of the blade during or after use as it is likely to leave marks on the filler, making it harder to rub down when it is dry, and wasting time and money.

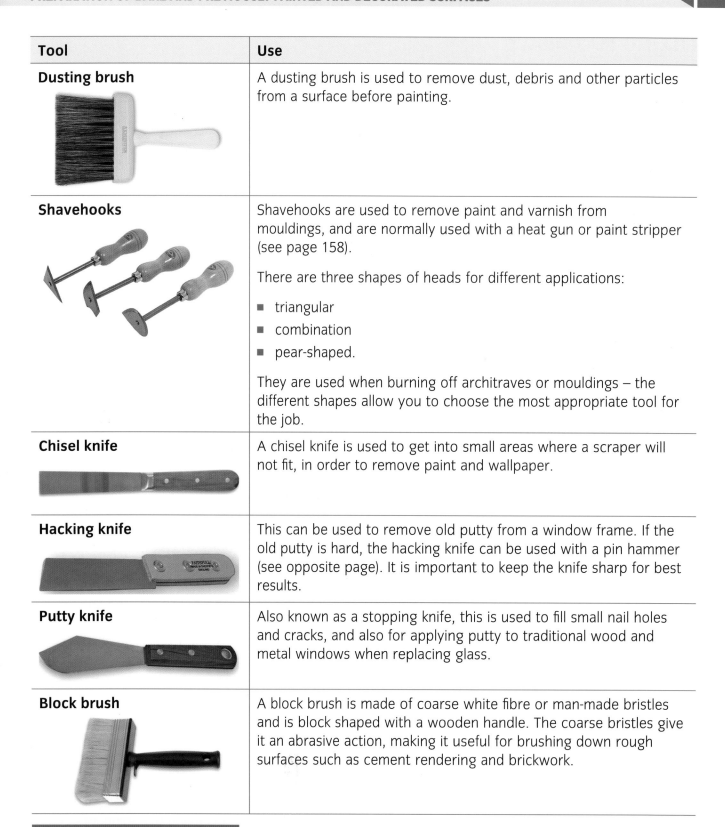

Tool	Use
Dusting brush	A dusting brush is used to remove dust, debris and other particles from a surface before painting.
Shavehooks	Shavehooks are used to remove paint and varnish from mouldings, and are normally used with a heat gun or paint stripper (see page 158). There are three shapes of heads for different applications: ■ triangular ■ combination ■ pear-shaped. They are used when burning off architraves or mouldings – the different shapes allow you to choose the most appropriate tool for the job.
Chisel knife	A chisel knife is used to get into small areas where a scraper will not fit, in order to remove paint and wallpaper.
Hacking knife	This can be used to remove old putty from a window frame. If the old putty is hard, the hacking knife can be used with a pin hammer (see opposite page). It is important to keep the knife sharp for best results.
Putty knife	Also known as a stopping knife, this is used to fill small nail holes and cracks, and also for applying putty to traditional wood and metal windows when replacing glass.
Block brush	A block brush is made of coarse white fibre or man-made bristles and is block shaped with a wooden handle. The coarse bristles give it an abrasive action, making it useful for brushing down rough surfaces such as cement rendering and brickwork.

ACTIVITY

Some of the tools used for preparing surfaces for decoration are described on these pages. Can you think of any other tools and equipment you may need? Check your answers with your tutor.

Tool	Use
Wire brush 	A wire brush is used for removing loose rust and **corrosion** from metalwork.
Hammers  Claw hammer Pin hammer	The two main types of hammer used by decorators are the claw hammer, used for pulling out nails and driving nails in, and the lighter pin hammer, used on more delicate surfaces – for example, to drive pins in when replacing broken glass.
Nail punch 	This is a metal tool, used with a hammer, to knock in nails that are protruding from wood surfaces.
Rubbing block 	Rubbing blocks, also known as sanding blocks, are used to make handling and using dry, or wet and dry, abrasive paper easier. They may be made of wood, cork or rubber. Wood and cork are used with dry abrasive paper, and rubber is used with wet and dry.
Filling board 	A filling board is used for transferring filler from where it is mixed to the workstation. Decorators may make their own to suit their needs. A filling board is very similar to a plasterer's hawk.
Buckets and sponges  	Decorators use buckets of water and sponges for various tasks, including: ■ to wet and dry abrade a previously painted surface ■ to dampen wallpaper before stripping ■ to wash down a substrate before painting.

Tool	Use
Synthetic and natural paint brushes  Natural bristle brush  Synthetic bristle brush	Although there will be more information on brushes in Chapter 5, you may also need them for preparation work – for spot priming, for example. Natural pure-bristle brushes are made out of animal hair and are used mainly for applying oil based paint (gloss). Synthetic brushes are man-made fibres and mainly used for water-borne paints (emulsion).
Paint kettles  Plastic paint kettle Metal paint kettle	These are made from either plastic or metal and are used to decant paint for use. Plastic is generally used for water-borne paint and metal for oil based paint. Also known as paint pots.
Skeleton gun 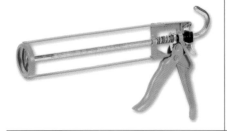	Sealants, caulk and mastic tubes are inserted into a metal frame called a skeleton gun in order to dispense them directly onto a surface.
Hot air gun 	A hot air gun, also known as a stripper, is used for removing paint from a surface. This is quicker than using liquid paint remover (LPR), and it is particularly suitable for using on timber. Aim the hot air gun at the surface, starting at the bottom so the rising heat will start to soften the paint above. As the paint softens, remove with a scraper, making sure not to touch the blade, as it will become hot.

ACTIVITY

What PPE is necessary when preparing surfaces for painting? Use the internet to find examples of a decorator's PPE, then list four pieces of equipment and the hazards that they will protect you from.

THE PREPARATION PROCESS

It is important to be aware of the necessary safety measures and precautions to take when you are preparing to decorate.

HEALTH AND SAFETY

You will already have covered many aspects of health and safety in Chapter 1, and should have a good understanding of what is meant by health and safety and how to work safely. This is a good time to take another look at health and safety though, specifically relating to the preparation of surfaces. Before starting work, whether on a building site, a domestic site or at college, it is important to consider:

- what causes accidents

- how to stop accidents happening

- reporting accidents

- risk assessment.

Risk assessment

Before starting any preparation work, you will need to do a risk assessment. Much of the work carried out on site can be hazardous, not only to yourself but to others. You face different hazards with every new site and every new situation. As discussed in earlier chapters, a risk assessment is not only the responsibility of the employer but of everyone working on site.

Here are some things to think about when carrying out a risk assessment:

- Is the work across an exit or on steps?

- Will the work involve using a stepladder? If so, is it secure?

- Will you be rubbing down? If so, is the correct PPE supplied?

- Do you know how to use the tools and equipment safely?

- Will you be using any hazardous substances?

Although many health and safety precautions are common to all trades, there are some things that are particularly important to a painter and decorator. For example:

- As a decorator you will come into contact with many chemicals and irritants, so you will need to apply barrier cream to protect the skin from contaminants that may cause infections or irritations. Do this at the start of every day.

Caution sign

ACTIVITY

With a pen and paper, walk around your site or college workshop and see how people are working, and what materials and equipment they are using. Are they working safely? What could go wrong? Write down your findings and discuss them in groups or with your tutor.

INDUSTRY TIP

You should always report accidents and near misses to your employer/foreman, no matter how small. Accidents that result in death, major injury or more than seven days off work, or are caused by dangerous practices, must be reported to the Health and Safety Executive (HSE).

Latex glove

Gauntlet gloves

- It is important to wear goggles, a dust mask and overalls when rubbing down, as the dust this creates can get into your eyes, be breathed into your lungs and irritate your skin. Make sure that the work area is well ventilated and dampen the floor when sweeping up. When working in a room that cannot be ventilated it may be necessary to wear a ventilator.

- Light cotton or latex gloves will protect your hands when you are rubbing down, and are comfortable to use. Gauntlet gloves should be worn for heavy-duty work such as washing down walls or using LPR.

- When using LPR to remove old paint films, be aware that the paint remover may be toxic and highly flammable. Check the manufacturer's instructions (see COSHH, Chapter 1, pages 9–11), make sure that the work area is well ventilated and wear a mask and goggles (see Personal Protective Equipment (PPE) at Work Regulations 1992, Chapter 1, pages 20–23) and rubber gloves, as paint stripper can burn.

- Be aware of how to lift heavy weights safely (stepladders, paint tins, wallpaper, etc) and don't be afraid to ask for help. Some items may need more than one person to lift them (see Manual Handling Operations Regulations 1992, Chapter 1, pages 17–19).

- For some jobs a secured stepladder will not be sufficient – you may need to use a scaffold tower. Make sure you don't over-stretch yourself!

- Although you will always need to wear toe-cap boots wherever you are working, it is unlikely that you will need a hi-viz jacket or a hard hat for a domestic job. However, if you are working on a building site these will be required.

- Tools and equipment must be regularly tested, and toxic and flammable materials stored correctly.

PROTECTING THE WORK AREA

When working on a building site or in someone's home, anything that is not being worked on should always be protected from damage. Items that will need protecting include:

- flooring, such as carpets, rugs, tiles, wooden floors and patio floors
- ceiling light fittings
- door furniture such as locks, handles and hinges
- curtains and rails
- sofas and chairs

- tables and any other furniture
- wall lights and fittings
- patio areas
- plants and plant pots if working outside.

Before starting work it is important that you check to see what needs covering or removing, as any damage you cause can be very costly to your pocket and your reputation.

It is important to protect any furniture that cannot be removed

MATERIALS USED FOR PROTECTING SURFACES, FURNITURE AND WORK AREAS

One of the most common sheet materials you will use as a decorator is a dust sheet. Dust sheets can protect surfaces against paint and paste splashes, small particles from rubbing down, or other small spillages.

There are also a number of other materials that can be used for protection. As with all tools, materials and equipment, it is best to choose good-quality products, as cheap alternatives do not always provide such good protection.

All items will need to be protected and some will need to be removed from the work area before work starts. Items that can be removed, for example curtains, curtain poles and curtain tacks, and **door furniture** should be stored safely so that they can be returned after the work has been completed.

Door furniture

Anything attached to the door, such as handles, knobs, locks, letterboxes, fingerplates and hinges

Cotton dust sheets

The best-quality dust sheets are cotton **twill** sheets. They are generally used to protect floors and furniture, and come in different sizes. They can be folded to give better protection. You can also buy dust sheets in a narrow width made especially for treads and rises on staircases.

Twill

A woven material

Advantages of twill dust sheets	Disadvantages of twill dust sheets
■ When new or clean, they give a very professional image. ■ When used to cover the floor they will remain in place when walked on (in some places may need taping down with masking tape). ■ Available in different sizes.	■ Expensive to buy and clean. ■ Can absorb chemicals such as paint stripper. ■ Paint spillage may soak through the dust sheet. ■ Possible risk of fire when burning off old paintwork.

Narrow dustsheets are used to cover staircases

Plastic dust sheets can be thrown away after use

Polythene/plastic dust sheets

Polythene or plastic dust sheets can be used in the same way as cotton dust sheets. However, they are waterproof and can be thrown away after use.

Advantages	Disadvantages
■ Inexpensive to buy. ■ Paint spillage will not soak through the sheet. ■ Do not absorb chemicals such as paint stripper.	■ Do not look as professional as cotton dust sheets. ■ Do not stay in place as easily as cotton. ■ When wet they can become slippery.

Tarpaulins

Tarpaulins are made from a number of different types of material, including:

- PVC-coated nylon
- rubber-coated cotton
- heavy cotton canvas
- nylon scrim.

The most common size used by decorators is 6m x 4m. Because tarpaulins can protect against moisture they are best used when washing down a surface or stripping off old wallpaper.

Masking paper and masking tape

Masking paper and masking tape can also be used to protect items. Masking paper is smooth brown paper that comes in rolls. It is secured using masking tape and is especially good for covering floors, furniture and around window frames.

Masking tape can also be used around small items, such as wall light and socket fittings. Adhesive tape and waterproof tape may also be required for external use.

A masking paper dispenser can be used to cover large areas

PREPARING BARE AND PREVIOUSLY PAINTED SUBSTRATES

Before painting a surface it is essential to ensure that the finish is as good as it can be and that the paint will stay on the surface – both in the long term and the short term. For example, paint that is applied to a greasy surface will not adhere, while paint applied over flaking paint will not stay on for long.

The following are some of the preparation processes that you will need to undertake.

Wet and dry abrading

Wet and dry abrading is used to remove defects to make a smooth surface for decorating. See pages 152–154 for types of abrasives used in preparation. When abrading new timber it is important to remember that you should not rub against the grain – this can result in furring of the timber and will leave scratches on the surface. This will show through the final result when painted. This process is covered in more depth on page 174.

Scraping

Where abrading or dusting off is not sufficient to remove defects and nibs, the surface will have to be removed using a stripping knife. This may be used on its own, with a hot air gun or with LPR. Scraping is also used to remove wallpaper, as described on page 167.

Degreasing

The surface must be dry and free from grease before painting. Any grease can be washed off using white spirit. Previously painted non-ferrous metals will need to be abraded, and any rust should be scraped back to a firm edge before painting.

Knotting

You may notice on bare timber that some surfaces have a number of knots, where the branches were formed during the growth of the tree. Before painting the timber you will need to seal it, as knots contain sap that will bleed through the paint surface.

Knotting solution can be used to seal knots as well as a number of other stains, such as felt-tip pen marks, tar splashes and resin. Don't forget to use the appropriate PPE when using knotting solution, as it is highly flammable.

Knotting solution is best kept in a knotting bottle or a glass container, which will prevent the knotting solution evaporating and drying out. Always make sure that the surface is clean and dry before applying the knotting solution with a brush, taking care to cover the knot or stain entirely. The knotting solution should dry quickly, and when it is completely dry the surface coating can be applied. The brush should be cleaned with a cleaning solvent (see the manufacturer's instructions).

Priming

For interiors, softwood and acrylic (water-borne) primer is used. Universal wood and metal primer is used for both interior and exterior timber, and both soft and hardwood as well as most metals. Alkali-resisting primers are used for plastered surfaces, brickwork and **rendering**, and they contain alkali salt. To prime a surface is to apply a first coat of paint. This is covered in detail in Chapter 5.

Knotting solution

Seal knots with knotting solution

Rendering

A sand and cement mix covering to brickwork

Stopping

Stopping should be used for exterior work, as it is stable in damp conditions. The stopper is pressed into the holes and cracks with a small filling knife and then levelled off.

Some new timber may shrink when exposed to the weather or moisture. Once the timber is dry it is ready to be filled, as described below.

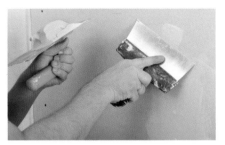

Fill nail holes before painting

Filling

You may come across a number of other defects such as protruding nail heads, usually caused by a carpenter or joiner securing timber but not punching the nails below the surface. These will need to be punched in below the surface using a nail punch.

Once you have dealt with protruding nails they can be filled, along with any other nail holes, dents and cracks, with a suitable filling agent before painting.

Rust removal

Ferrous metals are likely to rust – depending on the extent of the rust, it can be removed with a wire brush. Abrasive paper, a scraper or a mechanical wire brush may be required if the rust is severe.

Remove rust with an abrasive

New metalwork will need to be cleaned down using white spirit to remove oil residues and grease. Always use a lint-free cloth to avoid small, fluffy particles of cloth spoiling the surface.

Raking out

Timber that has been affected by damp can rot away and go soft and mushy. This needs to be raked out using a shavehook before being allowed to dry out completely. The process for making good timber affected by wet rot is described fully on page 173.

Undercutting

Undercutting is similar to raking out, but you take the cutting wider, in a square or circle, to give a larger area to fill or stop.

Wetting in

This term not only means wetting in of wallpaper before stripping it off, but also the wetting in of cracks and holes before applying filler – this helps the filler stick to the surface. You may use diluted PVA for this.

Caulking

Some surfaces are prone to shrinking and movement. For example, cracks and holes filled with powder filler may split open, and in these cases you would use caulking. Caulk is a waterproof filler and sealant used to fill cracks and gaps. Is it is sometimes called painter's mastic. Mastic is an acrylic type of caulk and is applied using a mastic gun which holds and dispenses the mastic from the tube.

Mastic (or caulk) is applied around door frames, window frames and around the edges of ceilings and walls. Excess mastic can be removed using a filling knife. When mastic is dry it feels like rubber (it can expand and contract with any movement or temperature change) and can be painted or papered over.

Dry lining (taping and joining)

Dry lining is where plasterboard is attached to studwork with galvanised clout nails to form partition walls. Joints and nails will need to be made good to ensure they do not show through. This method is detailed on page 175.

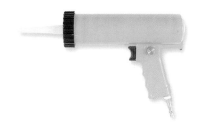

Mastic gun

REMOVING OLD PAINT SYSTEMS

Previously painted woodwork should be washed down using sugar soap and warm water, and then rinsed off using clean water. This will remove grease and dirt and the woodwork may then be ready for painting. The removal of contamination using cleaning agents is covered in depth on page 171. Some surfaces will require abrading, so should be rubbed down using wet and dry and then rinsed off before paint is applied.

REMOVING OLD PAINT SYSTEMS WITH HOT AIR GUNS AND LPRS

Some previously painted surfaces may require burning off with heat, using a hot air gun/stripper. This is the quickest method of removing coatings from timber surfaces. As always, it is important to wear appropriate PPE, including protective gloves, overalls, goggles and a mask. If you are removing old paintwork containing lead you will need to take extra care. Burning off lead can give off fumes that may be **carcinogenic**, so a respirator must be worn. The use of lead paint started to be phased out in the 1950s but the law banning its use did not come into effect until 1978. If you suspect that old paintwork contains lead you can test it with a kit before proceeding.

Taping and joining

Carcinogenic

Cancer causing

Hot air gun/stripper

Advantages of using a hot air gun/stripper	Disadvantages of using a hot air gun/stripper
■ Unlikely to scorch when burning off timber. ■ When used on window frames there is less chance of glass cracking.	■ Slower than LPG. ■ Needs power to run. ■ Effectiveness can vary, for example when using in high winds.

Hot air gun used to remove paint

Respirator

Removing paint with chemicals (LPRs)

There are some basic rules to follow when using liquid paint strippers:

- Read and follow the manufacturer's instructions.

- Remove ironmongery from the surface to be stripped, eg door handles.

- Protect surrounding areas from any splashing or contamination.

- Protect yourself with the appropriate PPE.

- Always make sure that the work area is well ventilated, or protect yourself by wearing breathing apparatus.

Sometimes pressure builds up in the metal container holding the paint remover, which can cause gas and liquid to spurt out when the cap is removed. This could result in damage to the eyes and skin, so when opening the can slowly unscrew the cap, letting the pressure escape before fully removing it.

Avoid getting paint stripper on your skin or in your eyes, as this will cause burning and eye damage. If you do get stripping solution on you, rinse it off using cold water and seek medical advice.

INDUSTRY TIP

No smoking – paint stripper is highly flammable.

Liquid paint remover

ACTIVITY

Look for containers of paint stripper in your college or workplace, and read the labels. What do they tell you? Make a list of the PPE required, how to use and how to store it.

Water-borne paint stripper must be poured into a metal paint kettle before using (it can eat right through a plastic one). Apply it to the surface using an old paint brush. After a while the paint will start to blister, showing that it is ready to remove with a stripping or scraping knife. The amount of time that this takes will vary depending on the thickness of the paint.

REMOVING EXISTING WALLPAPER

Before a new wall covering can be applied, the existing covering will need to be removed. There are many types of wallpapers on the market, but most can be removed using water and a stripping knife. Vinyl wallpaper is mostly used in kitchens and bathrooms because it can resist steam and moisture, and must be treated differently. The top layer needs to be peeled off dry before proceeding as below. The following steps describe how to remove existing wallpaper.

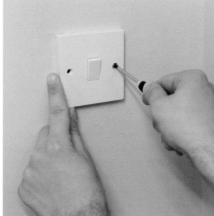

STEP 1 Cover the floor with dust sheets to protect it from water damage, making sure that you secure the sheets with masking tape. The sheets may become very wet, so use a wet floor sign to alert people to this hazard.

STEP 2 It is dangerous to use water where there is electricity, so turn electricity off at the mains before loosening light switches and plug sockets so that you can strip off the paper behind them. Only switch the electricity back on once you are sure that the surfaces are dry.

STEP 3 Fill a bucket with warm water and a small amount of washing-up liquid. Begin wetting the walls in, working from the bottom to the top. Apply the soapy water to the wall using a large (150mm) flat paint brush.

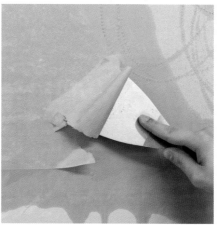

STEP 4 When the wall is thoroughly wet, leave the water to soak in and penetrate the wallpaper, softening the paste used to stick it to the walls. You may need to wet in a second time if it is hard to remove, or use a wallpaper scorer to help with water penetration.

STEP 5 Now use a stripping knife to remove the paper. If the wallpaper is still hard to remove you may need either to soak the walls again or allow more time for the water to soften the paper. Remember let the water do the work! Clear away the wallpaper as you go.

INDUSTRY TIP

If wallpaper is hard to remove, try adding an egg-cup full of vinegar or fabric softener to a bucket of hot water. This will help break the surface tension of the water, allowing it to penetrate the wallpaper easily.

MAKING GOOD

Once you have removed all of the wallpaper you will need to make the surface ready to receive the new coating. This is called making good, as it will give you a good, sound surface to work on. The following steps show how to make good the surface.

STEP 1 Wash down the walls to remove any excess paste, using clean warm water and a sponge. You may need to change the water several times. Leaving paste on the walls may cause problems such as cissing (see page 169) when filling or painting.

STEP 2 You will need to wait for the walls to dry before making good (see page 175 for more information on how to make good). While you are waiting, clear the remaining removed wallpaper from the floor. Remember to work safely – wallpaper can be a hazard, because the paste is very sticky and slippery.

STEP 3 Once the walls have dried, rub them down using a medium-grade abrasive and then dust off the wall area ready for filling.

STEP 4 Mix the filler to the right consistency: it should be like whipped cream. Use a spot board (a 350mm square of plywood) to mix on. Only mix as much as you need at any one time because, once mixed, the filler will start to set. Transfer the filler to a painter's hawk and then wash off any excess filler from the mixing board, ready for it to be used again.

STEP 5 With a filling knife, start to fill holes and cracks. Hairline cracks may need cutting open or raking out using a stripping knife, as the filler will only lie on top of the crack and will not stick to the plasterwork. Never use a filling knife to rake out, as this will damage the blade, resulting in a poor quality finish of the filling.

STEP 6 When the filler has dried, rub it down and dust off before redecorating. Check to see whether the filling needs a second fill, and if so repeat the process.

INDUSTRY TIP

Never over-fill (by putting too much filler on), because filler shrinks and you will need to do a second fill. Remember, you will have to rub it down once it is dry, and you don't want to make extra work for yourself.

Your finished work is only as good as your preparation. It is no good being a good painter and decorator and having good skills in applying paint coatings if the preparation is of a poor standard. Not only will your work not look good – it may not stand the test of time.

CORRECT DEFECTS IN SURFACES AND SURFACE COATINGS

As discussed in the previous section, there are many defects that affect substrates. Before painting or decorating on these surfaces, the defects must be rectified. Many common defects are covered on pages 151–152, but below are some more defects relating to surface coatings that will need treating before the preparation is complete.

Runs

Runs are defects on a painted surface where paint has been applied too thickly or unevenly. The paint flows downwards and stands proud of the rest of the surface.

An example of a run

Curtains

Similar to runs, this is a defect that occurs in paint coating particularly when applied to a vertical surface, and is due to uneven application. It takes the form of a thick line of paint like a draped curtain. They are also known as sags.

An example of a curtain defect in applied paint

Cissing

This is a term to describe when a coat of paint, varnish or watercolour refuses to form a continuous film and leaves the surface partially exposed. The main cause of this is when paint is applied over a greasy surface that has not been washed down or de-greased.

Flaking

This is a defect primarily due to poor adhesion (sticking), where the paint film lifts from the surface and breaks away.

Bittiness

This is when bits of grit, fluff and other foreign bodies contained in the paint spoil the appearance of the finished paint film. Examples of this happening are when the lid of a tin of paint has not been put back on properly or a surface has not been dusted off after rubbing down.

An example of bittiness

Chalking

Chalking is where a paint surface breaks down and becomes loose and powdery. It is caused by the weather so usually occurs on outside walls. It requires rubbing down with abrading paper before priming and repainting.

An example of chalking

Efflorescence

This is the appearance of a fine white powder that forms on the surface of brickwork and plaster. Both of these materials contain salts. As the materials dry the moisture evaporates and the salt is drawn to the surface, leaving a white powder on the bricks. The powder should be removed using a stiff brush on the dry bricks. Do not wet the surface, as the efflorescence will return when the bricks dry.

ACTIVITY

Start to take notice of your surroundings. Whenever you see paintwork, have a look for defects.

INDUSTRY TIP

Decontamination suggests the removal of pollutants or poisons, but in painting and decorating the term refers to anything that will spoil the finish, such as dust, dirt, old or stale paste, silicone and resin exudation.

INDUSTRY TIP

Remember to look at COSSH regulations for use, storage and PPE required for all solvents used. These things will be clearly marked on the container, so take particular care if you are given a chemical to use that has already been decanted into another container, such as a paint kettle or roller tray.

Fungicide

A substance that destroys fungi

Treat mould before decorating

A proprietary de-greaser

Efflorescence on brickwork

Efflorescence on plasterwork

MATERIALS, TOOLS AND EQUIPMENT NEEDED FOR RECTIFICATION AND DECONTAMINATION

Along with the tools, equipment and PPE covered in the first two sections you will also use some of the following materials to rectify defects.

Fungicidal washes

An area that has become infected with mould, mildew or other fungal infestations will need treating with a **fungicidal** wash before decorating, or else the stains will show through the final finish and the fungi will continue to grow. You will need to follow the manufacturer's instructions for applying the wash, and wear PPE which will include a mask, goggles, gloves and overalls.

Once dry, the area will need to be decontaminated by thoroughly washing down with clean water.

De-greasers

All previously coated surfaces must be free of grease and oil before painting, but the term de-greasing usually refers specifically to bare metal. Surfaces can be de-greased using white spirit, methylated spirit or a proprietary de-greaser. Apply with a lint-free cloth and allow to dry.

Stain blocks (proprietary and non-proprietary)

Some stains on surfaces to be painted are likely to bleed through, or not be fully covered, if not treated with a stain block. Examples include felt-tip pen, damp patches caused by leaking pipes and food spillages. If these cannot be removed with detergent or white spirit, a stain block will need to be applied with a brush and allowed to dry completely before painting. Remember to read the manufacturer's instructions before using.

Primers/sealers

As mentioned earlier, a primer is a first coat of paint. Primers will be covered in more detail in the next chapter. It is important to use the correct primer for the job – here are the most common ones and their uses:

- alkali-resisting – for plastered surfaces, brickwork and rendering
- aluminium wood – for hardwood, especially resinous timber, and for use over previously varnished or wood-stained surfaces. It can also be used to seal damp proof courses (DPCs)
- acrylic – for interior and exterior softwoods, old and new plaster, cement, concrete and hardwood. It should not be used on metal
- stabilising solution – for unstable or powdery paint surfaces.

Shellac/patent knotting

You will need knotting to seal knots and resinous areas in timber. See page 163 for full instructions for using it.

Cleaning agents

As you have seen, it is essential that all surfaces are clean and grease-free to ensure a good finish. On previously painted surfaces you will use hand-hot water and either sugar soap, washing soda or detergent (a small squeeze of washing-up liquid is good, because it is readily available). Stubborn marks may require a dilution of household bleach in cold water. The surface treated with all these cleaners will need to be decontaminated with clean water before decorating. Solvent wiping involves using white spirit, methylated spirit or acetone on a cloth to de-grease and clean an area. This is convenient because the surface does not need to be decontaminated after use.

Remove any cleaning agents applied by using clean water before decorating

Chemical stripper

Paint stripper was covered on page 166, but there are other chemical strippers available. On previously painted substrates it is usually sufficient to make the surface good by cleaning and abrading, but if the surface of the paint has broken down and blistered it may be necessary to strip the paint off. Information on applying stripper is detailed on pages 166–167.

RECTIFICATION PROCESSES

This section covers the processes used specifically for rectifying defects in surfaces and surface coatings. Before you begin the rectification process, ensure that you:

- have protected the work area (see pages 160–162)
- have undertaken a risk assessment
- are wearing the correct PPE
- follow any relevant environmental and health and safety regulations.

Use a scraper to remove wallpaper after wetting in

Cleaning

Contaminants must be removed from surfaces before painting and decorating. Put simply, this means that the surface must be clean and free from dust, dirt, grease, old paste, silicone, resin, sugar soap and detergents. The materials and methods used are covered in the previous section.

Scraping

Scraping is used to remove wallpaper after wetting in and to remove paint systems after applying an LPR.

Brushing

Brushing is used to remove dust and powdery residue from painted surfaces after rubbing down and for removing efflorescence from brickwork and blockwork. Remember not to wet the surface, or the powdery salt substance will return when it dries.

REPAIR AND MAKE GOOD SURFACES

The final step in preparing a surface for decoration is to repair and make good the surface. You are aiming to achieve a blank canvas on which to apply paint or wallpaper. As you have probably realised by now, the preparation can take longer than the finishing coats.

MATERIALS, TOOLS AND EQUIPMENT

As well as the materials tools and equipment already mentioned, here are a few more that you might need for repairing and making good surfaces.

Multi-purpose two-part filler

Ready-mixed lightweight filler

This is used for minor repairs to plastered surfaces, mouldings and coving.

Tinted stoppers

Tinted stoppers include:

- acrylic coloured timber filler

- oil based stained stopper

- plastic wood

- wood putty.

These are stoppers that are used on timber, particularly if it is to be stained or varnished, as white stopper would show through. They come in a variety of colours to match the colour of the wood.

PVA primer/sealer

This is a type of glue that can be used straight from the container or diluted for use on walls and ceilings. It makes a good surface for paint to stick to and makes it easier for wallpaper to slide into place. It may be used in making good to coat cracks and holes before filling.

Sand and cement

This is used for making good large cracks or holes in exterior rendered walls. A coat of PVA can be used before filling with the sand and cement mixture.

Expanding foam

This is used to fill large cracks, particularly settlement cracks and around window frames. Using a skeleton gun, the foam is squirted into the area to be filled and it will expand to fill the void. Any excess will leak out on to the surface. When completely dry this can be cut out using a Stanley knife.

Expanding foam is used to fill cracks and gaps

MAKING GOOD PROCESSES

Defective areas such as open joints in joinery, splits, indentations, open-grained timber, resinous timber, putties, holes, cracks, gaps, stale paste, rust and corrosion need to be made good before decoration.

Before any work begins, make sure that you have followed the correct preparation procedures as covered earlier in this chapter, including protecting the work area, conducting a risk assessment and ensuring that you follow environmental and health and safety regulations.

RAKING OUT TIMBER AFFECTED BY WET ROT

Some previously painted surfaces may be affected by wet rot that can occur in damp timber, such as timber frames. Wet rot is a fungus that destroys the timber as it grows, and develops in wet and moist conditions. Before you can work on an area affected by wet rot, all moisture will need to be removed. Once it has dried out, the timber will be treated as follows.

1 Defective timber can be raked out using a scraper or shavehook (see tool list on page 156). Allow the surface to dry out, then, using a clear wood preservative, flood (thoroughly cover) the exposed timber. Allow to dry and then **spot-prime** the affected areas with wood primer.

2 Fix wood screws (non-ferrous) into the timber to give support to the area and give the filler something to stick to.

3 Apply a coat of two-pack filler and allow it to dry.

4 Apply a second coat of filler to the surface and allow it to dry. Use abrading paper to rub down the filler so that it is **flush**.

Note: If the surface has been affected too badly, the timber may need to be cut back and replaced by a carpenter.

Wet rot

Spot-prime

To apply appropriate primer to sections of surface area that have been made good, to prevent the next coat from sinking into the filler

Flush

When two surfaces are even, on the same level, with no raised edges

WET AND DRY ABRADING

Wet and dry abrading is done when you want a first-class paint finish. This is particularly important on doors.

STEP 1 Cover the surrounding area with waterproof dust sheets and secure them in place. Put out a wet floor sign to warn people that the surface may be slippery. Gather the equipment and PPE you will need, particularly rubber gloves and overalls. You will also need a bucket with warm water and a little detergent, wet and dry abrasive and a rubber sanding block.

STEP 2 Wrap the wet and dry abrasive around the sanding block and dip it in the soapy water. Using soapy water helps the abrasive to glide over the surface. Starting from the top, on a small area at a time, rub down with the abrasive in a circular motion. Continue on to the next small area, dipping the block in the water frequently.

INDUSTRY TIP

Remember, you are not trying to remove the paint, just make it smooth for painting over.

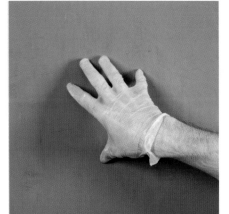

STEP 3 When you have covered the whole area, check all over for lumps, bumps and rough edges with your fingertips (as they are more sensitive than your hand), repeating as necessary until the surface feels as smooth as glass.

STEP 4 When you are satisfied that the surface is uniformly smooth, rinse with clean water – you may have to change the water several times. The surface will need to be dry before painting, so while you are waiting clean up the work area and your tools.

APPLYING CAULK AND SEALANTS

Decorator's caulk or mastic is applied using a skeleton gun around door and window frames to make a smooth waterproof finish. (See pages 165–166.)

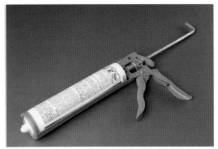

Caulk in a skeleton or mastic gun

MAKING GOOD TROWELLED FINISHES

These include interior plaster and exterior rendering.

Plastered surfaces

Like timber, plastered surfaces can be affected by cracks, nail heads and open joints, and should be treated in a similar way.

New plaster should never be rubbed down using abrasives, as this will scratch the surface and will show though once painted. You should use a stripping knife to remove any nibs, then dust the surface using a dusting brush before painting or making good (filling).

Previously wallpapered old plasterwork will need to be stripped of its wall covering using the same method as before.

Making good plasterboard

Plasterboard is very porous and will soak up any moisture, causing it to go soft or blister. Applying a coat of sealer to the surface will stop moisture from penetrating. When plasterboard is used on walls there will usually be joints where the sheets of plasterboard butt together – these will need making good so they cannot be seen. They will need taping and then filling so the joints do not break open. As with new plasterwork, the surface of the plasterboard should never be rubbed down with abrasive paper. This will not only scratch the surface – it will lift the plasterboard surface and will severely damage the finish. Gently use a filling knife to remove surface nibs.

Plasterboard that has been wallpapered may need to be stripped off. The method for this is the same as for removing wallpaper from a plastered wall. It is important not to over-soak it, as it will blister.

Once all the making good has been done, and the surface rubbed and dusted down, it is time to continue with painting or wallpapering.

External rendering

External surfaces need to be treated differently from interior surfaces, because they are exposed to the elements. Holes and cracks should be filled with a mixture of sand and cement, diluted with water to make a paste that will stick to the wall. Diluted PVA painted on before filling will help the sand and cement adhere. Level off the surface with a knife or trowel and allow to dry.

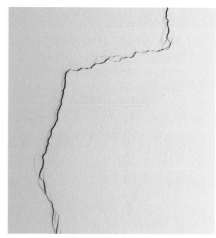
Crack in plasterwork

Tape and then fill the joints between plasterboards

INDUSTRY TIP

When stripping off wallpaper from a plasterboard surface, do not dig into the surface face. This will let water and moisture soak into the plasterboard, damaging the surface and making extra work when filling the surface before decoration.

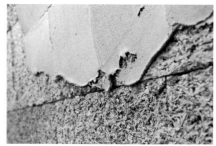
External rendering

RE-GLAZING TIMBER FRAMES (WINDOW OR DOOR PANELS)

To fit glass into a frame rebate it needs to be sandwiched between two layers of putty. The following will show you how to reglaze a timber window pane.

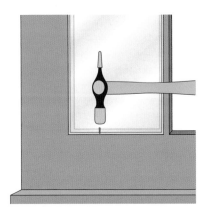

STEP 1 First you need to get the putty to the right consistency. Work the putty by kneading it between your fingers for a few minutes.

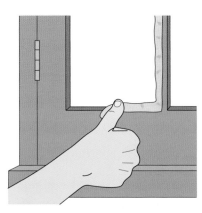

STEP 2 Roll the putty between your fingers to make a long sausage shape, and push the putty (bedding) around the frame rebate firmly with your thumb.

STEP 3 Offer the pane of glass up to the rebate and press it in around the edges to make good contact. Put light pressure on the glass until the excess putty oozes out and the bedding putty is 2–4mm thick. *Warning*: do not push the glass from the centre, as it may break.

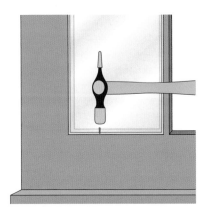

STEP 4 Tap glazing sprigs into the rebate to hold the glass firmly while the putty sets, using a pin hammer. The glazing sprigs must be flush with the glass.

STEP 5 Apply the face putty to the remainder of the rebate using your thumb.

STEP 6 Smooth the putty using a putty knife, running the flat edge of the knife along the glass. The top of the putty should be below the sight line so when painted the paint will just touch the glass, sealing the gap.

STEP 7 Remove any excess bedding putty with a putty knife.

STEP 8 Paint the putty as soon as it is hard enough to stand the pressure of a paint brush. This should be done within two weeks – otherwise, it may crack up or even be eaten by birds.

REPLACING OLD AND DEFECTIVE PUTTY

When removing old paint from window frames, some of the putty may be damaged and break away. Before replacing the putty the timber will need to be primed (see Chapter 5). Once the primer has dried, any defective or missing putty can be replaced:

1 Remove any loose or defective putty from the glass using a small stripping knife or shavehook.

2 Give it a light rub-down with a medium abrasive and dust off the area.

3 Prime any bare timber and allow to dry.

4 Work the putty into a stiff dough, push into the rebate with your thumb, smooth with a putty knife and remove any excess putty with the knife.

5 Paint as soon as the putty has hardened enough to stand the pressure of a paint brush.

Removing old putty

Case Study: Lucy and Tomas

Lucy and Tomas decided to set up their own decorating business, so they put an advertisement in the newspaper. They were soon asked to price up decorating a living room for Mrs Khan. They visited the site and made a rough estimate, without measuring, of what materials they would need and guessed that it would take three days. Mrs Khan accepted the price.

When they arrived they found all the furniture in the room and all the curtains on the rails, which took them some time to remove and cover up. Lucy started to wet down the wallpaper but it soon became clear that stripping it off was going to take longer than they expected. It was late when they finished, so they left the discarded wallpaper to clear up in the morning.

The next morning some of the wallpaper had stuck to the dust sheet, so it took longer to clean up. They rubbed down the walls, which were very dry and made a lot of dust. The filler did not stick because they had forgotten to wash the paste off the walls after stripping the wallpaper and they had forgotten to bring a mastic gun to use around the doors and window frames. By the end of day two they still had not finished the preparation and they started to realise that working for yourself is not as easy as they first thought. In the end the job took five days and was finished to a high standard so the client was pleased, but they had underestimated the cost of the materials and the amount of time it would take. They earned very little from that job but it did teach them some valuable lessons.

Work through the following questions to check your learning.

1 Knotting is applied to softwood structures to do what to the timber?

   a   Undercoat.

   b   Prime.

   c   Seal.

   d   Stain.

2 What is the **best** material to use to fill around the tops of skirting boards, window frames and door frames?

   a   Filler.

   b   Stopper.

   c   Caulk.

   d   Putty.

3 Where is the **best** place to start when washing down a wall surface to be decorated?

   a   At the top of the wall.

   b   At the bottom of the wall.

   c   Anywhere on the wall surface.

   d   Furthest away from the door.

4 Which one of the following is **best** used for exterior work?

   a   medium-density fibreboard (MDF).

   b   Hardwood.

   c   Chipboard.

   d   Softwood.

5 Which one of the following is the correct method of decontaminating timber after using a paint stripper?

   a   Sanding it down.

   b   Wiping it down with old rags.

   c   Drying it off.

   d   Washing it down with water.

6 When should solvent-borne paint stripper be used?

   a   When there is a thin layer of paint to be removed.

   b   When the paint is flaking.

   c   When the surface is to be varnished.

   d   When there is a thick layer of paint to be removed.

7 How can efflorescence be removed from a surface?

   a   By washing it off with warm water.

   b   By wiping it down with rags.

   c   By brushing off with a stiff brush.

   d   By burning it off.

8 What causes wet rot?

   a   Cold weather.

   b   Windy conditions.

   c   Moist and warm conditions.

   d   Dry conditions.

9 What should you do **first** when removing vinyl wallpaper from a surface?

   a   Peel off the top layer.

   b   Score the paper first.

   c   Wet it in.

   d   Dry strip it.

10 What tool should be used to remove paint from mouldings?

   a   A stripping knife.

   b   A filling knife.

   c   Shavehooks.

   d   A wire brush.

11 What material should be used to wash down a previously painted surface?

   a White spirit.

   b Sugar soap.

   c Washing-up liquid.

   d Methylated spirit.

12 When using water-borne paint remover, which of the following is an advantage?

   a It does not scratch or scorch the surface.

   b It raises the grain of the timber.

   c It can soften plastic surfaces.

   d It has to be cleaned off before the surface can be painted.

13 Which of the following should be protected by a dust sheet before work can start?

   a Curtains and rails.

   b Electrical sockets.

   c Ceiling light fittings.

   d Floors and carpets.

14 When should a risk assessment be carried out?

   a At the end of a job.

   b In the middle of a job.

   c Before work starts each day.

   d When you think it needs doing.

15 Which one of the following will ensure that you produce the **best** paint finish?

   a Working safely.

   b Thorough preparation.

   c Good-quality tools, equipment and materials.

   d Using a tack rag.

16 What is meant by flaking paint?

   a Where the surface is covered with fine cracks.

   b Paint that has been applied too thickly.

   c Paint that has been applied over a greasy surface.

   d Where the paint film lifts from the surface and breaks down.

17 Which of the following is a ferrous metal?

   a Cast iron.

   b Copper.

   c Aluminium.

   d Lead.

18 What PPE should you wear when rubbing down?

   a High-visibility jacket, goggles and head protection.

   b Goggles, dust mask and overalls.

   c Ear defenders, toe-cap shoes and goggles.

   d Overalls, gloves and knee-pads.

19 What tool is used for stripping a surface of wallpaper?

   a Filling knife.

   b Stripping knife.

   c Sanding block.

   d Shavehooks.

20 Who **must** be informed in the event of a serious accident?

   a The supplier.

   b The British Safety Council.

   c The Health and Safety Executive.

   d The client.

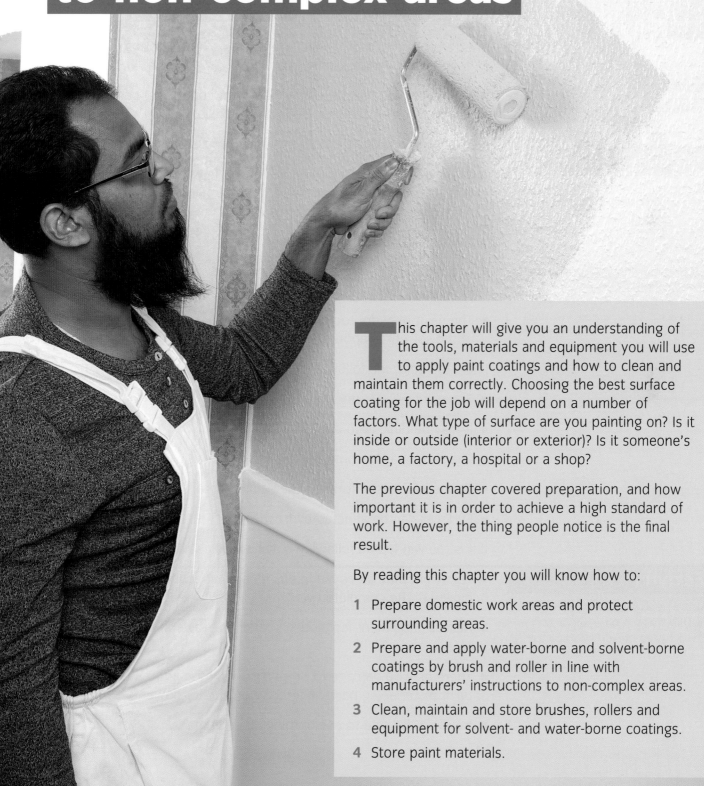

Chapter 5
Unit 118: Applying paint systems by brush and roller to non-complex areas

This chapter will give you an understanding of the tools, materials and equipment you will use to apply paint coatings and how to clean and maintain them correctly. Choosing the best surface coating for the job will depend on a number of factors. What type of surface are you painting on? Is it inside or outside (interior or exterior)? Is it someone's home, a factory, a hospital or a shop?

The previous chapter covered preparation, and how important it is in order to achieve a high standard of work. However, the thing people notice is the final result.

By reading this chapter you will know how to:

1 Prepare domestic work areas and protect surrounding areas.

2 Prepare and apply water-borne and solvent-borne coatings by brush and roller in line with manufacturers' instructions to non-complex areas.

3 Clean, maintain and store brushes, rollers and equipment for solvent- and water-borne coatings.

4 Store paint materials.

Weather conditions, such as snow, are likely to affect your finished work

PREPARE DOMESTIC WORK AREAS AND PROTECT SURROUNDING AREAS

Before starting any job you need to do your own risk assessment – not only to make sure that you and those around you are safe, but also to make sure that your finished work will be of a high standard.

There are many factors to consider when using paint, as different conditions may affect your finished work. These include:

- external – rain, snow, sleet, overcast sky, wind, storms, sea mist, pedestrians, vehicle traffic, pollution

- internal – dust, grease, damp, poor light conditions, occupation (if part of the area is being used), public areas

- location – rural areas, industrial areas, coastal areas.

All paint relies on the temperature to enable water and solvents to evaporate into the atmosphere so that the material can dry. If the conditions are not good, problems can occur during drying.

If it is too warm, the following may happen:

- Applied paint becomes too thin and does not cover the previous coating.

- The paint may dry too quickly while you are applying it as a result of the solvent evaporating during the oxidation process.

If it is too cold, the following may happen:

- The paint will not dry.

- It may be difficult to apply the paint.

- The paint may become too thick to apply.

- Condensation can form on the painted area.

- Surfaces can be affected by frost.

If it is too windy, the following may happen:

- Paintwork may be coved in dust/debris, affecting the standard and quality of the completed work.

- Access equipment (eg ladder, scaffolding towers) cannot be used safely.

- There may be damage to property during the application of the paint material (eg paint splattering on cars or flower beds below).

- It will not be safe to use burning-off equipment.

If it is too wet, the following may happen:

- The film finish may be impaired in some way (eg loss of gloss, **flashing**).

- Paint may not adhere (stick) to the previous coat of paint.

- It may be unsafe to work.

- It may delay the completion of the job.

Always make sure that the work area is well ventilated if working inside, not only when rubbing down or painting but also when burning off, because as the paint softens it starts to give off fumes again.

Flashing

A defect that occurs in flat and eggshell finishes and looks like glossy streaks or patches

PREPARING WORK AREAS

You should already have an understanding of the materials and equipment needed to protect a work area, as some of this was covered in Chapter 4. Here is a little more detail.

PROTECTING WORK AREAS BEFORE AND DURING WORK

When working in someone's home, it is very important to remember that any part of the house you enter needs to be protected from damage or spillage. Items that will need protecting include:

- flooring, such as carpets, rugs, tiles, wooden floors, patio floors

- access walkways to the work area

- ceiling light fittings

- door furniture such as locks, handles and hinges

- curtains and rails

- sofas and chairs

- tables and any other furniture

- wall lights and fittings

- patio areas

- plants and plant pots if you are working outside.

Where possible, portable items should be stripped from the room and stored during the painting and decorating process.

- Remove all moveable items from the room and store them in other rooms, making sure that access routes are not blocked. Furniture that is too large to be moved should be relocated to the centre and covered with protective sheeting.

Remove items and furniture from the room, if possible

INDUSTRY TIP

It is no good carefully sheeting up the living room where you are painting, but forgetting about the route to that room from your van outside, or to the kitchen where you will need to fetch water. If it is impossible to protect the whole area, you may need to wear disposable shoe covers.

Remember to turn electricity off at the mains before loosening light fittings

- Home office equipment such as computers and printers that cannot be removed from the room must be covered carefully and unplugged (check with the client first).

- Take care, if working in a kitchen, that hazardous surfaces such as gas and electric hobs are not turned on, causing a fire hazard.

- If the carpet is to be lifted, roll it up with the underlay and place it in the centre of the room. Cover using protective sheeting.

- Remove all curtains, nets and blinds and carefully fold them up, and if possible store them in another room to stop any damage occurring. If there is more than one window you may have to label them so you know where to hang them at the end of the job.

- Remove all curtain rails and fittings and store them in a safe place together, ready for refitting.

- Switch off the electricity supply at the mains if possible before loosening light fittings and switches. Do not leave them loose when you are away from the work area, as this could be dangerous when the mains is turned back on.

- Remove all ironmongery (furniture) from windows and doors to be painted.

- Mask up where needed, but remember not to leave masking tape on longer than necessary.

- Cover floors with dust sheets and secure them with masking tape.

USE OF DUST SHEETS

The work area needs to be protected as soon as you start to prepare surfaces for decorating, so the use of dust sheets was covered in the previous chapter. Traditional cotton twill dust sheets are the most widely used kind, but there are other types on the market that may be more suitable for specific jobs. While amateur decorators may be happy to use old bedsheets, they may not be thick enough to stop paint seeping through onto floors and carpets. Plastic or polythene sheets are cheap and can be disposable but paint and other liquid spills stay wet for a long time so there is a risk of treading paint all around the house. Using heavy-duty dropcloths will ensure that floors are adequately covered.

Heavy-duty canvas dropcloth

Adhesive plastic covering is available for floors. It comes on a roll and can be disposed of after use. The advantage of this is that it does not require additional taping to secure it.

If you are working outside you will need to consider the following:

- Protecting flower beds – if you need to access doors or windows from the outside, make sure that you do not damage plants and

Adhesive plastic covering

ornaments. Cover with light polythene dust sheets if necessary to stop paint or debris falling on plants and pathways.

- Terraces or patios may need protecting – not just from paint and debris, but also from steps or scaffolding. Use tarpaulin to protect the ground, as it is waterproof and harder wearing than cotton dust sheets.

- PVC guttering and pipes can be removed if required by unclipping from retaining clips, so that you can paint behind them.

- Make sure that there is no danger to the public and householders, and use warning signs where necessary.

ADDITIONAL TOOLS

Many of the tools that you will need for preparation have been covered already, but there are a few more that might be useful at this stage.

Screwdrivers

You will need a selection of screwdrivers to remove light fittings, switches and door furniture:

- slotted – for straight slotted screws

- cross-head – for cross-head (or Phillips) slotted screw heads

- Pozidriv – similar to a Phillips screwdriver but has more points of contact.

Different types of screwdriver

Pliers or pinchers

These are used to remove picture hooks from walls.

Brooms, dustpans and brushes, shovels

These are very important tools for a painter, not only for clearing up when you have finished, but also for clearing the area before you start work.

Pliers   Pinchers

Masking tape

Masking tape is a self-adhesive paper which comes in 55m lengths and 12mm, 19mm, 25mm, 38mm or 75mm widths. It has a variety of uses. Interior tape is used mainly for masking items that cannot be removed and stored, but it can also be used for taping down dust sheets to wooden floors or carpets to stop them moving and prevent tripping accidents. It can be used to protect narrow surfaces from paint or paint remover. The longer masking tape is stuck to a surface the more strongly it adheres (sticks), so take care when removing it. It is available with different strengths of adhesion – so, for example, a seven-day masking tape will be safe to leave on for seven days and will still peel off without damaging the surface. A low-tack masking tape can be used for signwriting and borders. This does not adhere as strongly to surfaces and is less likely to pull off the underlying

Masking tape

paint. Waterproof masking tape can be used for exterior work, such as masking up door furniture, window frames or fascia boards, and particularly to cover surrounding areas when painting rendered, brick or pebbledashed walls.

OTHER FACTORS

Other factors to consider when preparing the work area include:

■ Access – can you gain access when you need to, and can you get equipment and materials in easily? Can you get to running water to wash equipment, dilute paint and so on? Are people going to need to use the area you are working on, and will that cause any danger to you or them (for example when working on stairs or hallways)?

■ Public areas – you may be working in a domestic environment, but the property may still be accessed by visitors. You may need to put up barriers to prevent people entering your work area for their own safety.

Use barrier tape to prevent the public from entering the work area

ENVIRONMENTAL HEALTH AND SAFETY REGULATIONS

As explained in Chapter 1 the way you work is governed by certain regulations, which you should keep in mind while working. Many of the materials you will be working with are considered hazardous to health and need to be treated with caution (see COSHH, pages 9–11). For example, all paints contain vapours that are known as **volatile organic compounds (VOCs)**.

Volatile organic compounds (VOC)

Materials that evaporate readily from many sources; an example of which is the solvents used in the manufacture of many coatings. The measurement of volatile organic compounds shows how much pollution a product will emit into the air when in use

VOCs

These are vapours that evaporate into the air at room temperature from chemical substances, including those in cleaning products, cosmetics and paint. VOC emissions contribute to air pollution and affect the air we breathe. The measurement of volatile organic compounds shows how much pollution a product will emit into the air when in use. The paint industry is trying to reduce emissions, and many low-odour paints are now being produced. The European Parliament has set maximum VOC levels for different paints and varnishes (EU directive 2004/42/EC) and insists that containers should have a VOC content label so the consumer can compare products and choose an alternative if necessary. You can also ask your supplier for a copy of the data sheet.

If you are using a product that gives off vapours, you may need to put up a notice to warn people and make sure that you are using appropriate personal protective equipment (PPE). (See Chapter 1 for more information about PPE.)

Look for the VOC label on the products you use

Disposal of waste

You need to be very careful when disposing of hazardous waste:

- Do not pour it down the sink.

- Try not to buy more paint than you need for a job, and consider applying another coat if you have some left over.

- Empty emulsion tins must be washed out and can then be disposed of in the household waste.

- Check with your local authority for how to dispose of oil based paints and varnishes.

- Rags and cloths that have been used for applying chemical solvents should be allowed to dry and then disposed of carefully, as they can be a fire risk.

Old paint needs to be disposed of correctly

Cuts, abrasions, burns and dermatitis

Be particularly careful if you cut, graze or burn yourself when preparing or painting, as chemical substances can enter open wounds and cause infection and even blood poisoning. Make sure you cover the area with a clean waterproof dressing. **Contact dermatitis** can be avoided by applying barrier cream before every job and wearing gloves where necessary.

You will also need to be aware of safety risks such as dust inhalation, working with electricity and working at height, and produce a risk assessment. You can find out more about health and safety risks in Chapter 1.

Contact dermatitis

A type of eczema that can cause red, itchy and scaly skin, and sometimes burning and stinging. It leads to skin becoming blistered, dry and cracked, and can affect any part of the body, but most commonly the hands

Apply barrier cream to avoid developing contact dermatitis

PPE

PPE you may need includes:

- dust masks
- goggles
- toe-cap boots
- hard hat
- high-visibility jacket.

PREPARE WATER-BORNE AND SOLVENT-BORNE COATINGS TO NON-COMPLEX AREAS

Have you ever stopped to think about why it is necessary to paint anything? When asked, many painters and decorators don't really know why. Most people say that it is to make things look nice, and that answer is not wrong, but making something look nice is not all that a painter and decorator does.

REASONS FOR PAINTING

There are four reasons why a paint coating would be applied to a surface, so before moving on, take a little time to see if you can think of them. To help you, remember that we use the word DIPS.

Each letter stands for one of the reasons for painting:

- **D**ecoration
- **I**dentification
- **P**reservation
- **S**anitation

Decoration

We all have our own taste – what we like and do not like – but one reason for decoration is to make things look nice. You might not like the colours that the client has chosen, but you still have to apply them to the best of your ability. With experience you might be able to advise the client if you know colours do not work together. There is a whole science around the use of colour, as some colours are said to make people feel different emotions. For example, pale blue can be calming, red can make you anxious and sunny yellows can make you happy. Red walls would not be ideal in a hospital, and white or pastel colours in a nightclub would probably not give the right effect.

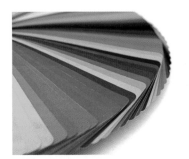

Colour cards

Identification

Different colours or types of surface coating can be used to identify areas or components. For example, pipework may have a British Standard colour painted on it to show whether it is carrying gas, water or other liquids. Setting industry standards ensures that all manufacturers use the same colours for identification so that mistakes are not made.

ACTIVITY

Start to take notice of the paint colours around you: in shops, offices, classrooms, doctors' waiting rooms, your own home. Are the colours appropriate for the area? If you could change the colour, what would you change it to, and why?

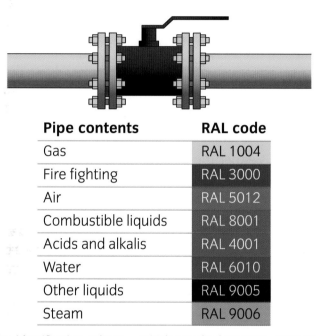

Pipe contents	RAL code
Gas	RAL 1004
Fire fighting	RAL 3000
Air	RAL 5012
Combustible liquids	RAL 8001
Acids and alkalis	RAL 4001
Water	RAL 6010
Other liquids	RAL 9005
Steam	RAL 9006

Pipeline identification colours – British Standard BS 1710: 1980 (Part 1)

Preservation

Painting can stop metal corroding and wood rotting, particularly when either is exposed to weather. An exterior door that has not been painted or has lost its paint coating will rot and need replacing, which will cost far more than regularly maintaining the door with paint or varnish. Corroding metal can also cost lives.

Sanitation

Coating substrates with paint prevents germs and dirt penetrating the surface, and this makes them much easier to wash and keep clean. This is particularly important in hospitals, shops and manufacturing, or where food is being prepared.

Testing kit

Pigment is used to colour paints

Key

A surface that is slightly rough, to help paint adhere to it

PAINT

There are two main types of paint:

- Water-borne paint – this means that the liquid part of the paint is water.

- Solvent-borne paint – this means that a chemical has been used instead of water to dissolve the other components of the paint.

When paint is applied to a surface, the water or the solvent (depending on the type of paint being used) will evaporate into the air, leaving a solid film that forms a protective and decorative layer on the surface.

Water-borne paint consists of three parts:

- Thinner – this is either the water or solvent part of the paint that dissolves the other components and makes it possible to apply the paint to a surface.

- Binder – this is a resin that forms the film of the paint. The binder determines how long the paint will last and the type of finish it will have (eg gloss, eggshell, flat).

- Pigment – this gives colour to the paint and is also responsible for the paint's ability to cover the surface.

Oil based paint contains a fourth element known as the drier, which speeds up the drying process.

Paint dries in one of two ways:

- Evaporation – the water or solvent turns into a vapour in the atmosphere and disappears.

- Chemical reaction – as the liquid part of the paint evaporates, the binder particles are drawn together, causing them to fuse and bind the pigment into a film.

TYPES OF SURFACE COATINGS

The combination of layers of paint is known as a paint system, and may consist of many different paints. The foundation coat of paint on a new surface is the primer or sealer, and it forms a **key** between the surface and the paint. The first coat bonds to the porous surface where it sinks in and grips on to it – or if the surface is non-porous, the paint film will lie on the top of it. The second coat to be applied is known as the undercoat, and this is followed by as many finishing coats as necessary.

Primers

A primer is the first coat of paint applied to a surface. The main purpose of a priming coat is to make the surface suitable to receive further coats.

Primer	Description	Method of application	Uses
Acrylic primer/ undercoat	▪ Water-borne paint thinned with water – used both as a primer and an undercoat. ▪ Usually available in white, but some manufacturers supply other pastel colours. ▪ Paint brushes and equipment will need to be cleaned with water.	▪ Brush, roller or spray.	▪ Can be applied to both exterior and interior surfaces. ▪ Can be applied to woodwork (softwood) old and new plaster, cement, concrete, hardboard, building boards. ▪ Not to be used on metal as acrylic primer contains water which may cause metal to rust. ▪ Can also be used as a matt finish for interior ceilings and walls.
Etch primer	▪ Designed for re-treatment of clean ferrous metals to ensure adhesion of the paint system to the surface. ▪ Paint brushes and equipment will need to be cleaned using the manufacturer's recommended cleaning solvent.	▪ Brush or spray.	▪ For pre-treatment of untreated surfaces such as aluminium, galvanised iron, zinc, copper, brass, lead, tin, clean iron and steel.
Alkali-resisting primer	▪ Primer that has been designed for surfaces that are alkaline in nature. ▪ Paint brushes and equipment will need to be cleaned with solvent (white spirit).	▪ Brush, roller or spray.	▪ To prime new and old building materials that are of an alkaline nature, eg plaster, brickwork, concrete blockwork.

Primer	Description	Method of application	Uses
Stabilising solution	■ Stabilising solution comes either clear or coloured. ■ The clear solution has better penetrating properties and is easier to apply. ■ Paint brushes and equipment will need to be cleaned with solvent (white spirit).	■ Brush or roller.	■ To stabilise old powdery surfaces before painting. ■ Can be used to seal plasterboard before paperhanging.
Lead-free wood primer	■ A general-purpose wood primer. ■ Available in white and pink. ■ Provides good adhesion for the undercoat. ■ Non-toxic, unlike lead-based primers (although lead-based primers are not sold any longer, they may still be found on some old paintwork). ■ Paint brushes and equipment to be cleaned with solvent (white spirit).	■ Brush.	■ Harder wearing than water-borne paint, so can be used on exteriors. ■ Can also be used on interior surfaces, particularly where children and pets may come into contact with the surface. ■ Good for hospitals, nurseries and places where food is stored.
Aluminium wood primer	■ This is a dull metallic grey oil based primer. ■ Paint brushes and equipment will need to be cleaned with solvent (white spirit).	■ Brush.	■ Used for resinous timber. ■ Used to seal surfaces previously treated with wood preservative. ■ Can also seal old bitumen-coated surfaces.

Primer	Description	Method of application	Uses
Zinc phosphate metal primer	■ A special rust-inhibitive (stopping) primer. ■ Paint brushes and equipment will need to be cleaned with solvent (white spirit).	■ Brush or roller.	■ Suitable for all ferrous metal surfaces.

Undercoats and finish coats

Undercoats are designed to give a sound base for the finish.

A finish coat (top coat) is the coat of paint that will be seen at the end of the job. There are many types of finish coat, and choosing the best one for the job often comes down to personal taste.

Opacity

The ability of paint to hide a surface – the higher the opacity the better the paint is at covering the background colour

Undercoat/finish coat	Description	Method of application	Uses
Oil based undercoat	■ A heavily pigmented oil based paint that dries to a matt finish and comes in a variety of colours. ■ Good adhesion to the primer and good **opacity**. ■ Paint brushes and equipment will need to be cleaned with solvent (white spirit).	■ Brush, roller or spray.	■ Over previously painted surfaces, timber, plaster concrete and metalwork. ■ Gives body and colour to a paint system and can be used over all primed surfaces both inside and outside.
Matt emulsion	■ A water-thinned paint suitable for painting ceilings and walls. ■ Easier to apply than oil based paints. ■ Matt emulsion dries to a flat/matt finish – small imperfections do not show, as no light is reflected. ■ Paint brushes and equipment will need to be cleaned with water.	■ Brush, roller or spray.	■ Mainly used for walls and ceilings. ■ Suitable for use over plaster, plasterboard, hardboard, brickwork, cement, rendering and wallpaper.

Undercoat/finish coat	Description	Method of application	Uses
Vinyl silk emulsion	■ Similar to matt emulsion paint, but with less opacity, and dries to a sheen finish. ■ Paint brushes and equipment will need to be cleaned with water.	■ Brush, roller or spray.	■ Uses the same as matt emulsion, but dries to a sheen finish which can be easily wiped down and is harder wearing. ■ Suitable for bathrooms, kitchens, hospitals and schools.
Gloss finish	■ Interior and exterior decorative paint, used as the main protective coating in the decorating trade. ■ Dries to a very high-gloss finish. ■ Excellent flow when **laying off**. ■ Very good flexibility, allowing the paint to expand and contract when dry. ■ Good weather resistance. ■ Paint brushes and equipment will need to be cleaned with solvent (white spirit).	■ Brush, roller or spray.	■ Decorative finish for interior and exterior surfaces. ■ Can be used on all woodwork, plaster and metalwork.
Eggshell/semi-gloss finishes	■ Interior decorative paint that dries with a sheen, also known as a silk or satin finish. ■ This is a solvent-borne paint and will dry to a harder finish than vinyl silk. ■ Paint brushes and equipment will need to be cleaned with solvent (white spirit).	■ Brush, roller or spray.	■ Decorative finish for interior surfaces, including ceilings, walls, softwood, hardwood and metal surfaces.

Laying off

Finishing off an area of paintwork with very light strokes of the brush in order to eliminate brush marks

Undercoat/finish coat	Description	Method of application	Uses
Masonry paint	■ A durable paint used for exterior walls (not timber surfaces). ■ Good opacity and alkali resistant. ■ The finish is tough, durable and flexible. ■ Paint brushes and equipment will need to be cleaned with water.	■ Brush, roller or spray.	■ Used to protect surfaces against the weather while also giving a good decorative finish. ■ Used on new and old cement rendering, concrete, brickwork, pebbledash and other types of masonry.
Low-odour eggshell	■ A water-borne coating for interior use, which dries to an eggshell finish or a soft semi-gloss finish. ■ Paint brushes and equipment to be cleaned with solvent (white spirit).	■ Brush, roller or spray.	■ Decorative finish coat for all interior surfaces. ■ Used where there is poor ventilation (toilets, kitchens, etc) so it has low odour and is non-toxic. ■ Requires no undercoat and dries quickly so that a second coat can be applied when required.

Clear finishes and wood preservatives

Paint does not always need to provide colour. For example, timber needs painting in order to preserve it, but it is often important to let the grain of the wood show through, so a variety of clear finishes, glazes and wood preservatives are used.

Wood staining on floorboards

The following table covers varnishes and preservatives you may come across.

Material	Description	Method of application	Uses
Emulsion varnish	■ A milky white material that provides a clear washable surface when dry. ■ Can be thinned using water. ■ Grease and food-stain resistant. ■ Washable and resistant to mild chemicals. ■ Non-toxic. ■ Paint brushes and equipment will need to be cleaned with water.	■ Brush, roller or spray.	■ Protective coating on wallpaper.
Polyurethane varnish	■ Clear surface coating available in gloss, matt or eggshell finish. ■ Use the manufacturer's recommended solvent to thin it. ■ Water, chemical and heat resistant. ■ Good adhesion. ■ Paint brushes and equipment will need to be cleaned using manufacturer's recommended solvents.	■ Brush or roller.	■ Protecting new and stained timber. ■ Used to protect paintwork, furniture and special decorative finishes like marbling and graining. ■ Although hard wearing not really suitable for exposed exterior surfaces.
Oil-resin varnish	■ A liquid coating that becomes a clear and protective film when dry. ■ Hard wearing and suitable for external use. ■ Water and weather resistant. ■ Dries to a high-gloss finish. ■ Paint brushes and equipment will need to be cleaned with solvent (white spirit).	■ Brush or roller.	■ Protecting new and stained timber. ■ Used to protect paintwork, furniture and special decorative finishes like marbling and graining. ■ Suitable for external use.

Material	Description	Method of application	Uses
Quick-drying varnish	■ A fast-drying, high-quality varnish that is easy to apply and has a very low odour. ■ When applying it has a milky white appearance but when dry it forms a clear finish. ■ Available in high-gloss or satin finishes. ■ Paint brushes and equipment will need to be cleaned with water.	■ Brush, roller or spray.	■ Gives good protection and decoration for interior timber and re-coating a previously coated surface that is in good condition.
High build wood oil	■ A highly durable **micro-porous**, **translucent**, semi-gloss finish that comes in a variety of colours (wood tones). ■ Forms a very flexible film once dried that can withstand changes in timber without cracking. ■ Paint brushes and equipment will need to be cleaned with solvent (white spirit).	■ Brush or roller.	■ The flexible micro-porous properties of high build wood stain makes it particularly suitable for the protection and decoration of exterior timber surfaces like window frames and doors.
Universal preservative	■ Clear solvent-borne liquid. ■ Takes 16 to 24 hours to dry under normal conditions. ■ Contains fungicide. ■ Paint brushes and equipment will need to be cleaned with solvent (white spirit).	■ Brush or roller.	■ Applied to new softwood that has not been treated with a preservative and suitable as a coating for weathered timber surfaces. On old timber the surface needs to be sound. ■ Stir well before use and apply one generous coat, paying particular attention to the end grain and joints.

Micro-porous paint

A paint that leaves a breathable film that allows moisture and air to be released but prevents moisture, like rain, getting in

Translucent

Allows light to pass through, but prevents images from being seen clearly

Material	Description	Method of application	Uses
Protective wood stain	■ A specially formulated protective wood stain. ■ Paint brushes and equipment will need to be cleaned with solvent (white spirit).	■ Brush and lint-free rag.	■ This can be used on both exterior and interior surfaces on softwood and hardwood as a decorative treatment. ■ Not to be used on painted or varnished timber. ■ Apply two coats of the wood stain by brush and lint-free rag. Allow to dry overnight in between coats.

PAINT SYSTEMS

Below are examples of the order of paint for paint systems.

Paint system	First coat	Second coat	Third coat	Fourth coat
New, unpainted surfaces to be painted with oil based or water-borne paints	Primer/sealer	Undercoat	Gloss	
	Primer	Undercoat	Eggshell	
	Sealer	Emulsion	Emulsion	
	Emulsion	Emulsion		
	Special primer	Undercoat	Top coat	Top coat
	Sealer	Stain	Varnish	
Previously painted surfaces	Undercoat	Gloss		
	Undercoat	Gloss	Gloss	
	Undercoat	Eggshell	Eggshell	
	Emulsion	Emulsion		
	Acrylic undercoat	Acrylic gloss		

APPLICATION TOOLS FOR SURFACE COATING

There is a wide selection of brushes and rollers on the market, which are used to apply paints, stains and clear coatings. The following will give you an understanding of which tool to use for a particular job.

Chapter 4 covered the tools and equipment needed for preparing surfaces for decoration, and stressed the importance of buying good-quality tools and equipment. This is also the case for the tools and equipment required for applying surface coatings.

BRUSHES

All brushes are made up of five parts:

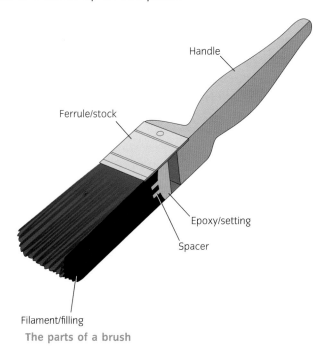

Handle

Ferrule/stock

Epoxy/setting

Spacer

Filament/filling

The parts of a brush

- Handle – usually made of a hardwood such as beech, sealed to make handling and cleaning easier and to stop water soaking into and damaging the wood. It can also be made from plastic.

- Ferrule/stock – this is a metal band that holds the filling and the handle together.

- Epoxy/setting – an adhesive which cements the filling by its roots into the stock.

- Filament/filling – these are usually natural bristle or synthetic man-made hairs, eg nylon.

- Spacer – small wood, plastic or cardboard strip that creates a reservoir to carry paint.

Natural bristle brushes are usually made from pig, hog or boar hair and are particularly suitable for applying oil based paints. Synthetic or man-made bristles are more springy and are better suited to applying water-borne paints.

Flat paint or varnish brushes

Available in pure bristle or synthetic hair, the cost of these brushes varies according to the quality and the quantity of the filling. They can be used for applying most types of paint and varnish coatings to a variety of surfaces, including doors, window frames and ceiling and wall areas.

Varnish brushes

Two-knot washing-down brush

Pure bristle flat wall brush with copper ferrule

Two-knot brush

Block brush

Set of fitch brushes

Wooden-handled radiator brush

Metal-handled radiator brushes

Washing-down brushes

These are relatively cheap two-knot brushes, available in one size only, and used for washing down with sugar soap or detergent.

Flat wall brushes

These are available in a wide range of varying qualities, and may be either man-made or pure bristle. The quality is dependent on the weight and length of the filling. This type of brush is used to apply emulsion to large flat areas such as ceilings and walls, and may also be used to apply adhesive to wallpaper.

Two-knot brushes

These brushes are available mainly in pure bristle, and the knots are usually bound in copper wire, as it does not rust. They are used to apply water-thinned paints to rough surfaces such as cement, rendering and brickwork. They are also used to apply cement-based paints, as the bristles are not attacked by the alkali in the cement, and for washing down surfaces when using a cleaning agent such as sugar soap.

Cement paint brushes (or block brushes)

These brushes have man-made filling or coarse white fibre that has been set in a polished wooden handle. Cheaper block brushes are available in plastic. This is an inexpensive brush type for applying masonry finishes and cement paints to a rough surface such as cement rendering or brickwork.

Fitch brushes

These are available with pure bristle or synthetic filling, which is usually white and set in a round or flat ferrule. They are used for fine detailed work in areas that are difficult to reach with a paint brush.

Radiator brushes

These have a bristle filling attached to a long wooden handle, or a wire handle that can be bent to fit into awkward areas. They are used to apply paint to areas that are difficult to reach with a paint brush, particularly behind pipes, radiators and columns.

ROLLERS

Applying paint to a large flat surface may be quicker using a paint roller. Specially shaped rollers are also available for painting corners, but sometimes it can be easier to use a paint brush. The standard type of roller used by decorators is a cylinder roller, which consists of a straight cylinder with a fabric cover called a sleeve.

The choice of roller will depend on the type of coating being used and the type of substrate to be painted. There are many types, including very smooth rollers for applying finishing paints to flat doors and lambswool rollers for applying paint to a textured surface such as pebbledash. It is important to select the appropriate roller for the job. When working on ceilings or high walls, an extension pole attached to the roller may enable you to avoid using scaffolding.

Mohair

Rollers made from natural mohair are very expensive, but you can now buy synthetic mohair rollers, which are more affordable. Short-haired rollers are used to apply gloss paint to a smooth surface, medium-haired are for applying emulsion and long-haired rollers are for pebbledashed surfaces.

Medium-piled mohair sleeve

Short-pile lambswool

Lambswool roller sleeves are made from the wool of sheep and are used to apply water-borne or oil based paint to a smooth surface such as plaster, plasterboard or metal.

Long-pile lambswool

These roller sleeves have a deep **pile**, which is well suited to applying water-borne paints to brickwork and pebbledashed surfaces.

Pile

The soft projecting surface of a fabric consisting of many small threads

Woven long pile

All woven rollers are made of synthetic filaments. Long-pile rollers are used mainly for applying emulsion and masonry paint to pebbledashed surfaces. They come in 330mm widths, so become very heavy when loaded with paint. All woven rollers are very similar to lambswool rollers but are much cheaper, so can be thrown away after use.

Woven medium pile

These are used for applying emulsion, primer, rust-protection paint and varnish to small surfaces or semi-rough surfaces.

Medium-pile woven fabric roller sleeve

Polyester long pile

These are synthetic fabric rollers, with a highly absorbent 18mm pile, used for applying water-borne coatings such as emulsion and masonry paint to rough areas.

Polyester medium pile

These are similar to polyester long-pile rollers, but with a shorter, 12mm, pile.

Woven short pile

The 6mm-deep pile is used for applying emulsion, primer, rust-protection paint and varnish to small surfaces.

Small paint roller

Decant

To transfer a liquid by pouring from one container into another

Contaminate

To pollute or infect

Consistency

Related directly to the viscosity of a coating, which can be altered by the addition of thinners or solvents

Small rollers

100mm rollers can be bought in long-, medium- and short-pile versions and can be made from natural or synthetic material. They are used for applying paint to small areas, for example flush doors, panels, furniture and small wall areas. They can also be used for applying paint behind a radiator.

PREPARING PAINT FOR USE

Once the surface is prepared and you have chosen the paint system to apply there is still some work to do before you start to paint. The covering you are going to use will usually come in a large container, so the paint will need to be **decanted** into a paint kettle, a roller tray or a bucket.

DECANTING PAINT

If the container of paint has not been used before, you must do the following:

- Remove any dust from the lid of the paint container. It may have gathered dust by being stored close to someone rubbing down.

- Open the lid using a paint tin opener. Never use the edge of a paint scraper or filling knife, as the blades are easily damaged.

- Stir the paint with a paint stirrer or palette knife until all the sediment is dispersed and the required **consistency** is achieved.

Paint stirrer

Palette knife

- Pour the required amount of paint into the paint kettle or roller tray.

- With your brush, remove any paint that may have gathered in the rim of the paint container and then wipe it clean using a rag.

- Replace the lid of the paint container so that the remaining paint does not become contaminated.

If the containers of paint have been previously used, remove any dust from the lid of the paint container and open it as described above. Also bear in mind the following points:

- The air trapped inside the container when the lid was last replaced may cause a skin to form on the surface of the paint. If there is a skin present, it can be removed by cutting it away from the edge of the inside of the container. Lift out the skin intact if possible and dispose of it.

- Search the paint for lumps and debris by straining. Place a paint strainer on a paint kettle and pour the required amount of paint through the strainer to remove any bits of skin or contamination that may be present from the last time the container was opened.

- Remove the strainer and clean it or dispose of it.

- Clean the rim of the container using a rag and then replace the lid.

Traditional strainers will need cleaning after each use, otherwise they will clog up when the paint dries. Single-use disposable strainers are available, but these do work out more expensive. For a cheaper option you can use old tights or stockings to strain the paint, and then dispose of them.

The **viscosity** of the paint will have to be checked to make sure the paint is the correct thickness to apply to the surface. Paint that is too thick will be hard to apply, and paint that is too thin will not give sufficient coverage. Check the manufacturer's instructions before thinning out paint.

If the paint inside an old tin is still usable it will need to be opened with care

Traditional paint strainer

Viscosity

The ability of a liquid or coating to flow; the more viscous it is, the slower it flows

APPLY WATER-BORNE AND SOLVENT-BORNE COATINGS TO NON-COMPLEX AREAS

PAINTING LARGE AREAS

When painting large areas, such as ceilings and walls, there are a number of things to consider.

What do you need to reach the work areas?
If you are working on a ceiling or a high wall you may need some form of scaffolding to reach the work area, or you may be able to manage with a pair of steps. The important thing is to plan how you are going to reach the whole area to be covered, because once you have started you will need to keep the edge going so that paint will flow into itself and not leave fat edges.

Is the surface flat or textured?
This will determine what tools and equipment you will need to carry out the painting.

What is the drying time of the paint?
The manufacturer's instructions on the paint container will tell you how quickly the paint will dry. If the drying time is quick and you have a large area to paint, you may need a second person to help. The instructions will also tell you how long to wait before giving the surface a second coat.

Scaffold tower

Will you need more than one person to paint the work area?

Remember that you will need to keep the edge wet to ensure that you produce a solid paint film by eliminating brush strokes. You may need to work with a partner to achieve this.

Is the surface porous or non-porous?

This may affect the drying time, the consistency and the amount of paint required. See Chapter 4, page 151, for more about porosity.

What should you use to apply the paint?

For small areas such as doors, window frames and pipes you may need only a brush, but for larger areas you may need a roller for the area and a brush for **cutting in** around the edges. If two of you are working on the same area, one may cut in and the other may apply the paint using the roller.

Where should I start?

When painting large areas, plan where to start and where to finish to ensure that the edge does not dry off before the next application of paint. Look at the area that is going to be painted, and remember that you will need to keep the edge wet – so whether it is a ceiling, wall, or door always start at the narrowest part.

APPLICATION OF PAINT COATING TO CEILINGS AND WALLS

CUTTING IN

When painting an area with a large brush or roller it is difficult to get into the corners and around obstructions, so before you start you will need to use a small brush to make a neat line around door frames, windows, mouldings and internal angles. Professional decorators rarely use masking tape to cut in around windows and other obstacles, as it is time consuming and paint sometimes seeps under the tape anyway. You will develop the skill to paint straight lines neatly – it may take a while to have the confidence to paint freehand, but practice makes perfect.

Once you have cut in the edges you can then fill in the area with a large brush or roller.

WATER-BORNE PAINTS

When applying water-borne coatings such as emulsion paint to ceilings or walls by brush, work in stages as shown on the next page. However, do not lay off in the conventional way, as you would when painting a door (see page 207). Cross-hatching is the best method when applying emulsion, to minimise the effect of brush marks (tramlines) created by the brush.

Cutting in

The process of producing a sharp neat paint line between two structural components in a room, such as a wall/ceiling, architrave/wall, etc

---

INDUSTRY TIP

Goggles are not needed when painting ceilings.

Decorator painting a ceiling

ACTIVITY

Draw lines with a pencil on a piece of hardboard and practise cutting in along the lines. Hold your brush like a pencil to start with, but you may develop your own style later on.

Cutting in

THE CITY & GUILDS TEXTBOOK

When matt emulsion dries, the light is **refracted** rather than running down the brush marks, thus making the paint appear more **opaque** and matt.

Vinyl silk emulsion highlights defects of both the surface and the brush marks, but it is easier to keep clean than matt and can be wiped over with a cloth.

If you are using oil based paint on ceilings you will need to follow the same process you used when applying paint to walls.

In order to keep the wet edge to a minimum in terms of both time and area you will need to work on small sections at a time by mentally dividing the wall into small squares.

This is the sequence for one decorator applying paint to a wall:

One decorator paints sections 1–6	5	3	1
	6	4	2

Example area 2.5m × 5m

If two decorators are working on a large wall, one would cut in while the other decorator filled in with a roller.

This is the sequence for two decorators applying paint to a ceiling:

One decorator paints 1–3, above, at the same time as the second decorator paints 1–3, below	3	2	1
	3	2	1

Example area 2.5m × 5m

As explained earlier, make sure you keep the edge wet. The size of the brush you use will depend on the size of the area being painted. Remember, you are aiming to keep the edge wet and at the same time to apply an even coat.

When using brushes and rollers on large surfaces such as ceilings and walls:

- cut in the edges first at the ceiling or wall line
- cut around obstacles such as electrical fittings and any fixtures
- use a suitable-sized paint brush for the cutting in.

Refract

To deflect light from a straight path

Opaque

Not transmitting light – the opposite of transparent

INDUSTRY TIP

Make sure you learn the sequences for working on your own and working with a partner.

APPLICATION PROCEDURES

The following instructions describe application procedures in different situations.

APPLYING SOLVENT-BORNE PAINTS BY BRUSH TO NON-COMPLEX AREAS

STEP 1 Apply the first application of coating to the surface using the cross-hatch method. Work in areas of approximately 300mm square along the surface and then continue down or across the surface.

STEP 2 Lay off the applied paint in the short direction, overlapping each brush stroke by a third of the width of the brush. The paint will flow into itself and make an invisible join.

STEP 3 When applying the paint, you will need to put light pressure on the brush to make the bristles work the paint to an even application.

STEP 4 Finally, lay off in the final direction, lengthways. You do not need to load any more paint on to the brush for the laying off process.

APPLYING OIL BASED AND ACRYLIC PAINTS BY BRUSH TO DOORS

If you are painting a door that opens towards you into the room, you will need to paint the edge with the lock and fittings on first. When you are painting a door that opens away from you, you will need to paint the hinge edge first. Paint the edge before the face of the door, as once the face has been painted there may be a build-up of paint on the edge, which will be less noticeable when the paint has dried.

Here are some factors to consider when applying paint coatings to doors:

- Is it an external door? External doors are often made from hardwood to help protect them from the weather and should be coated with an oil based paint. Remember that paint will dry quicker outside.

- Is it an internal door? Internal doors are more likely to be made from softwood and not affected by bad weather, so can be painted using either oil based or acrylic paint.

- Is the surface flush or panelled?

- Is the surface PVC or metal?

- Are there any glazed (glass) areas?

The traditional sequence of painting a flush door starts at the top left-hand corner and ends at the bottom right, as shown on the diagram.

Sequence for painting a flush door

Always rub down between coats to remove **nibs**, and then use a dusting brush to remove any fine dust remaining on the surface.

Panelled doors

When painting or varnishing a panelled door, follow the sequence shown in the diagram. Start at the top left panel to help avoid fat edges forming. Remember to lay off following the direction of the grain.

ACTIVITY

Take a flat piece of timber that has been primed (about 700mm × 1000mm should do) and practise this method of applying oil based paint before attempting a real door.

Nibs

Small particles of foreign matter, such as paint skin or grit, that have dried in the film of a coating and which cause it to feel rough

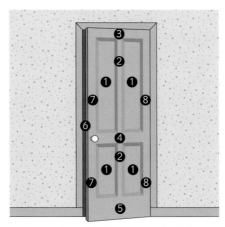

Sequence for painting a panelled door

PAINTING LINEAR WORK

All rooms have some form of **linear** work, consisting of the following surfaces:

- door frames
- skirting boards
- mouldings.
- dado rails
- picture rails

When painting these surfaces, use a small cutting-in brush and make sure that the surfaces are not overloaded with paint, as this could result in runs and sags, spoiling the finished look of the surface.

FERROUS AND NON-FERROUS SURFACES

If the surface needs priming, use the appropriate primer followed by an undercoat and finishing coats.

The method for applying paint is the same for all surfaces:

1 Lightly rub down with fine abrasive.

2 Dust off.

3 Apply the coating and lay off to form an even coat of paint.

Painting a skirting board

VARNISHING OR STAINING TIMBER SURFACES

Although this can be a separate specialist job, you may be called on to varnish a timber surface such as a door or a skirting board. On surfaces that are to be covered with opaque paint the undercoat and primer will not show through the finishing coats, but this is not the case with translucent or **transparent** coverings. Stains and varnishes protect timber surfaces without obscuring the beauty of the grain. It is therefore important that these surfaces are prepared in a different way from wood that is painted.

WOOD STAINS

Wood stains can be used on exterior and interior timbers and when applied they soak deep into the timber surface to emphasise the grain of the wood. They come in a variety of colours, from natural wood shades to vibrant colours intended to change the appearance of the timber. They can be sealed with clear varnish or polish after application.

A natural wood stain is used to emphasise the timber

Wood stain application

Before applying the wood stain make sure the surface is dry, then lightly rub down using fine silicon carbide paper, with the grain. Remove dust and apply the stain with a brush and a lint-free cloth. Lay off following the direction of the grain so that the wood stain flows and forms an even finish.

VARNISH

This is a transparent liquid that is applied to a surface to produce a hard, protective, transparent coating. Varnish can be clear, and is also available already stained in wood colours.

Varnish application

The aim is to produce an even level film free from runs, sags and pin-holing and with no dust or bittiness. It is important to apply the varnish firmly and confidently. If the coating is rubbed out too thinly and is bare in places it will be impossible to obtain an evenly distributed film, and this result in runs and a poor appearance. Previously varnished surfaces should be lightly rubbed down to de-nib them, then dusted off and the surface wiped over with a tack rag. Knots should not be sealed with knotting solution, as this will show through the varnish. Some surfaces will require more preparation so will need sanding, then should be wet abraded using silicon paper.

Varnish provides a protective coating to wood

Apply paint evenly to avoid runs in your finish

An example of bittiness in applied paint

POST-APPLICATION DEFECTS

As decorators we aim to produce a perfect finish, but mistakes can be made that need correcting. Chapter 4 listed many of the common defects you may find when preparing previously painted surfaces. These and other defects are covered here in a little more detail, focusing on what causes them and how to avoid making them in the first place:

- Cissing – take care not to pick up grease on the bristles of the brush, as this can cause cissing (when the paint does not form a continuous film on the surface). Check also that there is no grease on the substrate. If an area has cissed, allow it dry before wiping off, degreasing and repainting.

- Orange peel – this texture may be left by certain roller sleeves when applying paint to the surface. Make sure that the pile on the roller is not too thick for the job – however, most rollers will leave a slight orange-peel effect. If a smooth, flat finish is required it is best to use a brush.

- Ladders and excessive brush marks – these are paint defects in which the laying-off brush lines can be seen after the final laying-off process has been completed. When laying off, use light brush strokes so the paint flows into itself. To rectify these defects you will need to wait until the paint is thoroughly dry, not just touch dry. The surface will then need to be wet and dried before being recoated (see abrading in Chapter 4). Try not the break through the surface of the paint film when rubbing down, or you may have to undercoat the area again.

- Runs – this is a defect caused by over-application of paint, which at first sags and then turns into runs before drying. Paint needs to be applied evenly and laid off so that it flows into itself. Rectify in the same way as ladders.

- Sags and curtains – these are similar to runs, and should be rectified in the same way as ladders.

- Excessive bits and nibs – these may occur if the paint has not been strained or the surface not dusted down properly after rubbing down. They may also happen as a result of other tradespeople doing their job, or just walking by if there is dust on the floor. If the paint is the problem, stop and strain it – the problem will not just go away. Dust off the surface if necessary and make sure you don't paint while someone is sweeping up around you. Bits and nibs on the surface will have to be thoroughly rubbed down when completely dry before you apply the next coat.

- Fat edges – this is a fault of application whereby a thick ridge of paint occurs on a corner or **arris**. It can be avoided by laying off at the corners with an almost dry brush. This can be a particular problem when painting doors, as paint tends to build up on the edges.

- Ropiness – also known as ribbiness or tramlines. This occurs when paint does not flow evenly and is usually caused by faulty workmanship. It could happen as a result of applying the paint unevenly or over-brushing the paint until it starts to set (not keeping the edge alive/wet).

- Misses – these are areas that have been missed when applying paint, generally through carelessness. When dry, the area will have to be re-coated and then checked to make sure the area is uniformly covered. If not, re-coat.

- Skid marks – these are usually caused by overloaded rollers skidding over the surface.

- Paint splatters and specks on surrounding areas – this could be a result of over-vigorous brush strokes or having too much paint loaded on the brush. Make sure that surrounding areas are protected before starting work. Remove splatters with the appropriate solvent – water for emulsion, white spirit for gloss paint.

Arris

A sharp external edge, such as the edge of a door

Misses are generally caused by carelessness

CLEAN, MAINTAIN AND STORE BRUSHES, ROLLERS AND EQUIPMENT

As with all tools and equipment, there is little point in buying good-quality paint brushes and rollers if you do not clean and store them properly.

CLEANING PAINT BRUSHES AND ROLLERS

Tools that have been used for oil based paint will need cleaning with a different solvent than tools used for water-borne paint, but the aim is the same – to remove all of the remaining paint from the filling and stock of the brush. This is the process:

- Identify the type of paint that has been used, whether it was oil based or water-borne paint (you may not have been using the brush yourself).

- Pour excess paint from the kettle or roller tray back into the paint container and wipe the brush on the container to remove as much paint as possible (some decorators use a piece of board to wipe their brush on).

- Wash the brush in the correct solvent – for oil based paint use white spirit or the manufacturer's recommended cleaner. Use water for water-borne paint.

Cleaning oil based paint equipment

Follow this process when cleaning oil based paint equipment:

- Pour the cleaning agent (white spirit) into the paint kettle and use a vigorous pumping action to remove paint from the stock. Repeat until there is no evidence of any colour coming from the brush.

- Spin the brush between your two hands to remove as much of the solvent as possible (paint brush spinners can help with this job).

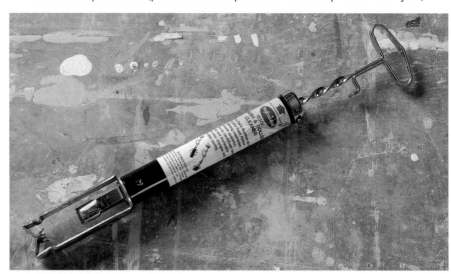

Paint brush spinner

Clean off water-borne paint with warm soapy water

Steeped

Soaked in liquid

- Wash the brush in warm soapy water until you get a clean lather, then rinse thoroughly in clean water.

Cleaning water-borne paint equipment

Follow the same process as for oil based paint, but use warm soapy water instead.

Cleaning rollers

Rollers take longer to clean than paint brushes, and the longer the pile the more time consuming they are. Using cheaper roller sleeves that can be thrown away at the end of a job can be cost-effective.

If you cannot clean up your brushes and rollers at the end of the day, they can be **steeped** in water or solvent until they can be cleaned properly. Do not leave them there for too long, though, as the liquids will evaporate and the brushes and rollers will dry out, making them unusable.

Cleaning other equipment

Excess paint from used kettles, roller trays and roller buckets should be wiped back into the paint container, and the item should be washed with the appropriate solvent. Once these items have been cleaned they should be stored in a dry area, as damp may cause metal to rust.

STORING EQUIPMENT

STORING PAINT BRUSHES

Clean paint brushes should be stored in a cool, dry place. Excessive heat may cause the bristles and setting material to shrink, resulting in loose ferrules and bristles. In damp conditions mildew may develop on the bristles, which will damage the brush.

Never store the brushes with the filling pointing downwards, as this will bend the bristles and ruin the brush.

A brush keeper is used to store brushes in a wet state. The brush is kept in a bottle of solvent with an evaporating wick. The fumes from the solvent replace the air inside the brush keeper, preventing the brushes from drying out.

STORING ROLLERS

Rollers should be stored at a moderate temperature in a place where they cannot be contaminated by chemicals, oil or grease. If possible, hang them up so that the air can flow around the roller sleeve. If you cannot hang them up, stand them upright, as storing them on flat surfaces may crush the pile.

STORING PROTECTIVE SHEETING

Cotton dust sheets and other protective sheeting should be given a light shake once finished with (although not near wet paint!) and folded up ready for use. If sheets are wet or damp they should be allowed to dry before being folded and stored to prevent mildew forming on them. All protective sheeting should be stored on shelves off the floor. It is important to keep sheeting clean and dry because it will be used to protect floors another time. If need be, send it away to be cleaned.

Sheeting such as tarpaulin, PVC-coated nylon, rubber-coated cotton and heavy cotton canvas should be stored in the same way as cotton dust sheets. Rubber tarpaulin can be wiped clean using a sponge and warm water and allowed to dry before being folded and stored.

If protective sheeting is not used for some time it will need to be checked for damp. If there are signs of damp, unfold and air-dry it before re-folding and storing it.

Paint brush storage system

Allow tarpaulin sheets to dry before folding for storage

> **INDUSTRY TIP**
>
> Always check that tools are clean before use. Kettles, buckets and roller trays should be wiped out before use to remove dust particles.

CARE OF PPE

It is very important to keep your PPE clean and in good condition. Check it daily to make sure that it will do the job it is intended to do.

Safety boots/toe-cap boots

After use wipe away dirt and grime with a cloth, as some solvents may harm the leather. Clear the treads and clean as required.

Hard hats

A hard hat should be cleaned at least once a month or as often as necessary to remove oil, grease, chemicals and sweat. Soak in a mild solution of soap and hot water, rinse with clean water, wipe and let the air dry it. Sunlight can damage the hat, so check for cracks and splits and replace the hat if necessary.

High-visibility jackets

Wearing a high-visibility jacket is meant to make it easier for other people to see you, so you must keep it clean. Wiping it clean with a damp rag should be sufficient.

Goggles

There are lots of jobs that will require you to wear goggles (rubbing down, washing down cleaning solvents from brushes, etc). Wash them in mild soapy water to keep the lenses free from grease and dirt.

Protective gloves

Make sure that there are no tears or splits in rubber gloves, as solvents and chemicals may seep through and harm the skin (they can cause rashes and dermatitis). Cotton or latex gloves are good for light work. Wash cotton gloves regularly, or wear disposable latex gloves. Remember always to apply barrier cream, even when you are wearing gloves.

Dust mask

Your dust mask will need changing regularly depending on the type of work you are doing. For example, when you are doing heavy rubbing down or sanding the mask will need changing more often than for light rubbing down.

For more information, look back at the PPE section in Chapter 1.

Check your hard hat before use

Applying barrier cream

Remember to change your dust mask

Deteriorate

To make or become worse

Flash point

The temperature at which a material gives off a vapour that will ignite if exposed to flame. Chemicals with a low flash point are labelled as highly flammable

STORE PAINT MATERIALS

New or partially used materials and tools and equipment will need storing correctly to ensure safety and so that they do not **deteriorate**. They should be stored in such a way as to protect your own health and safety and that of others. Many chemicals used by decorators have a low **flash point**, and if they are kept in hot conditions they are likely to explode or catch fire.

The storage area should be dry, well ventilated and frost free all year round but should not contain any naked flames, for example gas heaters or boilers, as many materials are flammable. For the same reason you should not smoke in a storage area.

INDUSTRY TIP

Do not smoke around highly flammable materials.

INDUSTRY TIP

Be careful how you lift items from storage areas. Look back at the guidance on manual handling in Chapter 1, pages 18–19.

Check the use-by dates on water-borne paints

Here are some things to consider when arranging storage areas:

INDUSTRY TIP

Always check manufacturer's instructions on storage.

- The storage area should be fitted with sturdy racks, with large and heavy material stored on the bottom shelves. Never store powder filler or textured finish materials on concrete floors, as floors can remain cold and damp even in warm weather and the products will be unfit for use. Small containers of filler that have been opened can be stored in airtight plastic containers.

- Oil based paints (undercoat, gloss and varnish) and water-borne paints (emulsions and masonry paints) should be stored on shelves and clearly marked with the labels turned to the front. Use them in date order.

Ensure the correct fire extinguishers are available

- Oil based materials should be **inverted** at regular intervals to prevent settlement of the pigments and separation of the ingredients. Check that the lids are on firmly before doing this.

Inverted

Turned upside down

- Some water-borne paints, such as emulsions and acrylics, have a limited shelf life – check their use-by date.

- Some paints are susceptible to livering, where the paint thickens to a jelly-like condition (like raw liver) as a result of oxidation during storage.

- Never stack materials so high that there is a danger of them falling. Don't over-reach to try to get a product from a high shelf – you don't want it falling on you and covering you in paint.

- Appropriate fire extinguishers should be available in case of a fire. (See fire extinguishers and their uses in Chapter 1, page 39.)

- Make sure that lids and caps are on tightly to limit the escape of VOCs into the air.

Check lids are on tightly before storage

Case Study: John and Nils

Decorators John and Nils were sent to an address by their employer and told to prepare and paint a bedroom. The client was out so they let themselves in and went upstairs to find the bedroom. They found two tins of paint in one of the rooms, so started to prepare for painting. They were told to paint two coats of emulsion on the ceiling and walls and one coat of undercoat and a coat of gloss on all woodwork.

While John started to de-nib the ceiling, Nils went to make tea. After their drink they started painting the ceiling. It was a large room so they worked on it together to keep the edge wet. They then painted a coat of paint on the walls. They worked very hard, as there was much to do, and when they were finished they washed their brushes and kettles and went home.

That evening John and Nils received a call from their boss to say that the client was outraged and wanted them back to put the damage right the next day.

What could they have done wrong?

At first glance it seems as if John and Nils did very little wrong, as the room was well painted. It was unfortunate that communication with their employer and the client was poor – no real harm was done, as they did not make a mess. The only problem was that they had painted the wrong room!

The paint had been stored in one room but it was meant for the bedroom next door. So, however good your decorating skills, make sure your communication skills are good too and if you are not sure what to do – check.

Work through the following questions to check your learning.

1 Which one of the following is **not** classed as a finishing coat?

   a Eggshell.

   b Undercoat.

   c Varnish.

   d Gloss.

2 When should barrier cream be applied?

   a When washing up brushes.

   b When cutting in.

   c When taking a break.

   d When starting the job.

3 Which one of the following is a water-borne paint?

   a Emulsion.

   b Eggshell.

   c Gloss.

   d Oil based undercoat.

4 What is a fat edge?

   a Where paint has run down a wall.

   b Where grease has stopped the paint from adhering.

   c Where a thick ridge of paint forms on a corner.

   d Where paint has been applied without being diluted.

5 Which one of the following is **best** used to protect flower beds when working outside?

   a Tarpaulin.

   b Cotton dust sheets.

   c Heavy-duty canvas dropcloths.

   d Polythene dust sheets.

6 Which one of the following is the **correct** order of painting?

   a Primer, undercoat, gloss.

   b Sealer, emulsion, eggshell.

   c Emulsion, undercoat, gloss.

   d Undercoat, gloss, eggshell.

7 Why is pigment used in paint?

   a It helps with the drying of the paint.

   b It gives colour to the paint.

   c It helps to thin the paint.

   d It binds the components of paint.

8 Which one of the following is another name for bristles?

   a Stock.

   b Setting.

   c Filling.

   d Spacer.

9 When applying paint to a large wall, where is it **best** to start from?

   a The top of the wall.

   b The right-hand side.

   c The narrowest part.

   d The left-hand side.

10 Why is it good practice for two painters to work together on a large area?

   a To get the job done quicker.

   b So they have someone to talk to.

   c So that there is less chance of splashing.

   d To keep the edge wet.

11 Which one of the following is classed as linear?

   a Skirting boards.

   b Walls.

   c Doors.

   d Ceilings.

12 What is the cause of a defect known as 'orange peel'?

   a Leaving grease on a surface.

   b Poor laying off of the paint.

   c Not removing nibs from the surface.

   d Using a roller to apply paint to a surface.

13 Which one of the following brushes is **best** for painting rough surfaces?

   a Fitch brush.

   b Block brush.

   c Flat brush.

   d Varnish brush.

14 What can cause dermatitis?

   a Brush marks.

   b Not wearing goggles.

   c Safety boots being too loose.

   d Not wearing gloves.

15 What is the **first** thing you should do before opening a container of paint?

   a Clean the lid to remove dust.

   b Check that you have a strainer ready to use.

   c Shake the container to mix the paint.

   d Check that it is the right colour.

16 What does 'opaque' mean?

   a Covering the previous coat.

   b Not transmitting light.

   c The thickness of the paint.

   d The applied paint not drying.

17 Which one of the following should be used to remove surface nibs before painting?

   a Aluminium oxide abrasive.

   b Glass paper.

   c Wet and dry.

   d Emery paper.

18 What can happen if you are painting in high temperatures?

   a The paint becomes too thick to apply.

   b The film finish can be impaired.

   c The paint will not dry.

   d The paint will dry quickly.

19 Which one of the following defects is caused by grease on a surface?

   a Runs.

   b Cissing.

   c Skid marks.

   d Sags.

20 When tarpaulin is stored damp, what might it do?

   a Stick to itself.

   b Not lie flat.

   c Perish.

   d Go mouldy.

Chapter 6
Unit 119: Applying foundation and plain papers

This chapter deals with many aspects related to paperhanging, especially the selection and application of foundation and plain papers. The information covers the tools and equipment required and the types of paste and adhesives used, as well as the range of papers described as foundation and plain papers. These and many other paper-type hangings are often referred to as wallpaper, although technically all hangings should be referred to as ceiling or wall coverings. This means that specialist materials such as grass cloth and lincrusta hangings can also be included. You will look at specialist materials in more depth at Levels 2 and 3.

By reading this chapter you will know how to:

1 Select, use, maintain and store tools and equipment.

2 Select and prepare adhesives.

3 Apply lining paper and wood ingrain to walls.

4 Store materials in line with manufacturers' instructions.

◀

INDUSTRY TIP

The terms wall coverings, wall hangings and wallpapers often refer to the same thing.

Wooden printing blocks

Machine printing

SELECT, USE, MAINTAIN AND STORE TOOLS AND EQUIPMENT

Like many hand skills, paperhanging or hanging of wall coverings is one that requires patience, practice and an eye for accuracy. The application of wallpapers dates from at least the medieval period, when wallpapers were seen as cheap alternatives to costly tapestries, silks, panelling and other decoration of the time. These early papers were usually hand block printed onto squares of paper and then matched on the wall. Later papers were machine printed and it then became possible to manufacture them in long lengths, similar to those still in production today.

Today many wall coverings offer us the opportunity to introduce colour, pattern, texture and finish into our interior decorative schemes. As discussed in previous chapters, it is important to know how to use and maintain the right tools for the job.

TOOLS AND EQUIPMENT

The first aspects to consider are the selection and use of the tools and equipment for hanging wallpaper. Listed below are the essential items for hanging foundation and plain papers, many of which you will be familiar with through previous chapters.

It is always important to keep tools and equipment clean and properly maintained. In most cases they will need to be cleaned after use, dried and stored in a well-ventilated and dry space. If tools are kept in a tool box, ensure that they are properly dried before putting them away.

Tool	Use, care and maintenance
Tape measure 	This is used for measuring lengths and distances. It is a retractable metal tape, usually 5m or 10m long. It should be wiped clean with a little oil to ensure smooth running of the tape inside the case. Allow it to dry before storing.
Folding rule 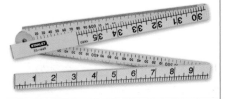	This is used for measuring lengths of wallpaper before cutting, also used for measuring widths of cuts. It is typically 1m long. It folds into four to make it easy to store in the pocket of overalls. Wipe clean with a damp cloth or sponge and allow it to dry before storing.

Tool	Use, care and maintenance
Plumb bob 	This is used for ensuring that first and subsequent lengths of wallpaper are hung vertically. A small weight, usually made from steel, is suspended from a length of cord. Make sure it is completely still before checking for **plumb**. Keep the bob clean, and untangle the line and wrap it around when not in use.
Chalk and line 	Marking chalk lines is particularly useful for setting out the first length of paper to a ceiling. The image on the left shows the self-chalking type of line, although it is possible to use a piece of string and chalk sticks (see page 271). The line needs to be rubbed with chalk each time it is used. Ensure that chalks and lines are kept dry. If you are using the self-chalking type, the container will periodically require topping up with chalk.
Paste brush 	This is a 125mm or 150mm flat wall brush used to apply paste or adhesive to wall or surface coverings. It is also used to apply size to **absorbent** wall and ceiling surfaces before hanging papers. These brushes are usually made from bristle or synthetic fibre. Wash with warm soapy water to remove any adhesive, rinse thoroughly in clean water, then hang to dry in a well ventilated room. If brushes are stored wet or damp they can be prone to **mildew**.
Paste table 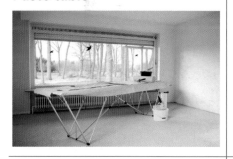	This is used to lay out wallpapers for measuring, cutting, matching and pasting. It is usually made from wood or plastic, and is typically 1.8m long and 560mm wide, about the width of lining papers – however, this can vary between different manufacturers. Paste tables are usually collapsible to make them easy to transport. Try to ensure the face and edges of the board are kept free of paste when in use to avoid transfer to the face of paper. Wipe down with warm soapy water when finished, rinse with clean water and allow it to dry before storing in a dry, well ventilated room.
Pasting machine 	A pasting machine can be used to apply paste to papers. This method can be extremely quick and ensures that the correct amount of paste is applied when correctly set up. Essentially the machine is filled with paste and the paper is pulled through rollers that apply the paste to the paper. When the correct length has been pulled through it is cut off ready for folding and soaking, before hanging.

Plumb

Vertical or perpendicular

Tool	Use, care and maintenance
Sponges 	These are used for wiping excess paste from surfaces. They are usually made of synthetic material that allows water to be absorbed so that the wetness can be transferred to the surface in a reasonably controlled way. Wash sponges with warm soapy water and then rinse clean. Allow to dry thoroughly before storing in a well ventilated area.
Buckets 	Plastic buckets are commonly used for mixing paste or size, and are then used as a container to hold the paste or size during application. They are also used to store water for use with a sponge to wipe paste off surfaces. Wash buckets clean with warm soapy water and then rinse clean before storing.
Seam roller 	This is used to roll down the edges of paper, or in corners or angles. Wipe it clean regularly when in use, and wash it with warm soapy water when you have finished. Rinse clean and allow it to dry – wait until it is fully dry before storing. A little oil may be applied to the spindle of the roller.
Paperhanging brush 	This is used to apply papers to walls to ensure that all air pockets are removed and that the paper lies flat without creases. It is sometimes referred to as a smoothing brush. Try to keep it clean and free of paste when in use. When you have finished, wash it in warm soapy water and rinse clean. Allow it to dry thoroughly by hanging it up before storing flat in a well ventilated place. As with paste brushes, if stored wet or damp these brushes can be susceptible to mildew.

Absorbent

An absorbent surface soaks up liquids. The more liquid a material can soak up, the more absorbent it is. **Sizing** will help to even out the absorbency so that papers do not stick too soon

Sizing

Applying a thin coat of glue size or thinned paste to an absorbent surface before hanging wallpaper

Mildew

Sometimes referred to as mould. A fungus that produces a superficial growth on various kinds of damp surface. Can be whitish in colour or black spots that multiply

Tool	Use, care and maintenance
Paperhanging shears 	These are used to cut lengths of wallpaper, and also for trimming around obstacles. They should be kept clean and sharp – they can be sharpened using a fine file or oilstone. They are also sometimes referred to as scissors. Shears can become clogged with paste and will require wiping clean to ensure that a good cut is maintained. Wash clean after use to remove paste, and store once dry to avoid the blades rusting. They can be lightly oiled around the pivot, but ensure that any excess oil is removed from the blades before cutting wallpaper.
Pencil 	This is used primarily for marking out lengths of paper and for putting tick marks onto the wall to assist with marking plumb. Some decorators will also use them for marking wallpapers at the top and bottom of hung lengths as well as around obstacles. An HB pencil (not too hard) is ideal. Ensure that you keep a point. However, marking for cutting can also be done with the back edge of the paperhanging shears. Using the back edge of the shears creates a crease line in the paper, thus avoiding the potential for leaving pencil marks.
Spirit level 	This is used for checking the vertical positioning of wallpaper, as well as horizontal borders. Be careful when transferring levels around a room, as this is not always the most accurate method for this. It is generally not as accurate as a plumb bob, but is particularly useful for short lengths of paper, such as over doors or windows. A spirit level is only truly accurate over the length of the bubble in the middle. Wipe clean when finished, and store.
Laser level 	Using a laser level is an extremely accurate method of checking horizontal and vertical levels. A relatively low-cost level will be more than adequate for decorating purposes, as long as it has the capability for providing horizontal and vertical laser lines and can also tilt and turn.
Straight edge  Straight edge  Straight edge with handle	Straight edges are used by some decorators, particularly for trimming waste paper when up against straight edges such as skirtings, door frames and ceiling edges. The two types shown, with a handle and without, are typically 600mm in length.

Tool	Use, care and maintenance
Trimming knife  Retractable blade Snap-off blade	Some decorators like to use trimming knives when cutting around obstacles. In the first instance it is best to learn the skills of using shears for cutting and trimming, as there will be occasions when knives are not suitable and may tear the paper. Two types of trimming knife are illustrated, and in both cases extreme care must be taken when handling them.
Sharps box 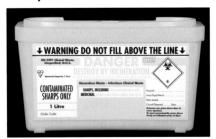	When using the snap-off type of knife, there will be sharp edges that are snapped off and should be immediately disposed of in a sharps box or container. When the container is nearly full it should be taken to the local waste disposal area for correct disposal.
Roller and scuttle 	Some decorators like to use a roller and scuttle filled with paste to speed up the process of pasting papers on the table. They are also useful for the types of papers that require the wall to be pasted instead of the back of the paper. You will still need to take care when applying paste to avoid getting it on the front of the paper.
Protective gloves or barrier cream 	Thin latex protective gloves are especially useful if you are sensitive to the fungicide in some pastes. This chemical additive can cause irritation, and in some cases dermatitis. Barrier cream is an alternative – it will provide some protection against irritation and should be used before carrying out any task. Always wash your hands with soap and water after papering tasks and before eating food to avoid **ingesting** any chemicals.

Ingest

To take into the body by mouth in the act of swallowing or absorption

INDUSTRY TIP

Avoid dropping a spirit level, as this can jolt the bubble and affect the levelling ability, making it inaccurate.

INDUSTRY TIP

Stretch string or a rubber band across the middle of the top of the bucket when pasting. This gives you somewhere to rest the brush when not in use.

INDUSTRY TIP

Use a piece of dry paper between the roller head and the wallpaper that is being rolled. This helps to avoid paste squeezing onto the surface of the roller and then being transferred to the face of the finished wallpaper and leaving marks.

GENERAL MAINTENANCE

Ensure that all tools are cleaned after use and allowed to dry. Generally, all tools will need to be stored in dry, ventilated areas. Many can be kept in drawers, or on shelves or storage racks. It is important to keep all metal tools free from damp to avoid them becoming rusty. Paste brushes and paperhanging brushes are best hung up to dry and stored in dry conditions to avoid them being attacked by mildew. Be careful when storing sharp tools, particularly in the case of snap-off or retractable knives. Make sure that they are fully retracted before storing.

ENVIRONMENTAL AND HEALTH AND SAFETY REGULATIONS

Although you need to be aware of the requirements of the Health and Safety at Work Act (HASAWA) 1974, and in particular site rules about wearing personal protective equipment (PPE), it is probable that most paperhanging activities will take place in a closed room environment. You will still need to comply with PPE requirements if you have to gain access across a site or within a refurbished property where wider site rules may apply.

Remember that you will be required to wear a safety helmet, hi-viz jacket, safety boots, gloves and goggles on some building sites as standard practice. However, it is usually permissible to remove these while paperhanging. Do check this with your supervisor or site agent first, though.

Other regulations that will need to be considered will include the Control of Substances Hazardous to Health Regulations 2002 (COSHH), particularly in relation to the handling of materials such as fungicidal paste. If any of the work is to be carried out at height you will need to adhere to the Work at Height Regulations 2005 (as amended). This aspect was covered in detail in Chapter 3 – be sure that you have assessed the risks and are working safely. Additionally disposal of waste products will need to be carried out in accordance with the proper requirements for segregation of potentially hazardous materials. Many of these points are covered later in this chapter, but also see Chapter 1.

Though many paperhanging tasks will take place without the need for wearing a hard hat, safety boots or goggles, gloves and barrier cream may well be necessary when handling some of the pastes containing fungicide. Overalls with a bib or a paperhanger's apron will be extremely useful, not only as protective clothing but also to enable you to carry a small number of tools, particularly a hanging brush and shears, in the pockets, making them efficient and easy to use.

Take extreme care when handling paperhanging equipment, particularly items with sharp edges such as the shears – and you will need to be especially careful if they are the type with very sharp points.

A painter's bib and brace overalls

An apron with a front pocket

SELECT AND PREPARE ADHESIVES

In the first section of this chapter the types and uses of tools and equipment were considered. This section looks at the types and uses of various **adhesives**. In general terms adhesives are considered in terms of their water content, as this is the main factor to consider when selecting an adhesive for a particular surface or paper.

Adhesive

In decorating and particularly paperhanging terms, adhesive is a material sometimes referred to as paste that can stick paper to ceiling and wall surfaces

TYPES OF ADHESIVES

As the types of paper being studied at Level 1 are relatively lightweight, the following four adhesive types are covered:

- starch paste
- cellulose paste
- ready-mixed adhesive (lightweight)
- overlap adhesive.

Type of adhesive	Description/use	Water/solid content	Advantages	Disadvantages
Starch paste	A starch paste is typically supplied in powder form and will be based on organic starches extracted from maize, corn, wheat, etc. It is easy to prepare and should be used when freshly made. It can be used on all types of paper, providing it contains fungicide. If no fungicide protection is indicated it is best not to use it for vinyl papers because of the potential for **mould growth** appearing under the surface of the paper.	Medium solid – low water.	- Relatively slow setting. - **Adheres** well to surfaces.	- Easily stains the face of the paper. - Encourages and supports mould growth if not fungicide protected.

Type of adhesive	Description/use	Water/solid content	Advantages	Disadvantages
Cellulose paste	Cellulose paste will generally produce the thinnest of pastes and is therefore only really suitable for lightweight papers such as lining paper and other lightweight foundation papers.	Low solid – high water.	▪ Fairly transparent and therefore less likely to stain the face of papers.	▪ Has less adhesion than starch paste. ▪ When cellulose paste has been standing around for a long period of time it will become thin and unusable.
Cellulose modified with starch ether	Suitable for all types of paper, including lightweight vinyls. Usually contains fungicide to reduce possibility of mould growth occurring.	Medium solid – medium water.	▪ Fairly transparent. ▪ Mixes easily to a smooth paste. ▪ Better adhesive properties than cellulose.	▪ Can mark the face of papers more than cellulose.
Ready-mixed adhesive (lightweight)	Typically a PVA-based adhesive. Ready mixed is a ready-to-use wallpaper and lining paper adhesive and has been designed to roller or brush directly from the tub for quicker application. No mixing or dilution is required. The adhesive has strong grab and easy slide for perfect wallpaper hanging.	High solid – low water.	▪ No mixing required. ▪ Easy to spread. ▪ Suitable for hanging all types of lining papers and wallpapers.	▪ More expensive than other types of adhesive.

Mould growth

Mould is made up of airborne spores that can multiply and feed on organic matter in pastes (starch pastes contain organic products such as wheat). It may vary in colour depending on the species of fungus, eg black, pink, green

Adhere

To stick to a substance or surface

Type of adhesive	Description/use	Water/solid content	Advantages	Disadvantages
Overlap adhesive	Resin-based adhesive supplied in tubes and plastic tubs. Commonly used for sticking overlaps of vinyl wallpaper. Can also be used for fixing borders.	High solid – low water.	■ Ready mixed. ■ Easy to apply.	■ Need to ensure any excess properly cleaned off as will show shiny marks if left.

INDUSTRY TIP

When mixing paste it is best to create a swirling effect in the bucket of water and then to sprinkle the dry adhesive into the centre while continuing to stir.

PREPARING ADHESIVES

When mixing pastes, particularly from powders or flakes, it is essential to get the consistency right and avoid lumps. If the paste is lumpy it will be difficult to flatten out when pasting and will be likely to show as lumps or blisters in the finished job. It is important to follow the manufacturer's instructions and adjust the consistency to suit the various types of paper. Do not over-thin the paste, as this is likely to cause problems after pasting such as over-stretching, over-soaking and possible delamination of duplex papers.

If pastes are being stored overnight, make sure they are covered to avoid contamination from dust and debris that may settle on the top.

If pastes are kept for too long they can become stale and unusable. Cellulose pastes in particular become thin, and starch pastes can also thin and start to smell.

Cellulose modified with starch ether is probably the most popular choice for decorators for general hanging of papers, including lining paper and woodchip, because of its good adhesion and low marking properties.

So-called 'all-purpose' pastes have been developed fairly recently. These pastes provide all the benefits of both starch and cellulose pastes. The thickness of the paste can be adjusted easily according to the type of paper hung. They can be supplied in powder form for self-mixing or ready mixed in tubs. Tub-based pastes are quite commonly used with rollers when pasting.

Follow correct disposal procedures to avoid contaminating the water course.

You must be aware of the environmental and health and safety regulations when mixing and using pastes and adhesives. It is especially important to ensure that COSHH is followed and that the correct PPE is worn. Although the mixing process is not generally a health and safety issue, it may be sensible to wear gloves to avoid any splashes onto the skin.

Some pastes and adhesives contain fungicide to reduce the likelihood of mould growth and this can cause irritation and even skin conditions such as dermatitis. It may therefore be sensible to wear thin gloves or barrier cream when handling this type of product. Ensure that hands are washed, particularly before eating food, to avoid ingestion, which could lead to stomach irritation or upset.

Manufacturers have a legal duty under health and safety law to provide information about their products, and it is important to obtain a safety data sheet for each product used. Always ensure that the manufacturer's instructions have been followed. Using the information supplied, a risk assessment can determine what the hazards are and how they can be reduced. Advice on first-aid measures, such as how to deal with any ingestion of the product, protective equipment required and disposal of waste products, should be given by the data sheet. In general pastes are not described as hazardous – however, any waste material should not be allowed to enter drains, soil or bodies of water but should instead be collected and disposed of in the appropriate skip on site or in the correct area at the local authority recycling centre.

Wash hands thoroughly, particularly before eating

ACTIVITY

Source a wallpaper adhesive data sheet (either by finding one at your college or workplace or by searching online) and answer the following questions:

- Does the adhesive contain fungicide?
- What does it say specifically about hygiene measures?

APPLY LINING PAPER AND WOOD INGRAIN TO WALLS

This section covers the application of foundation papers. The term 'foundation papers' describes papers that make a base for other layers, whether paint or further wallpapers. This chapter concentrates on lining paper and wood ingrain although glass fibre and various thermal linings may also be considered foundation layers in certain crcumstances.

INDUSTRY TIP

Glass fibre reinforced lining paper can be used for excessively cracked surfaces.

LINING PAPER AND WOOD INGRAIN PAPER

These particular types of paper are sometimes referred to as pulps, because they are manufactured mainly from wood pulp materials. In the machine process this material is mixed with large quantities of water and stretched until it forms an incredibly thin continuous layer, and is then processed until it is cut to width, dried and then rolled all in the same manufacturing process.

This section looks at the selection, measuring, cutting and application of lining paper and wood ingrain papers to wall surfaces.

INDUSTRY TIP

Thermal or insulated lining papers could be used to improve the insulating properties of surfaces and reduce potential condensation and mould.

LINING PAPER

Lining paper is a white pulp paper sold in various grades, such 800g/m² or 1000g/m², where the number of grams per m² will determine how heavy and thick it is. Typically rolls are 560mm wide and 10m long – however, it is possible to buy double-, treble- and quadruple-length rolls. The longer rolls can be more economical if you are carrying out a lot of lining, as the waste is minimised.

Lining paper has the following common uses:

- It is used to provide a uniform surface in terms of even **porosity** for the subsequent hanging of finishing papers.

- It is used to line non-absorbent surfaces such as oil-painted walls, again to provide a surface with even porosity. Hanging finishing papers directly on non-absorbent surfaces could lead to defects such as springing of joints, poor drying out (leading to blistering) and poor overall adhesion.

- It provides even porosity on surfaces where large areas of making good have changed the overall porosity of the surface.

Be aware that the preparation of the underlying surface needs to be of the highest standard, as any small defect – even small grit – can be amplified in appearance once the lining has dried. See Chapter 4 for information on preparing surfaces.

Do not allow lining paper to over-soak when hanging, as it will be more likely to tear, particularly the thinner grades.

WOOD INGRAIN PAPER

Often referred to as woodchip, wood ingrain paper is a pulp paper made up of two layers between which small chips of wood are sandwiched. It usually comes in 10m long by 530mm wide rolls although, as with lining paper, it is possible to obtain double, treble and quadruple rolls for better economy. Wood ingrain can be supplied in different grades of texture: fine, medium or coarse. The grade chosen will depend on personal preference for a more or less pronounced appearance.

Wood ingrain is usually coated with water-borne paints, or sometimes oil based paints, after hanging. Ingrain papers tend to mask irregularities in the underlying surface due to the pronounced texture of the woodchip appearance.

As with lining paper you should not over-soak the wood ingrain paper when hanging, as thinner grades may tear and possibly delaminate. Delamination is described later in the chapter (see page 239) and refers to the separation of the top and bottom layers of paper as a result of over-soaking.

To ensure good preparation of the underlying surface it is usual to apply a size coat prior to hanging foundation papers. Sizing will help paper adhere better, allowing for good movement when hanging so that it will slide into position, and helping to provide good **butt joints.**

Porosity

The state of being porous – when small spaces or voids in a solid material mean that it can absorb liquids

An example of springing of joints in lining paper

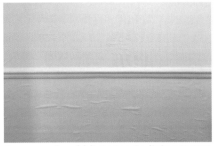

An example of blistering in lining paper

INDUSTRY TIP

When hanging paper as a foundation for other paper, it is usual to cross-line in the opposite direction to the finishing paper. This is typically horizontally, and it is done this way to avoid any joints in the paper lining up in the same place and making a weak bond, which is likely to cause lifting edges. If, on the other hand, it is used as a foundation for painting then it is hung in the traditional vertical manner.

Butt joint

Edges of lengths of paper that touch without a gap or overlap

HANGING TECHNIQUES AND PROCESSES

The following processes described will be mostly the same for hanging foundation, plain and most patterned papers. Some papers though, particularly specialist types, will require special hanging instructions. These will be dealt with at Level 2.

PLANNING

You need to consider a number of factors before beginning paperhanging:

- calculating the amount of paper

- starting and finishing points relative to the natural source of light or a feature wall

- hanging method (horizontal or vertical)

- paper selection

- type of paste required

- pasting method to be used.

Make sure you give sufficient thought to each of these factors before commencing work.

STARTING AND FINISHING POINTS

The starting point in many rooms will be to hang the first length away from the light, ie a window or other source of daylight. Working away from the light in this manner will minimise shadows appearing along the edges of the joints and therefore they will be less noticeable. The picture below shows pink wallpaper being hung away from the recessed window, as this is a source of daylight.

ACTIVITY

Produce a completed checklist of the planning items listed opposite for a practical task you are undertaking.

Start hanging paper away from the light

In some instances it may also be desirable to consider any focal points or features such as fireplaces or feature walls to give the best effect. It can be a good idea to **centre** paper over a fireplace to try to get an even pattern appearance.

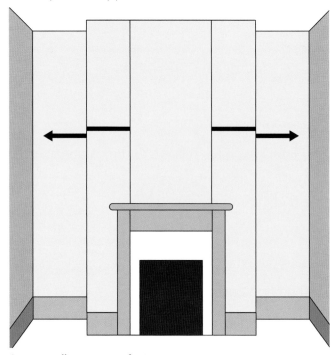

Centre wallpaper over features

The finishing point in many cases will be above the doorway entering the room. The main idea, particularly when using patterned papers, is to find an area where the loss of pattern will be less noticeable.

Marking starting lines

There will be a number of occasions when you will need to mark starting lines. These include the first drop to be hung, and after internal and external angles. It will also be necessary to provide a horizontally levelled line when cross-lining. This line should be marked approximately one length down from the ceiling line to ensure that all following lengths remain horizontal.

Starting lines are also marked when hanging paper horizontally

Few walls are truly square or perfectly vertical. To overcome this, and avoid the pattern going askew, it is essential to mark a vertical pencil line against a plumb line or long spirit level adjacent to where the first length is to hang. Allow the plumb bob to swing freely until it is at rest before putting a pencil mark down the wall behind the string. Measure the width of a roll or use a roll of paper to mark the wall, one width away from the corner, less 10mm, to allow a slight overlap onto the return wall or chosen starting point. Using a plumb line lightly pencil some guide marks from ceiling to skirting.

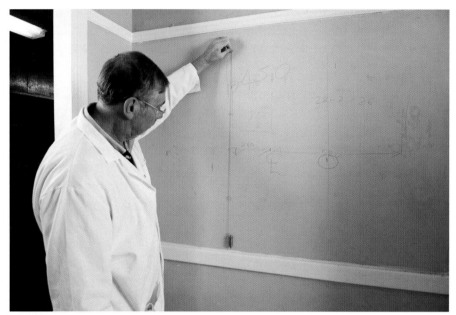

Use a plumb bob to mark straight lines

Measure your first length, allowing an extra 50mm at the top and bottom, and cut all lengths of paper on the table ready for pasting. Repeat the process on every wall.

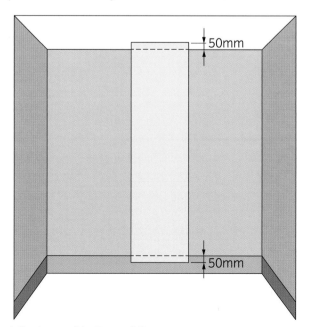

Allow 50mm at the top and bottom of the paper

MEASURING AND CALCULATING QUANTITIES OF WALLPAPER

Before starting the paperhanging project calculate how many rolls of paper are required so that you can buy enough.

There are a few methods used by decorators to calculate the quantity of paper required for a project, but at Level 1 the area method is used. Further methods will be shown at Level 2.

Area method

To use the area method, you need to divide the area of the room by the area of one roll of paper. Below we will look at the calculations you need to work out the quantity of paper for covering a whole room.

First you must calculate the area of the roll of paper. Remember from Chapter 2 that this can be done by multiplying the length by the width. If you are using metres as your unit of measurement, the area will be described in metres squared (m^2). Next, calculate the area of the room, which can be done in a similar way. It is useful to add together the distance around the room (the perimeter) and then multiply it by the height to give the total area. Finally, to work out how many rolls you need you then divide the room area by the area of a roll of paper. Here is an example.

Example

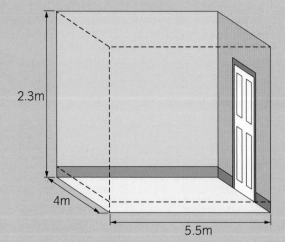

2.3m

4m

5.5m

Calculate the perimeter of the room by adding up the wall lengths.

Step 1

You are using a roll of paper that is 10m long and 525cm (or 0.525m) wide.

10m (length) × 0.525m (width) = 5.25m² (area)

Step 2

To calculate the perimeter of the walls, you need to add up the four lengths:

5.5m + 5.5m + 4m + 4m = 19m

Step 3

Now you have the perimeter of the room, you can work out the area using the following calculation:

19m (perimeter) × 2.3m (height) = 43.7m²

Step 4

Finally, divide the room area by the area of a roll of paper:

43.7m² ÷ 5.25m² = **8.32** rolls of paper

This total should always be rounded up to the next full number. In this case **9** rolls will be required.

INDUSTRY TIP

It is common practice to order an extra roll to allow for waste.

Wallpaper manufacturers will often provide a wallpaper coverage guide which uses the area method.

This method of calculation is useful for calculating the quantity of non-patterned wallpapers such as lining paper and woodchip, but for patterned papers more accurate methods will be needed.

To achieve a more accurate figure, the total area of such things as doors and windows would need to be deducted as well as making allowance for pattern repeat.

INDUSTRY TIP

Always measure twice before cutting lengths of wallpaper to ensure that no mistakes are made.

PASTING, FOLDING AND SOAKING PAPER

The following steps show you how to paste, fold and soak paper.

STEP 1 Apply paste up through the middle of the length of paper and paste out towards the edges of the pasteboard – first towards the top edge and then pulling the paper across and down towards the bottom edge (nearest to you).

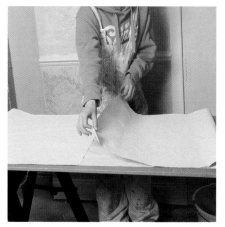

STEP 2 Once the length of paper on the paste table has been pasted, begin folding the paper, ensuring that the edges when folded are square to keep them from drying out.

STEP 3 Make sure that no paste gets onto the face of the paper or onto the paste table where it might be transferred to the face of the paper. Depending on the length of pasted paper, either the end-to-end folding technique or concertina fold may be chosen.

Once the paper has been pasted, it should be allowed to soak for an appropriate length of time. It is best to follow the manufacturer's instructions on timing.

Under-soaking

If paper is not soaked enough, this can result in air bubbles under the paper once it is hung. This is referred to as blistering in the list of defects. This defect occurs because the paper is still trying to expand, and as it will be stuck only in some places the paper will push outwards, forming bubbles or blisters.

Over-soaking

If the paper has been allowed to soak too long then it will have overstretched and possibly some of the paste will have started to dry. Further when paper oversoaks it will be much harder to handle and will more easily tear. Duplex papers such as ingrain (woodchip) can delaminate when oversoaked. This is where the top layer separates from the bottom layer. Both these aspects are included in the section on defects later in this chapter.

Take care not to under-soak or over-soak the paper

HANGING PAPER

The following steps describe one method of hanging paper.

STEP 1 Having pasted the paper and allowed it to soak, following the manufacturer's instructions, hang the top fold against the plumbed line and brush out from the centre, working down.

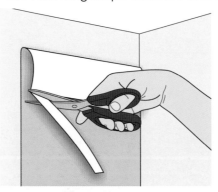

STEP 2 When the paper is smoothly brushed down, run the outer edge of your scissors along the ceiling angle, peel away the paper, cut off the excess along the crease, then brush back onto the wall.

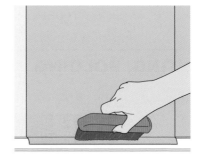

STEP 3 At the skirting, tap your brush gently into the top edge, peel away the paper and cut along the folded line with scissors or a blade as before, then brush back.

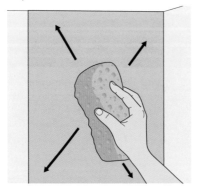

STEP 4 Using a sponge and a bucket of clean water, make sure you remove all the paste from the surface of the paper.

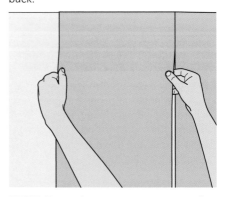

STEP 5 Cut the next piece, paste and soak as before. Hang it butting up to the first. Do not overlap.

PAPERING AROUND OBSTACLES SUCH AS SWITCHES

Be very careful when applying wallpapers over, under or around electrical switches, sockets and similar items. It is recommended that you turn off the supply at the mains.

INDUSTRY TIP

Some decorators prefer to slightly unscrew electrical fittings so the wallpaper can be tucked just behind, but you must ensure that the electricity is turned off before carrying out this step.

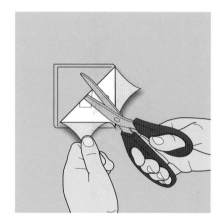

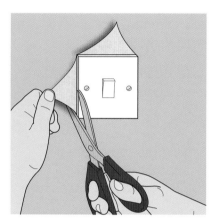

STEP 1 Smooth the wallpaper down very gently over the fitting and then, for square obstacles, pierce the paper in the centre, mark the corners and make diagonal cuts from the centre to each corner.

STEP 2 Press the wallpaper firmly around the edge of the fitting, lightly mark the outline and trim away the surplus.

STEP 3 For circular objects, such as ceiling centres or light fittings, make a series of cuts in a star shape. Press down around the outline, mark and trim in the same way.

PAPERING BEHIND RADIATORS

Ideally, you should drain a radiator and take it off the wall so that you can paper behind it. If that is not possible, first turn off the heat and wait for the radiator to cool. Paste the strip of paper to the wall above the radiator, then slit it from the bottom edge so that you can smooth it down on either side of the radiator's fixing brackets. Press the paper into place behind the radiator, using a dry narrow radiator paint roller.

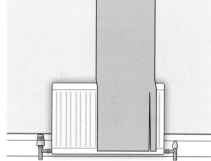

Wallpapering behind a radiator

PAPERING AROUND CORNERS

Allow a minimum of 5mm to turn into the corner. Turning only a little will minimise the amount of pattern lost. Sufficient turn should be given, however, to allow for the corner being out of plumb.

When applying paper to corners, ensure that the return piece is plumbed so that the paper hung on the return wall will remain vertical.

Papering around a corner

ACTIVITY

Visit http://dulux.trade-decorating.co.uk/ video/training_wallpaper_intro.jsp to see a complimentary training video for further knowledge on preparing for and later hanging wallpaper.

INDUSTRY TIP

Keep your paste table clean and clear of clutter to avoid getting into a muddle.

ACTIVITY

Study the defects and answer the following questions.

- Why are blisters caused?
- What causes polished joints?
- What can happen if the paper is out of plumb?

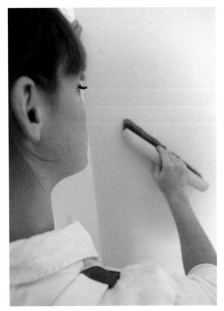

Excessive brushing can cause creasing

Avoiding problems when papering

- Read the manufacturer's instructions. Use the correct adhesive and follow soak times carefully to prevent shrinkage.

- Keep the face of the paper clean, removing adhesive with a sponge and clean water.

- Take care to apply an even amount of adhesive to the paper, particularly the edges.

- Make sure the wall is properly prepared, smooth and clean. Good preparation will ensure a better finish.

- Always use a sharp knife or scissors so as not to tear the paper.

- Marking the top of the paper on the reverse with a pencil will ensure that you don't hang a piece upside down. This can easily happen with a plain paper.

- Don't assume that a paper comes off a roll in the direction it will be hung. Look at the design to make sure you hang it the right way up.

- Have a black bag or empty cardboard box under the paste table to collect dry and wet waste off-cuts.

- It can be dangerous just to drop waste off-cuts on the floor, as they will be a potential slip or trip hazard.

DEFECTS

The following defects can occur through lack of care or incorrect application methods. Rectifying some of these defects will prove extremely costly – in many of the cases the defective wallpaper will require removal before hanging again.

Creasing
Excessive brushing may cause the surface of the paper to stretch. Then, when trying to keep plumb, there will be excess paper which is likely to crease. Also, paper over very uneven surfaces may stretch, again resulting in excess paper and potential creasing.

Overlaps
Overlaps can be caused by over-brushing, or over-soaking, which can also cause papers to stretch after hanging and result in overlaps. Careless use of the seam roller can stretch the paper, again resulting in overlaps.

Tears
There are a number of things that can cause paper to tear, but in all cases it is probably down to lack of care in the process of hanging. If very thin paste is used, this can cause over-wetting, which in turn

can make paper more likely to tear. Using blunt tools such as shears can cause paper to tear. Once papers have been soaked and are ready to hang proper care should be taken when handling, as rough handling can cause papers to tear.

Blisters

Blisters are usually caused by under-soaking or over-soaking, followed by careless brushing. Papers need to be properly pasted and smoothed as described (see pages 235–236) to ensure that no air bubbles or excess paste are left to make blisters on drying. Areas of paper that have been missed when pasting will be dry and therefore will not stick to the wall surface, also leading to blisters.

Polished edges

In most cases this defect is caused by poor use of the seam roller. If paste is allowed to get onto the face of the paper at the edges, and is then rolled, it is likely that the seam roller will polish this area and leave shiny marks. This can be helped or avoided by using a dry piece of paper between the seam roller and the face of the paper. Sometimes careless pasting can leave paste on the face of the paper edges and this can also give a polished effect when dry.

Open joints

Uneven surfaces can sometimes make it difficult for the lengths of paper to be properly butted together. If the paper is over-stretched to make them butt, on occasion the joints may spring back leaving an open gap.

Springing of joints

This often occurs due to lack of adhesion. This can be particularly noticeable when papering on non-absorbent surfaces such as gloss-painted walls. It can also occur when papers are over-stretched and will shrink back on drying to leave an open joint.

Loose edges

This defect is almost always a result of careless pasting techniques, where edges have been missed or there is inadequate general coverage. These dry areas will not stick to the surface and will lift.

Delamination

Delamination of duplex or two-part papers can occur if the paper has been allowed to over-soak or has been pasted with a paste that is too thin. The paste applied will soak through the first layer, softening the paper manufacturer's adhesive used to laminate the two layers together. Once this happens the two layers can separate.

Irregular cutting

Poor technique when using cutting tools such as paperhanging shears leads to a messy finish. It is advisable to practise cutting pasted paper before attempting to cut the real thing. Cutting to a line without tearing the paper or producing irregular cuts is a skill that demands patience.

ACTIVITY

On this page there are a number of defects listed. How could most have been avoided?

Careless use of the seam roller can lead to polished edges

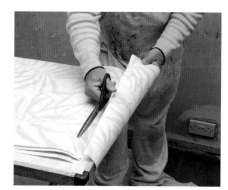

Cutting a straight line without tearing the paper will take practice

ACTIVITY

What type of treatment is required to prevent water stains from showing through finished paper? Specify a particular product that can prevent this.

Staining/surface marking

This is usually caused by poor pasting technique, where either the paste has got onto the face from the paste table surface or been allowed to wrap around the edges during application. Ensure that the paste table is kept clean at all times by wiping it regularly. Occasionally, water stains on the existing surface may be softened by the new paste and stain through the newly applied paper. This can be remedied by sealing any water stains before applying new paper.

Corners incorrectly negotiated

It is extremely important to plan well when paperhanging, especially with patterned papers. With good planning it is possible to lessen the impact of pattern loss when turning corners and going around various obstacles. Starting points for paperhanging are extremely important, as are the correct application methods when dealing with corners. Refer to pages 231–232 and 237 for more details.

Inaccurate plumbing

Inaccurate plumbing will lead to lengths of paper being out of plumb. On patterned papers, which you will cover at Level 2, this will be extremely noticeable, as the pattern will start to run out of position at the top of the wall. It is essential to ensure that the plumbing of the first lengths on turning corners is carried out accurately, and to ensure that the plumb bob has stopped moving before marking. Hanging lengths of paper following obstacles like windows and doorways also requires the use of the plumb bob to establish a truly vertical starting point again.

ACTIVITY

Have a look online for wallpaper advice sheets. What kind of information would you expect an advice sheet from a manufacturer to include?

Always check for plumb when turning internal and external corners

STORE MATERIALS IN LINE WITH MANUFACTURERS' INSTRUCTIONS

Consideration should be given to the physical types of materials when storing, bearing in mind that most will be badly affected by extremes of temperature, damp or direct sunlight. Many of the products that you might store are made of paper or are dry powder-based, and sometimes contained in cardboard packets. Any opened products will need to be properly sealed before storing, and bear in mind that they will have a limited shelf life before they become unusable.

Care should always be taken with the storage of wallpapers and adhesives, as they can be badly affected by damp, cold conditions. If it is too hot, papers can become too dry and if exposed to direct sunlight discolouration will take place. This will particularly affect patterned papers.

Always refer to manufacturers' instructions with regards to use, handling and storage. However, in most cases materials should be stored in warm, dry and secure conditions. If materials are bought in bulk it is probably a good idea to keep a stock book to keep track of when items are removed and require replacing. With all materials it is always best to check that the oldest stock is used first. Most materials, particularly adhesives, will have use-by dates for guidance.

Paste in storage

In the case of papers such as lining or wood ingrain paper, decorators will often store additional stock, as these products are used frequently. This will require a good racked storage system – wallpapers are best stored in racks and laid on their sides to prevent damage to their edges. Most papers are shrink wrapped in plastic to keep them clean before they are used.

Wallpaper in storage

Paste and adhesives should be stored in cool, dry, frost-free conditions, for example in drawers or in tubs stored on shelves. If pastes are allowed to get damp they will be unusable, as they will start to become solid.

ACTIVITY

Answer the following questions in pairs.

- What kind of storage conditions should be avoided?
- What would likely happen to papers if stored on their ends?
- Why are most papers shrink wrapped in plastic?

Case Study: Maya and Ron

Maya and Ron are in the process of decorating an empty town house, and they are about to hang lining paper in the lounge. Ron, who is the more experienced of the two, has asked Maya to start planning for hanging, and then to carry on hanging the lining paper. Ron can meanwhile get on with the task of preparing the kitchen.

During the morning Ron looks in to see how Maya is getting on. He is dismayed to see that Maya has hung a number of lengths vertically. The specification for this room states that there is a finishing paper to be hung after lining. Ron explains to Maya that the paper should have been hung horizontally and he thought Maya would know that. This has caused a problem because the lining will now have to be removed and rehung. Ron helps Maya to remove the lining paper and rehang it horizontally; this costs time and money but in the end provides a good foundation for the finishing paper.

This case study throws up a number of points to consider:

- How could this costly mistake have been avoided?

- Do you think Ron could have done anything differently?

- What could Maya have done differently to avoid this mistake?

- Why is it important to hang lining paper horizontally before hanging finishing papers?

Work through the following questions to check your learning.

1 What is the **best** thing to use for sharpening paperhanging shears?

   a Steel wool.

   b Wet and dry abrasive paper.

   c A fine file.

   d A coarse file.

2 What is a plumb bob used for?

   a Checking that paper is horizontal.

   b Measuring out angles.

   c Checking that paper is vertical.

   d Measuring out lengths.

3 A seam roller is normally used to do what?

   a Flatten blisters and wrinkles.

   b Squeeze out excess paste.

   c Roll down the edges of paper.

   d Flatten embossed paper.

4 Which one of the following **best** describes the term 'plumbing'?

   a Making something vertical.

   b Making something horizontal.

   c Getting the angle right.

   d Getting the pattern right.

5 Paperhanging brushes are mainly used for what?

   a Rolling down the edges of paper.

   b Squeezing out excess paste.

   c Flattening blisters and creases.

   d Removing pockets of air.

6 What can cause paperhanging shears to become blunt?

   a Cutting paper that is too thick.

   b Paste building up on the blades.

   c Paste on the paper.

   d Cutting paper that is too thin.

7 Mildew on paperhanging brushes is caused by what?

   a Not washing them after use.

   b Hanging them up to dry.

   c Washing them with soap.

   d Storing them before they are dry.

8 Which one of the following is the **most** useful item of clothing when paperhanging?

   a Boiler suit.

   b Apron with pocket.

   c Painter's jacket.

   d High visibility jacket.

9 Which one of the following adhesives has the **highest** water content?

   a Border adhesive.

   b Ready-mixed paste.

   c Starch paste.

   d Cellulose paste.

10 When cellulose paste has been standing around for a long period of time, what may happen?

   a It will become thick and need thinning.

   b It will become thin and need thickening.

   c It will become thin and not usable.

   d It will be unaffected by time.

11 Fungicides are used in some adhesives, but which one of the following health problems can be caused by their use?

   a Difficulty breathing.

   b Skin irritation.

   c Dizzy spells.

   d Loss of taste.

12 Where is the suggested starting point for paperhanging?

a   In a corner.

b   By the door.

c   By the window.

d   You can start anywhere.

13 Duplex paper is made in how many layers?

a   1.

b   2.

c   3.

d   4.

14 What is the name of the defect caused by the over-soaking of duplex papers?

a   Wrinkling.

b   Blistering.

c   Shredding.

d   Delaminating.

15 What is the name of the defect caused by poor use of the seam roller?

a   Springing joints.

b   Loose edges.

c   Polished edges.

d   Open joints.

16 What is the name given to paper containing fine chips of wood?

a   Blown vinyl.

b   Ingrain paper.

c   Embossed paper.

d   Lining paper.

17 Why do we vertically mark the starting point of the first length of paper?

a   To make sure the paper is plumb.

b   To make sure we have enough paper.

c   To make sure we know where to finish.

d   To make sure we have correct length.

18 Which one of the following is the likely cause of dry spots and loose edges on wallpaper after hanging?

a   Too much paste on the paper.

b   Too little paste on the paper.

c   Poor use of seam rollers.

d   Using paste that is too thick.

19 A dry room with a low level of light is ideal for storing which one of the following types of papers?

a   Lining papers.

b   Patterned papers.

c   Wood ingrain.

d   Non-patterned papers.

20 Why should rolls of wallpaper be stored in racks?

a   To make it easier to count them.

b   To prevent damage to the edges.

c   To enable you to see the pattern number.

d   To enable you to see the batch number.

Chapter 7
Unit 120: Producing specialist decorative finishes

This unit covers the skills and knowledge required to produce specialist decorative finishes, and you will draw on your experience of having prepared surfaces and painted them. You will develop your skills further by carrying out these decorative finishes, increasing your knowledge of a wide range of materials, tools and equipment.

Attention to detail, quality and cleanliness are most important, as this type of work is decorative and will be a focus for people to look at. Remember that not all painters can produce decorative finishes, and you will therefore be able to offer future employers and customers additional value with the skills you develop in this area of work. It will also enable you to increase your earnings, as you will be more skilled.

By reading this chapter you will know how to:

1 Produce quality finish ground coats for painted decorative work.

2 Produce broken colour effects using acrylic and oil based scumbles.

3 Apply single-colour stencils.

PRODUCE QUALITY FINISH GROUND COATS FOR PAINTED DECORATIVE WORK

It is possible to produce specialist finishes for decoration, and these can hide or mask minor surface imperfections, match other decoration and provide something different for the customer.

The advantages of these finishes are:

- Each job is **unique**.

- The colours and effects can be tailored to suit the customer's personal choice.

The main disadvantages are:

- It can be expensive to carry out this work, as it is labour intensive.

- It is difficult, if not impossible, to repair damage to the finished work.

- A smooth and level surface is ideally required to work on.

Although the work of preparing and **grounding out** the surface may seem to be the least productive or enjoyable aspect of painting and decorating, it is important to carry it out thoroughly. Any imperfections may be made more obvious by the materials used for the decorative finish.

Unique

The only one of its kind

Grounding out

Applying the ground coat for painted decorative work

Thorough preparation is important to avoid defects in the finish

SURFACES

The specialist finishes for which you will be developing skills are usually applied to walls, doors (eg kitchen cupboards or wardrobes) or items of furniture (eg boxes, picture/mirror frames) and the substrates will therefore normally be previously painted timber, previously painted plaster or previously painted plasterboard.

GROUND COATS

The paint applied to the surface on which decorative finishes will be produced is called the ground coat, and it is important that it has a quality finish with no defects or irregularities, no excessive brush or roller marks and good **opacity**. It should show through the broken colour of the **scumble** and add depth to the surface by being part of the colour scheme.

It is important therefore to be aware of the overall colour scheme, where the decorative effect will go, to make sure that the ground coat and scumble colours complement – or match if the customer wants – the surrounding area.

Water-borne or solvent-borne paint systems with an eggshell or low sheen finish are suitable for the ground coat, as matt or gloss finishes will adversely affect the **manipulation** process of the scumble for broken colour work. A matt finish will tend to absorb the scumble, while the manipulation tools will tend to skid around on a gloss finish. Pay attention to the compatibility of the ground coat material and the scumble type (ie how well they can be used together), and think about the location of the decorative effects with regard to durability. The colour relationship between the ground coat and the scumble is important – they should not be too different, to avoid a harsh finished appearance.

SAMPLE BOARDS

It is advisable to produce sample boards before carrying out the work, so the customer can see a variety of colour and effect combinations, and get an idea of what their chosen decorative scheme will look like. This may save you time and money in the long run, in case the customer changes their mind about the work that has been produced and says that the end product is not what they had agreed to. Make sure that you accurately record on the reverse of each sample all the materials, quantities and proportions as well as the tools used, so that you can **replicate** the effect. Ask the customer to sign the back of the sample board to confirm their choice.

Opacity

The power of the pigment to obliterate (hide) the existing surface colour

Scumble

A glaze (translucent product which will retain a design), to which a colourant has been added

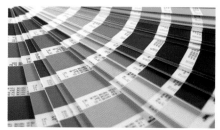

Colour charts can be used to check that colours are complementary

Manipulate

To skilfully handle or move

Replicate

To make an exact copy of

Ropiness

Another surface finish defect similar to brush marks, but where the marks are much heavier and coarser; being more pronounced, they are highly visible and unsightly

Key

A surface that is slightly rough, to help paint adhere to it

Adhere

To stick to a surface

Sinking

Reduction in the sheen of a paint film. This may occur when a section of making good has not been spot-primed and the film former has been partly absorbed by the porous filler

PREPARATION PROCESSES

To achieve the required quality finish for the ground coat, you need to abrade the surface thoroughly. Dry abrading may be appropriate as the first stage for poor, rough surfaces, but this should be followed by wet abrading (or wet flatting) to improve the finish by completely removing any application defects such as **ropiness**, runs or sags, and produce a finish that is very smooth but **keyed** to ensure that the ground coat **adheres**.

It may be necessary to make good any imperfections or indentations (see page 176), to ensure that the surface is level. The materials used for this will depend on the surface type and imperfection, including its depth. Repairs to timber may require a stopper; powder or ready-mixed filler will be appropriate for plaster or plasterboard, while shallow indentations will require fine surface filler.

It is important to select the correct abrasive type and grade for the stage of preparation. Use a coarser grade (eg 120) at first and finish with a fine grade (eg 400). The abrasive type must also be suitable for the dry method (eg aluminium oxide) or the wet method (eg silicon carbide) of abrading.

Areas that have been made good should be spot-primed to prevent the ground coat **sinking**. After the initial preparation, each coat of paint should be de-nibbed to remove any bittiness that may be present, followed by using a tack rag to wipe the surface and ensure that there is no residue or dust. For more information on preparation processes see Chapter 4.

Make good indentations by using filler

TOOLS AND EQUIPMENT REQUIRED FOR THE PREPARATION PROCESSES

You'll need a variety of tools and equipment for the preparation process. The following table explains what these tools will be used for.

Tools and equipment	Description and uses
Rubbing blocks	■ These hold abrasive paper and ensure that a flat, smooth finish is achieved. ■ Rigid blocks may be made from rubber or cork. ■ Flexible sanding sponges are suited to complex or curved surfaces, although the most hard wearing type is rubber.
Sponges	■ Used to wet the surface and then wash and wipe off the residue when using the wet abrading process. ■ Choose a synthetic decorator's sponge, as opposed to the type that is used for washing cars.
Buckets	■ Used to hold water for the wet abrading process. ■ Usually made of plastic.
Dusting brush	■ Used to remove dust and dirt from the surface and surrounding area before painting.
Work area protection	■ Dust sheets protect floors. ■ Masking paper and masking tape may also be required to protect adjacent surfaces.

PERSONAL PROTECTION

The personal protective equipment (PPE) required for the preparation process is described in the following table.

PPE	Description and uses
Dust mask	■ Used to filter the particles produced when dry abrading surfaces. ■ Types FFP1, FMP1 or P1 are suitable for these activities.
Disposable gloves	■ Used to protect the skin from harmful substances that may cause dermatitis or from drying out from frequent contact with water or water-borne substances. ■ There are different types available, including latex and nitrile (latex free). ■ Latex gloves are thin and close fitting. ■ Nitrile gloves are looser, but more puncture resistant than latex ones.
Overalls	■ Protects clothes, but must be removed when leaving the work area to prevent contamination being transferred. ■ Provide storage for small hand tools and equipment.
Safety footwear	■ Worn to protect the feet from falling items or from items puncturing the sole.
Barrier cream	■ Protects hands from contaminants, eg solvents that may cause dermatitis. ■ Some brands are water repellent.

THE PAINTING PROCESS
PREPARATION

Thorough preparation must be followed by careful paint application, using clean paint, clean application tools and a clean paint kettle or roller tray. This can be achieved by:

- dusting off the lid of the container prior to opening

- carefully removing and disposing of any skin that may have formed on the paint surface

- stirring the paint

- straining the paint if it was taken from a previously used container

- adjusting the consistency of the paint to take account of atmospheric conditions and/or surface conditions, by using the appropriate thinner (water for water-borne paint and white spirit for solvent-borne paint).

NUMBER OF COATS

The number of coats of paint required will depend on the following:

- whether priming is required, due to the method and extent of preparation of the surface

- whether a strong colour change from a previous coating is taking place

- whether the colour has poor opacity, eg certain yellows or blues

- whether the coating type is changing, eg from solvent-borne to water-borne.

TOOLS AND EQUIPMENT REQUIRED FOR THE PAINTING PROCESS

Using the right tools and equipment is the key to producing clean finishes.

Paint stirrers

These are used to ensure that all the ingredients in the container are dispersed evenly and that the coating is of a smooth consistency. Make sure you use clean, dry, smooth stirrers so they do not introduce contamination.

Strainers

These should be used for coatings taken from a previously used container to remove any contamination such as dirt or paint skin. If you are combining colours they also reduce the chance of there being any unmixed pigment. Proprietary strainers are most appropriate for larger quantities of paint or scumble. Fine mesh stockings are fine for straining smaller quantities, and are economical and disposable.

Paint stirrer

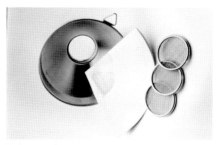

Paint strainer

Select the right brush for the coating you are using

Paint brushes

Natural bristle brushes should be used for solvent-borne coatings, and synthetic filament brushes for water-borne coatings. There is a range of sizes to choose from, taking into account the surface area to be coated.

Rollers

These should have a mohair sleeve so no texture is left in the wet film; a range of sizes is available depending on the surface area to be coated.

A mohair roller sleeve

Kettles and roller trays

Use galvanised kettles for solvent-borne coatings, and plastic pots for water-borne coatings. The size of roller trays should be appropriate for rollers being used.

Hair stipple brushes

These are often abbreviated to hair stipplers or stipplers, and are used to remove all traces of brush marks and leave a smooth, even finish. These brushes come in different sizes (dimensions are given in inches), and particular care should be taken when using, cleaning and storing them. When not in use, they should be laid on their sides rather than left standing on the bristle ends, as this may damage and distort the bristles. The effectiveness of the brush depends on the broad, flat area of bristle tips. Avoid build-up of paint or scumble on the bristles by frequently wiping the bristle ends with a cloth dampened with the appropriate thinner.

Use metal kettles for solvent-borne coatings

Hair stipple brush – 6 x 4

Hair stipple brush – 4 x 1

There are also rubber stipple brushes available, which are normally used for texture paint. If a bold effect is required, or the effect will be viewed from a distance, these may be used to manipulate the scumble. It is best to use this type of stippler with water-borne products, as cleaning solvents will cause the brush to deteriorate.

To maintain the condition of the brush, clean it as soon as it is no longer needed, to avoid the coating drying in the bristles. Place two or three trays of thinner with a pile of rags between them. Place the brush in each tray in turn, using the rags to absorb excess thinner between trays as the brush gets gradually cleaner. When all traces of paint or scumble have been removed, wash the brush in warm, soapy water and rinse it to remove any final traces of thinner and keep the bristles soft. Hang it up to prevent damage to the bristles and make sure it is fully dry before storing it, preferably in a box to protect it.

Tack rags/cloths

These are used just before applying coatings to pick up loose particles of dust, dirt and lint from the surface. Lint-free tack cloths are made from a continuous (non-fibrous) filament of synthetic yarn. They have finished edges and have been coated in a non-drying resin. When not in use, the tack rag or cloth should be stored in its polythene wrapping. Keep it clean and away from direct sunlight to prevent any drying of the resin.

DEFECTS

Some defects in the ground coat will be evident in the appearance of the broken colour effect:

- insufficient surface preparation
- using dirty/contaminated paint, application tools and equipment
- using inappropriate application methods

Bittiness in the ground coat is unsightly and the scumble can collect around this, making it appear a darker colour and spoiling the finished effect.

Heavy-handed laying off by brush will result in brush marks or ropiness and, as with bittiness, the scumble can collect in the uneven paint film. Careless laying off may also lead to misses in the ground coat, meaning the scumble will sink.

Poor opacity or inconsistent laying off can also leave an uneven ground coat colour which may be visible in the finished work.

To help reduce or avoid application defects in the ground coat, it is best to use either a roller with a mohair sleeve or a hair stipple brush to provide a finish free from brush marks.

ENVIRONMENTAL AND HEALTH AND SAFETY CONSIDERATIONS AND REGULATIONS

Attention to safe and healthy working practices is important because you, other people and the environment are all affected by your work activities. Legislation is in place to help protect all three. Environmental and health and safety regulations were covered in detail in Chapter 1, but it is important to be aware of how they relate to producing specialist finishes.

Tack rag/cloth

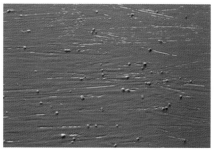

An example of bittiness in a ground coat

COSHH symbol for irritant

Volatile organic compound (VOC)

Materials that evaporate readily from many sources; an example of which is the solvents used in the manufacture of many coatings

ACTIVITY

Examine the packaging of your preparation and painting materials and identify whether the labels use the New International symbols or the European symbols. If you do not know the difference, go on to the HSE website and locate the information leaflet 'Working with substances hazardous to health' and find the section relating to the symbols. Compare the two types to familiarise yourself with the changes.

Reasonably practicable

Sensible, taking into account the trouble, time and money involved

CONTROL OF SUBSTANCES HAZARDOUS TO HEALTH (COSHH) REGULATIONS 2002

These regulations are intended to protect employees and others from the effects of working with substances that are hazardous to health. They cover substances that:

- produce gas, fumes, dust, mist or vapour which may be breathed in (inhaled)
- damage or contaminate skin
- could be swallowed (ingested) by being transferred from hands to mouth
- irritate eyes or could permanently damage eyesight
- may enter the body through a skin puncture (these are quite rare).

When working to produce your ground coat, you may be generating:

- dust, from the dry abrading process
- residue, from the wet abrading process – this could contain lead in an older (pre-1970) building
- fumes or **volatile organic compounds (VOCs)** when applying paints – and remember that, contrary to popular belief, water-borne coatings are not solvent free.

In addition to the use of dust masks, disposable gloves and barrier cream, all of which will help to protect you while you carry out decorating activities, you also need a good level of ventilation in the work area to ensure that there is no build-up of fumes or dust. All of the above are together known as control measures.

You must make use of any control measures and equipment provided, and comply with any special arrangements the employer (or your place of learning) has put into effect.

WORK AT HEIGHT REGULATIONS 2005 (AS AMENDED)

A place is considered 'at height' if a person could be injured falling from it, even if it is at, or below, ground level. These regulations are designed to prevent the deaths and injuries caused each year by falls at work.

The main principle of this piece of legislation is that everyone should do all that is **reasonably practicable** to prevent anyone falling. For further information about the Work at Height Regulations 2005 (as amended), see Chapters 1 and 3.

While producing specialist finishes, you may be required to work from stepladders or podiums/hop-ups. Chapter 3 deals with various types of access equipment, but it is worth remembering here that it is important to check the equipment for any defects before erecting it. Check that it is secure and on firm, level ground before starting to use it.

ELECTRICAL SAFETY

If you use an electrical sander to prepare the surface, use it in conjunction with a 110V transformer to reduce the risk of death by electrocution. Check all plugs, cables and connectors before use. They should be in good condition – if there is any sign of damage, this should be reported and the equipment must not be used.

DISPOSAL OF WASTE

As with health and safety, there is legislation to control the safe disposal of waste products, including coatings that are left over, used thinners, used rags and so on. The Environmental Protection Agency (EPA) is responsible for this, and you should ensure that you comply with its regulations governing different kinds of waste.

Your local authority will probably provide waste disposal services, and will give you guidance on how to dispose of your particular waste. There may be a charge for this, as it is seen as a commercial side of their business. You may therefore need to build the cost for waste disposal into the price you quote for any job.

RISK ASSESSMENTS

In order to work and use materials in the safest and healthiest manner, you will need to carry out risk assessments. As explained in previous chapters this is a simple look at what in the planned work could cause harm to people. You can then decide whether you have taken enough precautions, or whether you need to do more to prevent harm.

Working at height is any work where there is the risk of falling

Check electrical equipment before use

ACTIVITY

Select three materials you might use for decorative finishing work. Look at the EPA website to find the suggested safe disposal method for each one.

ACTIVITY

Undertake the first step of a risk assessment by listing all the hazardous activities and materials involved in the preparation and painting of a surface to produce a high-quality ground coat.

PRODUCE BROKEN COLOUR EFFECTS USING ACRYLIC AND OIL BASED SCUMBLES

This section is about producing broken colour effects by sponge stippling and two methods of rag rolling. A **translucent** coloured glaze called scumble is applied over a different-coloured ground coat to create the desired effect. The translucency of the scumble will allow the ground coat to be seen through it, and will be part of the colour scheme.

The two methods of rag rolling are as follows:

■ Subtractive method – scumble is applied in a continuous, even film to the ground coat, then manipulated using crumpled lint-free fabric or paper to break up and remove small areas of the

Translucent

Allows light to pass through, but prevents images from being seen clearly

coloured film. This is known as the subtractive method because you are taking away colour to produce the effect

■ Additive method – scumble that has been applied to crumpled lint-free fabric or natural sponge is pressed onto the painted ground coat. This is known as the additive method because you are adding colour to produce the effect.

These techniques are covered in more detail on pages 264–267.

SUITABILITY OF THE GROUND COAT

Before starting to produce any broken colour effect, check the suitability of the ground coat. You need a quality finish that has no visible defects (such as misses, ropiness, bits and nibs, brush marks or excessive orange peel), but you also need to check that the colour is appropriate, that it has good opacity and that the paint film is **hard dry**.

Hard dry

Describing a paint film that is hard enough to be worked on without damaging its finish

The relationship between the ground coat colour and the scumble colour will influence how pleasing the final result is, and totally different effects will be produced when a pale scumble is applied over a darker ground coat (eg light blue-green scumble over dark blue-green ground), as opposed to a darker scumble applied over a paler ground coat (eg red-purple scumble over a lilac ground). Whichever order you choose, the two colours should be of a similar tone and not too strongly contrasting. You will be learning more about colour, its use and schemes, in your second year.

MATERIALS

It is important to understand the materials used to create broken colour effects, which are oil based or acrylic (water-borne). Although this chapter discusses how to use different products and materials, you should always read the manufacturer's information to find out exactly how each one should be prepared and used, as there can be differences between products.

OIL GLAZE

ACTIVITY

Using the Internet to access manufacturers' information, find out which types of oil are used in the manufacture of paint.

This is a translucent **medium** (containing linseed oil, white spirit, extenders, beeswax and driers), which has little or no opacity.

Medium

The liquid ingredient that enables a glaze to be spread over a surface and dry as a film. A medium binds the colourant particles together and provides good adhesion to the substrate

You will be aware from Chapter 5 of how coatings flow out and dry as a smooth, level film, and that this is directly related to the **viscosity** of the coating. However, if you are producing a broken colour finish, you do not want the scumble to flow out, otherwise the effect will disappear before it dries. The inclusion of beeswax in oil based glaze enables the scumble to retain its shape (or pattern) after it has been manipulated.

Viscosity

The ability of a liquid or coating to flow; the more viscous it is, the slower it flows

This type of glaze is based on linseed oil, and so it has a natural tendency to yellow. This happens over time, but the effect is accelerated on surfaces that get hot, such as radiators, or where there is little light, for example behind pictures, furniture and so on. Potential customers should always be advised of the possibility of this happening, so they may make an informed decision on the range of products that are available.

Preparation

Oil glaze should always be thinned using white spirit (following the manufacturer's instructions) so that it can be applied as a fairly thin coat. Take care, though, not to over-thin it, as this will affect its ability to hold the pattern. Once it is the right consistency, colourant is added.

Working time

Oil glaze has a long 'open' or working time, which may be an advantage, particularly when you are working on large areas. However, the working time of any coating will be affected by the atmospheric conditions (eg heat, cold, damp) and you need to know how to adjust the material accordingly.

- Higher temperatures will shorten the drying time, but adding a small quantity of raw linseed oil will extend the working time.

- Lower temperatures will lengthen the drying time. The careful addition of a very small quantity of Terebine driers will speed up the drying process, which reduces the working time. However, if too much is added, the scumble will become brittle (cracking and losing adhesion) and the life of the decorative effect will be reduced.

When calculating the quantity of scumble you need for the size of area to be worked, you should always prepare more than is required. You should have plenty to:

- produce a sample board for the customer

- rub out and apply again if the effect is not as required or gets damaged while wet

- leave with the customer on completion of the job, for any minor repairs that may be required, or to enable a small area to be produced to match as closely as possible to the existing finish, for example if a radiator or pipework is replaced.

Bear in mind that it is difficult to repair damage perfectly. If the scumble is oil based, yellowing may already have started and so an identical match would be impossible.

Storage

Oil glaze is flammable, so it must be stored in cool, well ventilated conditions, with the lid of the container secured. When working indoors, glaze and thinners should ideally be stored in a metal, fireproof cabinet.

Raw linseed oil can extend the working time

ACTIVITY

Find out the type of fire extinguisher to use on a solvent-borne or oil based coating fire.

Store flammable liquids safely

Coalesce

In painting and decorating terms, where particles merge to form a film, particularly in water-borne coatings – the drying process is also known as coalescence

Acrylic glaze

ACRYLIC GLAZE

This is a liquid coating made up of small particles of acrylic resin dispersed (scattered) in water. It is milky in appearance, but when the water evaporates the particles **coalesce** to form a continuous, translucent film with a slight sheen. (For more about the drying process of emulsion paints, see Chapter 5.)

Manufacturers produce a range of acrylic glaze types, and the product information (technical data and safety data sheets) will help you select the most suitable type for the work. These products have a low odour and a working time of up to one hour. Tools are cleaned with water, and these glazes will not yellow over time. However, they may be prone to chips or scratches and are therefore most suitable for application to walls rather than woodwork. Because acrylic scumbles dry quite quickly, a higher skill level may be required to produce a quality broken colour effect on large areas.

It is important to remember that glazes, both oil based and acrylic types, do not contain any colourant, and they are not intended to be used as a clear protective film.

Preparation
The only preparation required is to add an appropriate colourant (see below) and adjust the consistency of the material to suit the atmospheric conditions and required working time.

Working time
Because it is a water-borne product, acrylic glaze has a shorter working time than an oil based glaze. The challenge for the decorator is often how to extend the working time, particularly when applying it to larger areas or in warm weather.

Decorators may use a number of methods to extend the working time of acrylic scumbles, which are not necessarily approved of by manufacturers. These include the addition of a small quantity of glycerine, or lightly spraying the surface with water before applying the acrylic scumble. While proprietary conditioners may help to maintain a wet edge for water-borne products, they also improve the flow of the material and help to reduce application marks. This latter characteristic is not a desirable quality for broken colour work, so if you do use a proprietary conditioner, take care to add a suitable quantity.

Using a wet rag rather than a dry one will help to break up the scumble and will also help to extend the working time of acrylic scumble.

One manufacturer advises that, if using emulsion paint as the colourant, the working time may be altered according to the ratio of acrylic glaze to emulsion paint. For example, 8:1 may give one or two hours of working time, while 4:1 will give about 45 minutes.

As time goes on, manufacturers are improving the open time of acrylic glazes and there is less need to use additives to extend the working time.

Storage
This water-borne product should be stored in cool, well ventilated, frost-free conditions.

SCUMBLE

This is glaze (either oil based or acrylic) to which colourants have been added, making a new material – a translucent coloured glaze.

It is easy to get confused about the correct name for these different products, particularly when some manufacturers call their glaze 'scumble glaze'. Remember the following:

A scumble contains colourant

- If the product is called 'glaze' or 'scumble glaze', it does not contain any colourant and is not suitable to be used on its own as a finish.

- If the product is called 'scumble', it contains colourant and is ready to be used for broken colour work.

Consistency
The scumble shouldn't be thick and sticky, but neither should it be too thin, otherwise its ability to hold an attractive decorative finish will be reduced. Broken colour effects should only have 'visual texture' which is two-dimensional and smooth, not 'tactile texture' which is three-dimensional and can be both seen and felt.

As well as understanding the difference between scumble and glaze, you also need to understand the difference between coatings that are translucent and opaque. The meaning of translucent has been explained in this chapter (see page 255), because it is an important characteristic of the glazes and scumbles already discussed. 'Opaque' means a solid colour finish, which **obliterates** the surface beneath. Paints and some timber treatments are opaque coatings.

Obliterate
To completely hide

Colourants
Good-quality colourants that are stable, lightfast and compatible with the particular glaze should be used. Because the glaze is translucent, even a small amount of colourant will appear as a strong colour. However, you need to add sufficient colour to ensure that the glaze is tinted as strongly as possible and will give consistent colour when applied thinly over the ground coat. Even though the glaze may appear very strong in the kettle or pot, when it is brushed out across a larger area it will be less **intense**.

Intense
Extreme, very strong or (here) high degree of colour

If you are using tube colour, it will be helpful to place a strip of the colour on a palette and then mix in a small quantity of the thinner (white spirit or water); this softened colour will be easier to mix into the glaze.

Acrylic paints can be mixed with a glaze to create a scumble

Whatever type of colourant you use, take care to fully mix and evenly disperse it throughout the glaze; if necessary, strain the scumble (using a fine mesh stocking or proprietary strainer) to ensure that there are no lumps of pure colour remaining.

Before starting to work, test the depth of colour on a small board or piece of card coated in the ground colour. Remember, you can always add a little more colour, but can never take it away.

The following colourants may be used in oil based glaze:

- artists' oil colours
- solvent-borne eggshell paint
- universal stainers.

The following colourants may be used in acrylic glaze:

- artists' acrylic colours
- proprietary acrylic colourants
- emulsion paint
- universal stainers.

For training purposes, poster colours may be used in acrylic glazes. Also note that some manufacturers advise against using acrylic eggshell as a colourant.

If solvent-borne eggshell or emulsion paint is used to colour a glaze, remember that the pigments used in those coatings are designed to obliterate the surface, a characteristic that is not desirable in the scumble – you should therefore use them very sparingly.

ACTIVITY

Name a colourant type that may be used in both oil based and acrylic glazes.

TOOLS AND EQUIPMENT

Refer to pages 252–253 for information about paint brushes, hair stipple brushes, mohair rollers, kettles and plastic pots.

LINT-FREE CLOTH

'Lint-free' means a cloth without fluff and loose fibres, for example cotton sheeting or mutton cloth. The texture of the cloth you choose will determine the effect produced.

Other products that may be used to produce broken colour effects include paper (tissue/kitchen paper), net curtain material, plastic film or bags. Any cloth used must be lint free, or the loose fibres will stick to the wet scumble and be unsightly.

Precautions

Cloths that have been used with oil based scumbles pose a fire risk – they may ignite as a result of spontaneous combustion. When not in use, these cloths should be:

- laid flat on a surface to dry by allowing the solvents to evaporate, or

- placed in a metal bin with a cover, or

- immersed in a bucket of water.

You should always take these precautions during lunch breaks or other short breaks, as well as at the end of the day.

CHAMOIS LEATHER

This type of leather is soft, supple, absorbent and non-abrasive. Although imitation chamois leathers or synthetic chamois leathers are available, they do not have quite the same natural qualities as the genuine article, which is expensive to buy.

Care

If the chamois leather has been used for oil based scumble, clean it in white spirit first (it is essential to wear gloves for this) to remove all traces of scumble. If an acrylic scumble has been used, rinse the leather thoroughly in warm water. Using a mild bar soap (not detergent, which will cause the chamois to become dry, brittle and less absorbent), lather the chamois, rinse it out and lather again with the bar soap, but do not rinse. With the soap still in the chamois, squeeze it dry and gently stretch it out; hang the chamois in an area protected from direct heat and sunlight.

Just before you use the chamois next time, rinse it in warm water to remove the remaining soap and squeeze out the water. Leaving the soap in the chamois between uses will help to keep it conditioned and preserve its qualities.

Paper towel can be used to produce a broken colour effect

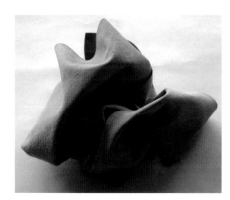

Chamois leather

ACTIVITY

Find out where natural chamois leather and imitation chamois leather come from.

Chamois leathers must not be placed in a sealed plastic bag or other container while still wet, as this will cause them to break down and make them unusable.

NATURAL SEA SPONGES

Sea sponges come from animals that live on the ocean floor; of the 5,000 sponge species, only seven are harvested and used for decorative, craft and cosmetic purposes. Sea sponges are soft and pliable, and their texture enables the creation of random and unique patterns. They may be used with oil based, water-borne and acrylic coatings.

Care

As with cleaning a chamois leather, the first stage of cleaning a sea sponge will depend on the type of scumble used – this will be followed by thorough rinsing in warm water until it runs clear. A natural sea sponge must be handled carefully. Gently squeeze it rather than wringing it out as you would a cloth, leather or synthetic sponge. Sea sponges are expensive to buy and should be dried before being stored in a location where they will not be damaged.

DRAGGING BRUSH

This brush is used to produce specialist finishes and is usually associated with **graining**, but it may also be used to produce a broken colour effect, which you will learn about at Level 2. The filling has either two rows of natural bristle, or one row of bristle and one row of stiff nylon, which replicates the split whale bone used in the past. The filling type influences the effect produced, with the one containing nylon producing a coarser effect than the bristle-only type. This tool is not used to produce any of the broken colour effects required in this chapter.

Care

The dragging brush is cleaned using the appropriate thinner for the material it has been used with. When all traces of the thinner have been removed, wash the brush in warm, soapy water and rinse it. It should be allowed to fully dry before being stored, preferably in a box to protect it against damage.

PALETTE

This is a rectangular timber or plastic board (sometimes with a hole to place the thumb through) on which a quantity of paint is placed.

SETTING OUT

You may be working from a scale drawing (perhaps showing panel areas on a wall), from verbal instructions, or you may be applying an effect to a specified architectural area such as a **dado**. If required, measure and mark out the area that is going to receive the broken

Natural sea sponge

Graining

Applying and manipulating an appropriately coloured scumble to imitate the appearance of a specific timber

Dragging brush

Dado

An area of wall immediately above the skirting in a room, and separated from the wall filling by a timber, plaster or plastic strip secured to the wall

colour effect, using appropriate tools such as a tape measure, chinagraph pencil, spirit level for horizontal lines and plumb bob for vertical lines, and chalk and line (or self-chalking line). Check the dimensions for accuracy throughout the setting-out process, and then apply masking materials.

PROTECTING ADJACENT AREAS: MASKING MATERIALS

When you are producing decorative effects, you need to think about the effect going right to the edge of the area and often into corners. The surrounding surfaces will need to be protected from the materials and tools you are using.

For the protection to be effective and not cause damage, you will need to select the appropriate kind of masking tape. The first factors to consider are as follows:

- the type of surface to be protected (smooth, delicate, rough, etc)

- the length of time it will need to be protected (one day, a week etc)

- the material you are protecting against (solvent, water, etc)

- whether it is for interior or exterior (consider temperature and weather, including **UV light**).

The masking tape will need the ability to:

- produce perfect, sharp edges

- hold straight lines over long stretches

- make precise curves

- be removed cleanly, without leaving residue or damaging the substrate.

Adhesive tape is made up of the backing (which may be paper, fabric or plastic film) and an adhesive (rubber based, acrylic based or silicone based). Different combinations of these materials produce a range of tapes. Tape is rated by how many days it may be left on a surface without leaving a residue when removed. The longer-rated tapes have less adhesive and are most suitable for smooth, delicate surfaces, such as a recently painted ground coat.

Application
If you are using separate masking tape and paper, the tape will need to be adhered to the edge of the paper, in manageable lengths. Alternatively a self-adhesive paper or pre-taped polythene sheet may be used, depending on the location and surface area of the work. First, accurately position the masking material lightly at the edge of the area to be decorated, then apply even pressure to the tape so

UV light

Ultraviolet rays from the sun, which can cause health problems (for example with the skin or eyes) and damage to materials

Masking tape

ACTIVITY

Find out which type of adhesive tape is most suitable when masking curves.

INDUSTRY TIP

Press the front of a thumbnail along the edge of the masking tape, to ensure that it is really well secured and to prevent creep.

Creep

Where masking tape has not been securely fixed to a surface and some scumble seeps beneath it – this will result in there not being a sharp edge to the broken colour effect

Take care when removing masking tape

that it firmly adheres to the surface. This will help to prevent any **creep** of scumble under the edge of the tape, which will lead to thick, blurred edges.

Removal

Masking materials should be removed as soon as is practicable after the work has been completed. When de-masking, take care to avoid the following:

- damaging the finished effect – it is almost impossible to invisibly repair and usually results in the scumble having to be rubbed out and the effect created again

- lifting the ground coat – should this occur, even shallow damaged areas will need to be filled (using fine surface filler) and spot-primed, before re-coating with the ground coat, feathering in the edges.

When removing masking tape, both the surface and the adhesive tape should be dry. It should not be pulled away from the surface, but instead needs to be pulled back on itself with a careful, even pulling motion. If you do not do this, the backing material may tear and leave adhesive residue on the surface, or the ground coat could be lifted.

Disposal of waste

Removed masking materials are a slip hazard if they are not placed immediately in a bin liner. If oil based scumble has been used, both masking materials and cloths are a potential fire risk (see page 261).

Storage

Tapes should be stored in a dry location, at room temperature, protected from direct sunlight and freezing temperatures. In these conditions they can be stored for at least 12 months. High temperatures will speed up the ageing process and will affect the usability of the tape.

APPLICATION TECHNIQUES

Having prepared your scumble (glaze plus colourant) and obtained the required consistency, you are now ready to produce a variety of broken colour effects. This section covers rag rolling (subtractive method), rag rolling (additive method) and sponge stippling.

RAG ROLLING: SUBTRACTIVE METHOD

This may also be referred to as the negative technique or ragging off.

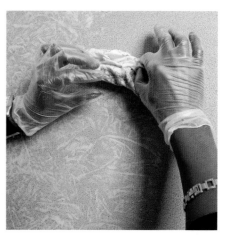

STEP 1 Apply the scumble using a well-worn brush (natural bristle may be used for oil based scumble, but synthetic filament must be used for acrylic scumble), and rub out to cover the surface evenly, being careful not to apply too much glaze.

STEP 2 Remove all brush marks from the scumble and produce an evenly textured finish using a hair stippler or mohair roller. A stippler is used by firmly striking the glaze at 90° with the bristle tips, using short, sharp, clean strokes, and moving it slowly across the surface until an even texture is achieved.

STEP 3 Crumple a piece of lint-free cloth (or chamois leather), and firmly but lightly roll this across the area, working in random, snake-like moves, slightly overlapping each time to avoid unrolled areas or tramlines (this is also called banding or tracking).

Before using a stippler or roller for the first time, prime the bristle tips or roller sleeve by drawing the rubbing-in brush across them a few times; this will help to reduce the **porosity** of the bristles' oblique pile and keep scumble from being absorbed by them, which could lead to areas of thin or removed scumble on the surface you are decorating.

You should repeat Step 3 until the entire surface has been rolled and an even effect achieved, with no **discernible** pattern. If a more detailed effect is required, either use a thinner type of cloth that will crumple with more broken edges, or roll the entire surface again to lift off more glaze.

If you are using an acrylic scumble, dip the cloth in water and wring it out before starting. This will help to break up the scumble and extend the working time.

Porosity

The state of being porous – when small spaces or voids in a material mean that it can absorb liquids

Discernible

Clearly seen

INDUSTRY TIP

When you perform Step 2, if the pressure of the striking action is too light, it will take a long time to remove the marks and even out the scumble. However, if too much pressure is applied there can be a tendency to drag the tool across the surface, and this will leave slip or skid marks in the scumble.

Crumple the cloth when rag rolling for an interesting pattern

At regular intervals, shake out and re-crumple the cloth, taking care not to fold it, because the more broken edges there are in the ball of cloth, the more interesting the pattern. To prevent the cloth becoming overloaded with scumble, periodically rinse it out in the appropriate thinner (white spirit or water), then wring it out well.

When working on large areas such as walls, consider the following:

- It is advisable for one person to apply and stipple the scumble, and a second person to create the effect. As each person's work is unique to them, the film thickness and pressure used when applying and stippling the scumble, and the way of crumpling the cloth and method of manipulating it, will also be unique. Roles should not be reversed partway through the job, as the final effect will be quite different and noticeable.

- It may be necessary to replace the cloth being used. The new one must always be from the same piece of material, as the texture and pattern being produced will be unique to that product.

- Getting into corners or small areas may require using a smaller piece of cloth, yet still producing the same effect.

RAG ROLLING: ADDITIVE METHOD

This may also be called the positive technique, or ragging on.

1 Place the prepared scumble in a container, and immerse the cloth or chamois leather in it and wring it out. It is advisable to press the cloth onto on a spare board or length of lining paper, to avoid applying too much scumble to the surface.

2 Roll the cloth over the surface in an irregular manner, making sure not to double-roll any areas, but also not leaving any part of the surface unrolled, otherwise tramlines or banding will result. If the amount of scumble being deposited on the surface begins to reduce, re-immerse the cloth in the scumble to re-load it, and wring it out.

The additive method

An advantage of this method is that there is no wet edge to keep open. However, it can be more difficult to achieve a uniform effect than with rag rolling (subtractive method).

SPONGE STIPPLING

This is also an additive method or positive technique. This decorative effect gives a multi-coloured, speckled appearance, with a minimum of two colours being applied to the ground coat, and three colours giving an extra dimension to the work.

An advantage of using emulsion paint for this effect is its speed of drying, particularly as two or three colours are being applied on top of one another and each colour must have dried before the next one can be applied. A large natural sponge should be used, particularly when working broad areas such as walls. Prepare it for use by immersing it in water and gently squeezing it out.

1 Place emulsion paint or prepared scumble in a roller tray or large dish.

2 Press one side of the sponge into the paint or scumble to load it.

3 Dab the loaded sponge on a spare board or length of lining paper to avoid applying too much to the surface. Alternatively, use thinned emulsion in a container, immerse the sponge and squeeze it out, then dab off the excess paint.

4 Stipple the paint onto the wall using a light dabbing action, turning the wrist (not elbow) each time to avoid any regular pattern being created. Take care not to drag or twist the sponge on the surface, otherwise skid marks may be created. The stipples should be placed close together, but not overlap.

5 When the first colour has dried, apply the next colour(s) in the same manner, always applying the lightest colour last of all. If minor damage should occur, apply a repair using the same colour as the ground coat to disguise it.

First colour applied overall

Second colour applied

APPLICATION FAULTS

Banding/tracking

This can occur if you don't slightly overlap areas while rag rolling or check the work carefully on completion.

Ensure you overlap areas when rag rolling to avoid tracking

Slip/skid

This fault can occur if you apply too much pressure or don't take enough care when evening out the scumble or producing the effect.

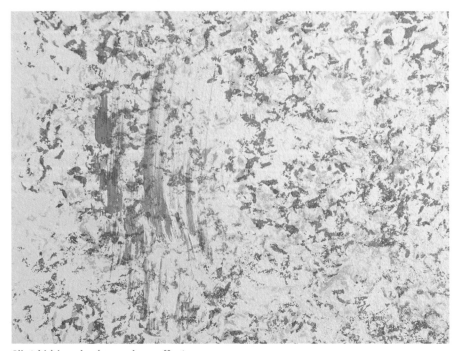

Slip/skid in a broken colour effect

PROTECTION OF THE FINISHED WORK

Broken colour finishes are delicate, and when they have been applied to areas that are subject to knocks and damage, such as doors, woodwork and certain wall areas, they need to be protected with a varnish that is compatible with the type of scumble used. An eggshell or flat varnish finish is most appropriate, as the light reflectance from any higher degree of sheen will detract from the decorative finish. The varnish should be applied as thin coats and built up, according to the durability required.

PERSONAL PROTECTION

You will need personal protective equipment (PPE) when you are carrying out any decorating work. The minimum precautions when producing specialist decorative finishes are as follows:

- Avoid products coming into contact with skin and eyes (wear gloves, and goggles if necessary).
- Ensure that there is good ventilation, using local exhaust ventilation (LEV) if necessary.
- Store and use products away from heat sources and flames.
- Do not eat or smoke in the vicinity of the work area.
- Wash hands before eating.

For more about PPE, see Chapter 1.

ACTIVITY

Using the Internet and manufacturers' information, find a non-yellowing varnish suitable for protecting oil based and acrylic scumble work.

APPLY SINGLE-COLOUR STENCILS

A stencil is produced when:

- a design or pattern is cut out of a thin plate of treated paper, card, acetate or metal
- the stencil plate is temporarily adhered to the surface being decorated
- colour is applied through the cut-out sections.

This produces a pattern on the surface and, by moving the stencil plate to different positions, you can produce identical versions of the pattern.

The main types of stencil plate are as follows:

ACTIVITY

Find out which types of metal are used to manufacture stencil plates.

- Positive – the actual design is cut out of the plate and is therefore applied as the colour. More intricate designs can be produced using this type.
- Negative – the surround or background of the design is cut out, so the design on the surface is the ground coat colour and the applied colour is the background. This often gives the design the appearance of a silhouette.

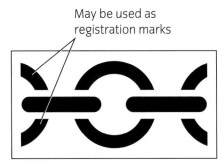

May be used as registration marks

A positive stencil design

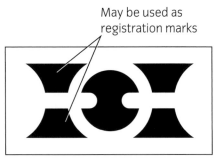

May be used as registration marks

A negative stencil design

Registration marks

Marks (or a very small cut-out section) made on a stencil which are lined up with chalk lines on the surface, and/or part of a previously applied stencil if using a multi-plate stencil, to ensure correct positioning before applying paint

A completed stencil effect

- Border or edge – this is a narrow band of integrated shapes, which may be either a positive or a negative plate.

- Multi-plate – two or more stencil plates are used to produce the finished design, with each plate being a different part of the design and for use with a different colour. It is essential that each plate is very accurately positioned, using **registration marks**, before the paint is applied.

Stencils may be applied in the following ways:

- single (or spot) design – both positive and negative types may be used

- linear border – eg around a room at dado rail or picture rail height

- frame – eg around a panelled area or on the top of a box

- overall wall decoration – with the designs being repeated at set distances, sometimes called a diaper pattern.

If the design for a stencil has not been carefully thought through, sections of the design will fall out when it is cut, because they are not physically linked to the rest of the design. These important links are called ties, and you will learn more about them at Level 2, when you will learn how to prepare, cut and repair stencil plates.

MATERIALS

Paints used to apply stencils should have the following properties:

- little or no flow

- quick drying, particularly if a border or multi-plate stencil is being applied

- reasonably good opacity

- compatibility with the surface – for example, using emulsion paint on a solvent-borne eggshell ground coat could result in cissing (see pages 169 and 210).

TOOLS AND EQUIPMENT

In addition to the standard decorating tools you will have learned about, such as a tape measure, ruler and chinagraph pencil (to prevent permanent marks), you will also need some more specialist equipment.

Chalk and line

This is thin string/cord that is pulled across a stick of chalk, which will coat it; proprietary winder chalk lines are also available. The coated line is used by pulling it taut between two points marked on a surface and then plucking or snapping it sharply so a thin, straight line of chalk is transferred to the surface. For short lengths, up to around arms' length, you should be able to strike the line on your own. For longer lengths, one end will need to be fixed in position on the surface.

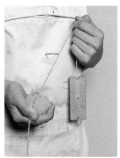
Chalking the line

Snapping a chalk line

Resulting chalk line

Spirit level and plumb bob

These tools, which you may usually associate with paperhanging, are important for **setting out** areas of different types of decorative effects. It is not considered good practice to use a spirit level for vertical lines; many surfaces are not flat and smooth and this will adversely affect the accuracy of the reading. A plumb bob, irrespective of how undulating the wall is, will still indicate an accurate vertical line.

Spirit level   Plumb bob

Set out

To put in a specified position or location – following a drawing, written specification or verbal instructions

ACTIVITY

Check the accuracy of a spirit level. If you do not know how to do this, find the information on the Internet and then carry out the check. Report the findings to your tutor if the reading is not accurate.

Stencil brush

This is a round brush with a filling of short, stiff bristles set in a metal ferrule on a short handle. Stencil brushes are available in a range of diameter sizes from 6mm to 38mm, and the size selected should be appropriate for the area of colour to be applied. Some decorators wrap masking tape around the lower half of the bristles to stop them

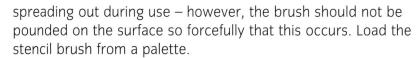

Stencil brush

spreading out during use – however, the brush should not be pounded on the surface so forcefully that this occurs. Load the stencil brush from a palette.

Paint must not be allowed to build up and dry on the bristles, which will happen quite quickly when you are using water-borne paints. Rubbing the bristle ends on a cloth dampened with the appropriate thinner will help to limit this. However, do not immerse the bristles in thinner, otherwise the viscosity of the paint still to be applied will be affected – if necessary, change to a clean dry brush. After use the stencil brush should be thoroughly cleaned in the appropriate thinner and then washed with soap and water. When it is completely dry, the bristles should be wrapped in paper, which is secured with masking tape or an elastic band – this will maintain the shape of the brush filling.

Scraper

This may be used to hold down the stencil plate close to where you are applying the paint, usually when using the lighter, treated paper-type stencil plates.

SECURING METHODS

Tape

See pages 185–186 for information about masking tape. Low-tack tape, as its name implies, has less adhesive on the backing, and is therefore most suitable when stencilling, as there will be minimal surface damage.

Proprietary spray adhesive

Spray adhesive

Aerosol spray contact adhesive is suitable for securing lightweight materials. An important principle of stencilling is that the stencil plate can be peeled off, repositioned and stuck down again (for up to 12 hours). Excess adhesive can be rubbed off with a clean finger or eraser once it has begun to dry. These products are expensive, and have been known to lift some of the newly applied ground coat when being repositioned, so they are best suited to stencil plates cut from acetate.

PLANNING CONSIDERATIONS

Before undertaking any stencilling work, it is essential to thoroughly plan the setting out and execution of it, taking into consideration a number of factors for a perfectly balanced effect.

If you are applying stencilling to a room, you will need to consider:

- room dimensions
- room shape
- the location and number of doors, windows and corners.

These can all affect the starting and finishing points and centralising of the design, particularly on feature areas such as the chimney breast, panels and so on. It is advisable to carefully note the dimensions of each wall and its features before you start, to enable you to work out balanced spacing for the plates. The setting out principles for stencilling are different from those you use for paperhanging (see pages 231–233). The finishing point with wallpaper should be the least obvious internal angle in a room. With stencilling you should aim to finish at a natural stopping point, which is a usually a feature such as a door or window.

If you are continuing a border stencil around an internal or external angle, the design must match on both sides. For this reason simple designs, in a single colour, may be the most appropriate to apply. However, you may decide to treat each wall as a separate section and to centralise the design on each wall. In these circumstances, you will need to give thought to the end of the stencil design and its finishing distance from the corner.

The term connections is used to refer to how many times the stencil is repeated to form a border. This is taken into account when planning out a room for a border. The gaps (connection spaces) can be changed depending on the length of the wall and the size of the stencil design, but the finished effect must be **aesthetically** pleasing and balanced.

The dimensions of the room will also influence the access equipment required for the work – both the height at which you will be working, and the length of the working platform required for a comfortable workstation, as stencilling can be a slow job. See Chapter 3 for access equipment types and usage.

When you are producing a frame around an area, the stencil design should really dictate the area size, not the other way round. In these circumstances there are two ways to negotiate the corners:

■ mitre joint – **bisect** the angle so the design will pivot on that line

■ stop and apply a corner feature – while a different single stencil design may be used as the corner feature, the natural flow of the design will continue better if a part of its design has been used to create the corner stencil.

The size of the stencil design should always be relative to its location. If it is too small, a large number of repeats will be needed, and this has cost as well as possible aesthetic implications. If it is too large, it may overwhelm rather than enhance the area, and if it has large areas through which colour is to be applied, the selection of appropriate tools and materials to produce an even colour is also a consideration.

A chimney breast

Aesthetic

Concerning the appreciation of beauty

ACTIVITY

List the most suitable type(s) of access equipment for applying a stencil at picture rail height.

Bisect

To divide into two equal parts

Feature corner stencil

SETTING OUT

Having carefully planned the positioning of the stencils, accurate measuring – including the correct use of a spirit level for horizontal lines and a plumb bob for vertical lines – is crucial. However, in buildings where architectural features may not be truly horizontal or vertical (eg older buildings), the setting out must produce an aesthetically pleasing effect, which may involve measurement only, and not the use of a spirit level and/or plumb bob.

The surface should be marked out with appropriate centre, horizontal and/or vertical guide lines, using chalk and line. This is then very lightly dusted off to remove any excess chalk.

The following steps show you how to set out and apply a stencil.

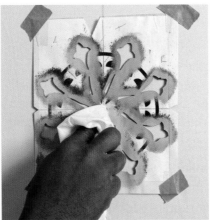

STEP 1 Place the stencil plate accurately on the surface, lining up registration marks with the chalked lines, and secure with low-tack tape. If you are using a proprietary spray adhesive, follow the manufacturer's instructions before adhering the stencil plate to the surface. The stencil plate should be secure enough not to move while the paint is being applied, which may cause smudging. However, it should be easy to remove and reposition without damaging the surface.

STEP 2 Before applying any paint, check whether a chalk line passes through the area to be stenciled. If so, remove it with a dry cloth, otherwise it will absorb the paint and create bittiness and uneven colour.

STEP 3 Pour a small quantity of paint onto a palette board and dab the bristle ends of the stencil brush onto the paint. Remove excess paint from the brush by stippling it out on a clean area of the palette board, spare board or length of lining paper – this will also ensure the paint is evenly distributed. You must do this every time you re-load the brush, to avoid a number of application faults.

STEP 4 Apply the paint through the cut-out sections of the stencil plate using a stippling action, keeping the brush at 90° to the surface, and moving it across the area until you have produced an even colour with a sharp outline.

STEP 5 Before removing the stencil plate, lift a small section of it to check that the depth of colour is correct, as it is very difficult to replace the plate exactly once it has been completely removed. Repeat the process and continue until the work has been completed. At this stage, the stencil plate should be cleaned, completely dried and stored carefully, keeping it flat or hung vertically.

When the applied stencils are dry, wipe off any remaining chalk lines with a clean soft cloth or damp sponge if necessary.

Do:

- Regularly wipe excess paint from the stencil plate (both front and back) using the appropriate thinner. This must be done carefully to avoid damaging the plate or getting it too wet.

- Use a scraper to hold down the stencil plate close to where the paint is being applied, particularly if the stencil plate is made from treated paper.

- Regularly check that the colour application is even; this may be done by partly closing your eyes and squinting at the work, to clearly see any differences there may be between each application.

- Carefully lift part of the stencil plate to check for both even paint application and correct weight of colour, before finally removing it. It can be difficult to re-apply the stencil plate accurately to touch up any areas. If applying a border stencil, or many repetitions of a single stencil design, this check should also be done to compare the weight of colour between the current stencil and those previously applied.

- Check the consistency of the paint on the palette and replace it if it is beginning to thicken or dry.

> **INDUSTRY TIP**
>
> When storing used stencil plates flat, separate them from other stencil plates with paper if possible, to avoid them snagging each other.

Do not:

- Be tempted to over-work the area, as this may lead to the applied paint beginning to lift off.

- Be heavy-handed in applying the paint, as this will cause creep.

- Dip your stencil brush directly into the container of paint – always load it from a palette.

APPLICATION FAULTS

Fault	Description and causes
Creep	- Paint getting beneath the stencil plate and blurring the edge of the design. - Caused by the application of too much paint, or paint that is too thin. - Not keeping the stencil plate regularly wiped clean. - Heavy-handed application, or the stencil plate not being secured/held tight to the surface.
Smudging	- Movement of the stencil plate on the wet paint – caused by careless removal of the stencil plate.
Paint lifting	- Caused by careless removal of the stencil plate or over-working an area during application.
Uneven colour and uneven weight of colour over repeats	- Failing to regularly check for even distribution of colour.
Bittiness	- Dirt and grit in the paint film. - Caused by insufficient checking of the surface cleanliness prior to starting work, not dusting off any excess chalk deposit or using dirty tools and equipment or contaminated paint.
Undue texture	- Excess paint applied to the surface. - Caused by not working the brush on spare board or paper immediately after re-loading it.
Buckled/curled stencil plate	- May be the result of the method used to make the stencil, leaving an insufficient margin around the design. - May be caused by not wiping off the stencil plate frequently enough or letting it get too wet when cleaning it off.

Case Study: Joe

Joe is a self-employed decorator who has been asked by a potential customer, Mrs Davies, to visit and discuss decorating her lounge using a decorative finish that would be unusual and individual. He has been recommended by an existing customer for whom he has undertaken painting and paperhanging work over the past 10 years.

Although Joe learned decorative finishes at college when an apprentice and helped his employer at the time with a few jobs which included some rag rolling and stencilling, he has only had a couple of commercial jobs of his own for rag rolling. He has a small portfolio of work, which includes some sample sheets produced when at college and photos of work he has undertaken over the years – mainly painting and paperhanging, but also the rag rolling jobs.

He visited Mrs Davies and showed her his portfolio, and she selected a rag rolled effect from one of his photos but requested a different colour combination. She chose to have a sea-green ground coat with a large and open white rag-rolled effect. Thanks to her friend's recommendation, Mrs Davies was happy to go away for a week's holiday and leave Joe to get on with the work, which he completed ready for her return.

He was surprised to receive a phone call from a dissatisfied Mrs Davies, asking him to visit her as soon as possible. On arrival she explained that the rag rolling was nothing like she had expected. It was too strong a contrast and very busy. She asked why it was so different from what she had seen in the picture. After a long conversation, Joe had to agree to remove the effect and hang wallpaper instead. The work would be undertaken in his own time but Mrs Davies would pay for the paper.

Joe learned an expensive (in terms of both time and money) lesson. He should have produced a sample board of the chosen colours and cloth to be used for Mrs Davies to approve before starting work.

A sample board being produced

A sample board hung in the room to be decorated

TEST YOUR KNOWLEDGE

Work through the following questions to check your learning.

1. What is the most suitable preparation process before applying a solvent-borne eggshell ground coat?
   a. To dry abrade using aluminium oxide.
   b. To dry abrade using glass paper.
   c. To wet abrade using emery cloth.
   d. To wet abrade using silicon carbide.

2. Why might a mohair roller be used to apply the ground coat for a decorative finish?
   a. To produce a fine textured effect.
   b. To reduce the appearance of brush marks.
   c. To reduce the number of coats required.
   d. To apply the paint quicker.

3. Which one of the following defects is **not** the result of a poor-quality ground coat?
   a. Skid marks.
   b. Uneven colour.
   c. Sinking.
   d. Ropiness.

4. Which one of the following statements is correct?
   a. Glaze contains coloured pigment and extenders.
   b. Scumble contains coloured pigment only.
   c. Scumble contains extenders only.
   d. Glaze contains extenders only.

5. What material may be used to extend the working time of an oil based scumble?
   a. White spirit.
   b. Solvent naptha.
   c. Linseed oil.
   d. Mineral oil.

6. A scumble used to produce a broken colour effect is what?
   a. Transparent, to protect the ground coat colour.
   b. Translucent, to show the ground coat colour.
   c. Opaque, to hide the ground coat colour.
   d. Transparent, to retain the ground coat colour.

7. Which one of the following materials is **not** suitable to use for producing broken colour effects?
   a. Chamois leather.
   b. Lint-free rag.
   c. Woollen cloth.
   d. Paper.

8. Which one of the following is **not** an advantage when sponge stippling with water-borne materials?
   a. Speed of drying.
   b. Ease of cleaning tools.
   c. Multi-application.
   d. Better colour range.

9. Which ingredient in an oil based scumble affects viscosity?
   a. Beeswax.
   b. Extenders.
   c. Coloured pigment.
   d. Terebine.

10. The reason for having one operative apply the scumble and remove brush marks, and a second operative produce the broken colour effect, is to do what?
    a. Enable a high work rate.
    b. Speed up the drying process.
    c. Produce a uniform effect over broad areas.
    d. Produce more skilled operatives.

11 Which one of the following should you do when mixing quantities of scumble for a piece of work?

   a   Mix slightly more than you've calculated for.

   b   Only mix the amount you require.

   c   Mix double the amount you require.

   d   Make the scumble thinner than usual.

12 Which one of the following coatings would be **most** appropriate to use as protection for broken colour work produced using oil based scumble?

   a   Acrylic eggshell varnish.

   b   Solvent-borne gloss varnish.

   c   Oil based translucent glaze.

   d   Solvent-borne eggshell varnish.

13 Which one of the following statements is correct?

   a   When using a positive stencil, the background is applied.

   b   When using a positive stencil, the design is applied.

   c   When using a negative stencil, the design is applied.

   d   When using a positive stencil, design and background are applied.

14 When setting out a linear border stencil to a wall, 2.3m above the skirting board, which one of the following is **not** a planning consideration?

   a   The room dimensions.

   b   Access equipment.

   c   The colour to be used.

   d   The number of repeats.

15 If a border stencil is to be applied to the lid of a large toy box, which one of the following factors will **not** be considered?

   a   Stencil size.

   b   Stencil spacing.

   c   Number of repeats.

   d   Width of ties.

16 What is an appropriate material for temporarily fixing stencil plates to a surface?

   a   Spray adhesive.

   b   Contact adhesive.

   c   PVA adhesive.

   d   Wallpaper adhesive.

17 Which fault is caused by failing to properly secure a stencil plate to the surface?

   a   Paint lifting.

   b   Creep.

   c   Uneven colour.

   d   Grinning.

18 A wall area has been marked out with chalk lines to receive stencils. Which of the following is aligned to these marks?

   a   Registration marks.

   b   Setting-out marks.

   c   Tape marks.

   d   Dimensional marks.

19 Dabbing a loaded stencil brush on a clean area of palette before use is done to do what?

   a   Distribute paint evenly.

   b   Mix the paint colours.

   c   Remove excess paint.

   d   Work in thinners.

20 The most likely effect of applying paint too heavily through a stencil plate is what?

   a   Crisp clean edges.

   b   Creep and poor finish.

   c   Poor opacity.

   d   Uneven application.

TEST YOUR KNOWLEDGE ANSWERS

Chapter 1: Unit 201

1 c Risk assessment.
2 d Blue circle.
3 b Oxygen.
4 a CO_2.
5 b Control of Substances Hazardous to Health (COSHH) Regulations 2002.
6 c 75°.
7 c Glasses, hearing protection and dust mask.
8 d Respirator.
9 a 410V.
10 b 80dB(a).

Chapter 2: Unit 101

1 c 15m.
2 a Open to interpretation.
3 b A section through a part of the structure.
4 a Strip.
5 c Raft.
6 c Damp proof course.
7 d Polystyrene.
8 d cement.
9 b 10°.
10 a Foundations.

Chapter 3: Unit 116

1 a Podium steps.
2 b To hold guard rails in place.
3 c To determine safe working practices.
4 c Windy weather.
5 a Someone trained and competent.
6 c Wooden steps.
7 b Falling from height.
8 b Having it footed by another person.
9 a Falling from height.
10 a Working from roof ladders.
11 d Report it to your supervisor and take it out of use.
12 a Work at Height Regulations 2005 (as amended).
13 d Any height above ground level.
14 b It is lighter.
15 d In a well-ventilated space, under cover.
16 b Length of shortest side × 3.
17 d Timber trestles.
18 b Employer.
19 c 75°.
20 c 1:4.

Chapter 4: Unit 117

1 c Seal.
2 c Caulk.
3 b At the bottom of the wall.
4 b Hardwood.
5 d Washing it down with water.
6 d When there is a thick layer of paint to be removed.
7 c By brushing off with a stiff brush.
8 c Moist and warm conditions.
9 a Peel off the top layer.
10 c Shavehooks.
11 b Sugar soap.
12 a It does not scratch or scorch the surface.
13 d Floors and carpets.
14 c Before work starts each day.
15 b Thorough preparation.
16 d Where the paint film lifts from the surface and breaks down.
17 a Cast iron.
18 b Goggles, dust mask and overalls.
19 b Stripping knife.
20 c The Health and Safety Executive.

Chapter 5: Unit 118

1 b Undercoat.
2 d When starting the job.
3 a Emulsion.
4 c Where a thick ridge of paint forms on a corner.
5 d Polythene dust sheets.
6 a Primer, undercoat, gloss.
7 b It gives colour to the paint.
8 c Filling.
9 c The narrowest part.
10 d To keep the edge wet.
11 a Skirting boards.
12 d Using a roller to apply paint to a surface.
13 b Block brush.
14 d Not wearing gloves.
15 a Clean the lid to remove dust.
16 b Not transmitting light.
17 c Wet and dry.
18 d The paint will dry quickly.
19 b Cissing.
20 d Go mouldy.

Chapter 6: Unit 119

1 c A fine file.
2 c Checking that paper is vertical.
3 c Roll down the edges of paper.
4 a Making something vertical.
5 d Removing pockets of air.
6 b Paste building up on the blades.
7 d Storing them before they are dry.
8 b Apron with pocket.
9 d Cellulose paste.
10 c It will become thin and not usable.

11 b Skin irritation.
12 c By the window.
13 b 2.
14 d Delaminating.
15 c Polished edges.
16 b Ingrain paper.
17 a To make sure the paper is plumb.
18 b Too little paste on paper.
19 b Patterned papers.
20 b To prevent damage to the edges.

Chapter 7: Unit 120

1 d To wet abrade using silicon carbide.
2 b To reduce the appearance of brush marks.
3 a Skid marks.
4 d Glaze contains extenders only.
5 c Linseed oil.
6 b Translucent, to show the ground coat colour.
7 c Woollen cloth.
8 d Better colour range.
9 a Beeswax.
10 c Produce a uniform effect over broad areas.
11 a Mix slightly more than you've calculated for.
12 d Solvent-borne eggshell varnish.
13 b When using a positive stencil, the design is applied.
14 c The colour to be used.
15 d Width of ties.
16 a Spray adhesive.
17 b Creep.
18 a Registration marks.
19 c Remove excess paint.
20 b Creep and poor finish.

INDEX

foundations 77–81
frames, re-glazing 176
friction 80
fungicidal wash 170

G

galvanised steel 149
gas 92
gloss finish 194
gloves 23, 160, 214, 224, 229
goggles 22, 160, 214
graining 262
ground coat 246–253, 256
ground conditions 113–114

H

hacking knife 156
hair stipple brushes 252–253
hammers 157
hand washing 34
hand-arm vibration syndrome
    (HAVS) 23, 31
hanging wallpaper see
    paperhanging
hard hat 22, 214
hardcore 82
hardwood timber 147
hatching symbols 48
hazardous substances 9–11, 33,
    186–187
hazards 5–6, 32–33, 123–125
head protection 22, 32
health and safety
    legislation 2–31
    sources of information 8
    see also risk assessment
Health and Safety Executive (HSE)
    2, 8–9, 102
Health and Safety at Work Act
    (HASAWA) 1974 4–8, 116
heights, working at 102–138
high build wood oil 197
high visibility (hi-viz) jacket 22,
    214
hollow floors 82
hop-ups 110
hot air gun 158, 165
hypotenuse triangle 66

I

imposed loads 77
improvement notice 8
indentations 151
inductions 6
inertia-operated anchor device
    129
injuries
    chemical burns 23
    reporting 12–13
    risk of 17
    statistics 2
insulation 33, 82, 94–95
internal conditions 182
internal walling 87–88
invoice 74

J

job sheet 72
joists 83

K

kettles 158
key 190
kinetic lifting 18
knots 151, 163
knotting solution 163

L

ladder stabiliser 111
ladders 25–26, 103–107,
    120–123, 210
    erecting 132–135
    securing 134–135
    storing 140–141
    see also access equipment;
        stepladders
lambswool insulation 95
lanyard 129
laser level 223
lashing 135
laying off 194, 204
lead 149
lead paint 190
lead-free wood primer 192
lead-in time 55
leaves 86

legislation, health and safety
    2–31
leptospirosis 12
lifting 18–19
    equipment 30, 131–132
    see also manual handing
Lifting Operations and Lifting
    Equipment Regulations
    (LOLER) 1998 30
light fittings 184
lightweight staging 109
lime 85
linear length 59–60
lining paper 230
lintel 84
lint-free cloth 261
liquid paint remover 154, 166
location drawings 49
lockers 16
locking bars 121
low-odour eggshell paint 195

M

making good 172–177
Management of Health and
    Safety at Work Regulations
    1999 116
mandatory signs 41
manual handling 131–132, 139
Manual Handling Operations
    Regulations 1992 17–19,
    131
masking tape 162, 185–186,
    263–264
masonry paint 195
mastic 165
materials
    calculating quantities 55–70
    sustainability of 92
    wastage 56
matt emulsion 193, 205
measurement, units of 57
mechanical handling 131–132
medium-density fibreboard (MDF)
    147
melanoma 23
metal surfaces 148–149
method statement 7
micro-porous paint 197
mild sheet steel 148

putty 155, 176–177
putty knife 156
Pythagorean theorem 66

Q

quick-drying varnish 197

R

radiator brushes 200
radiators, papering behind 237
radius 68
raft foundations 81
rag rolling 255–256, 264–267
raking out 164, 173
ready-mixed adhesive 227
registration marks 270
rendering 163, 175
Reporting of Injuries, Diseases and Dangerous Occurrences Regulations (RIDDOR) 2013 12
requisition order 73
resin exudation 152
respirators 23
rest areas 16
risk assessment 5–6, 113–116, 159–160, 182–183
roller and scuttle 224
rollers 200–202
    cleaning 212
    storing 213
roof ladders 104–105
roofs 88
ropes 121
ropiness 211
rubbing block 157
rungs 121–122
runs 169, 210
rust 151
    removal 164

S

safe condition signs 42
safety
    boots 214
    glasses 22
    harness 128
    helmet 22

notices 41–42
    see also health and safety
sample boards 247
sand and cement 173
sanitary conveniences 15
sanitation 189
scaffold boards 109, 121
scaffolding 27–30, 33, 109–110
    tower scaffold 27–28, 110, 126–127, 137–138
scales 46–47
schedules 52–53, 55
scraping 163, 172
screwdrivers 185
scumble 247, 255–256, 259–260
sealer 171, 173
seam roller 222, 239
second fix 147
section drawings 50
semi-gloss finish 194
services 90–92
settlement cracks 152
sewage 91
sharps box 224
shavehooks 156
sheathing ply 147
sheet material 147
shellac 154, 171
shrinkage cracks 151
sinking 248
site diary 74
site plans 49
size new plaster 88
sizing 222
skeleton gun 158
skid marks 211
skirting board 59–60
slate 89
sockets, papering around 237
softwood timber 147
solar panels 96
solid floors 82
solid walling 84–85
solvent-borne paints 190, 206
specialist finishes
    acrylic glaze 258–259
    ground coat 246–253, 256
    materials for 256–60
    oil glaze 256–257
    painting process 251
    rag rolling 255–256, 264–267

sample boards 247
scumble 247, 255–256, 259–260
setting out 262–264, 274–275
sponge stippling 267–268
stencilling 269–276
tools and equipment 249, 251–253, 261–262, 271–272
specifications 46, 51
spirit level 223, 271
splatters 211
splits 151
sponge stippling 267–268
sponges 157, 222
    natural 262
spray adhesive 272
stabilising solution 192, 154
staging 109
stain block 170
stale paste 151
standing ladders 104
starch paste 226
stencil brush 271
stencilling 269–276
stepladders 26–27, 106–107, 121–123, 135
stiles 121–122
stipple brushes 252–253
stone 85
stopping paste 155
stopping solution 164, 172
storing
    access equipment 140–141
    equipment 213
    paint 214–215
    paperhanging materials 241
straight edge 223
straw bales 93
strip foundations 78–79
stripping knife 155
substrates 146–150
    defects in 150–152, 169–172
    preparing 162–165
sunscreen 23
supplementary signs 42
suspended floors 82–83
sustainability 92–93
swingbacks 121
switches
    loosening 184

papering around 237
symbols
    drawing 48
    hazardous substances 11

T

tape measure 220
tarpaulins 162
tears 238–239
telephone messages 75
temperature 182
temporary bench mark (TBM) 47
tender 71
tie rods 121
tiling, calculating floor area 62–64
timber 93
    framing 86–87
    surfaces 147
timesheet 71
toe-cap boots 22, 214
toilets 15
tool box talks 6
tools
    application 198–202
    paperhanging 220–224
    preparation 155–158, 185
    rollers 200–202
    specialist finishes 249, 251–
        253, 261–262, 271–272
    see also brushes
tower scaffold 27–28, 110,
    126–127, 137–138
tramlines 204, 211
translucence 197
trench block 78
trench fill foundation 79
trestles 27, 107–109, 121–123,
    137
triangle, calculating area 65–67
tribunal 76
trimming knife 224

trip hazards 33
tubular scaffold 29–30
twill dust sheets 161
two-knot brushes 200

U

undercoats 193–195
undercutting 164
units of measurement 57
universal preservative 197
UV (ultraviolet) light 263

V

variation order 72
varnish brushes 199
varnishes 196–197
varnishing 208–210
ventilation 183
verbal communication 75
vibration white finger (VWF) 23,
    31
vinyl silk emulsion 194, 205
viscosity 203, 256
volatile organic compounds
    (VOCs) 10, 186–187
voltage 35
volume, calculating 69–70

W

walling 83–84
    external 84–87
    internal 87–88
wallpaper 230
    paste *see* adhesives:
        paperhanging
    removing 167–168
    see also paperhanging
washing-down brushes 200
washing facilities 15

washing hands 34
wastage 56
waste disposal 187, 255
waste management 116
water
    drinking 16
    penetration 151
    power 97
    services 90–91
water-borne paints 190, 204–205
weather conditions 114, 117,
    182–183
welfare facilities 15–16
Well's disease 12
wet edge 204–205
wet rot 173
wetting in 164
whiting 155
wide strip foundations 79
wind power 96–97
window frames, re-glazing 176
wire brush 157
wiring a plug 36
wood ingrain paper 230
wood stain 198, 209
woodchip *see* wood ingrain
    paper
work area, protecting 160–162,
    183–186
Work at Height Regulations 2005
    (as amended) 24–30, 102,
    112, 126, 254–255
work equipment *see* equipment
work schedules 55
working at height 102–138
written communication 71–74
wrought iron 148

Z

zinc phosphate primer 192

PICTURE CREDITS

Every effort has been made to acknowledge all copyright holders as below and the publishers will, if notified, correct any errors in future editions.

Affixit.co.uk: p272; **Alamo Hardwoods:** p151; **Alamy:** © Klaudia Faferek-Jaworska p175; **Alcolin:** p227; **Ann Cook:** pp xx, xxv, xxx, 157, 201, 222, 248, 249, 252, 261, 270, 273, 277; **APL:** pp 25, 104; **Australian Scaffolds:** p139; **Axminster Tool Centre Ltd:** pp xi, xvi, xvii, xviii, xix, xx, xxi, xxii, xxvii, xxviii, xxix, xxxvi, 20, 22, 23, 34, 36, 107, 111, 135, 137, 153, 154, 155, 156, 157, 158, 160, 165, 166, 170, 185, 188, 199, 200, 201, 202, 220, 221, 222, 223, 224, 225, 249, 250, 252, 253, 255, 257, 263, 271; **Beta Max Hoist Inc.:** p132; **Bjorn Heller:** p131; **BPS Access Solutions:** p105; **Brush Factory China:** p200; **Capital Safety:** p129; **Chase Manufacturing Ltd:** pp xxiii, 110; **City & Guilds:** pp xxx, 126, 150, 165, 229; **Clow Group Ltd.:** pp xiv, xxiv, xxix, 103, 104, 105, 106, 108, 134; **Construction Photography:** ©Adrian Greeman pp xxviii, 21, 56; © Adrian Sherratt p89; ©BuildPix pp xxxv, 11, 33, 173, 187; © Chris Henderson p34; © CJP p89; © Damian Gillie p85; © David Burrows p85; © David Potter p92; © David Stewart-Smith p91; © Grant Smith p13; © imagebroker p89; © Image Source pp 15, 16, 85;© Jean-Francois Cardella pp xix, 47, 170; © QA Photos/Jim Byrne p85; © Steve Aland p175;© Xavier de Canto p1; **Concreteideas.com:** p170; **CORAL Tools Ltd.:** pp xxviii; 221; **decoratingdirect.co.uk:** pp xxi, 200; **Decorating Warehouse:** pp 157, 222, 249; **Dreamstime.com**: © Dmitry Kalinovsky pxxi; **Eamonn Donnellan of Acclaimed Building Consultancy:** p152; **Fall Protection Solutions:** pp xx, 130, 131; **Fotolia:** © Alan Stockdale p39; **Hackney Community College:** pp xi, xiv, xviii, xxiv, xxvi, xxvii, xxix, xxx, xxxi, xxxii, xxxiii, xxxvi, 34, 101, 141, 145, 146, 163, 165, 166, 167, 168, 169, 171, 172, 174, 181, 184, 187, 190, 200, 202, 204, 206, 208, 210, 211, 212, 213, 214, 219, 224, 226, 228, 229, 230, 232, 233, 235, 237, 241, 245, 246, 251, 262, 265, 266, 267, 268, 271, 272, 274, 275; **Handover.co.uk:** pp xxii, xxvii, 251, 252, 258, 260; **Hawes Plant Hire:** p18; **Hire Station:** p108; **HSE.gov.uk:** p9; **Huntco:** p148; **If Images:** © Michael Grant p47; **iStock:** © Andrew_Howe p240; © Banks Photos p95; © deepblue4you p212; © Gannet77 p239; © pidjoe p242; ©ictor pp xxx, 109; ©JodiJacobson pp xix, 161, 249; **JSP Ltd:** pp xxiii, 129; **LFI Ladders:** p107; **Mad Supplies Ltd:** pp xxxvi, 200; **Malmesbury Reclamation:** pp xx, 148; **Mediscan:** p23; **Meteor Electrical:** pp35, 90; **PAT Training Services Ltd:** p37; **Photographers Direct:** © Robert Clare p253; **Prominent Paints:** p169; **Puresafety:** p257; **RIBA Product Selector:** p78; **RJW Engineering:** p161; **Roofco Limited:** p130; **Science Photo Library:** © Dr P. Marazzi/Science Photo Library p23; **Steroplast Healthcare:** p7; **Shurtape UK Ltd:** p264; **Shutterstock:** © 1000 Words p147; © 2happy p151; © 3drenderings pp xxvi, 203; © 7505811966 p128; © A Davis p186; © Alena Brozova p95; © alessandro0770 p93; © Alexander Erdbeer p13; © Alexey V Smirnov p152; ©Alina G pxxxii; © alterfalter p215; © Amy Johansson p130; © Andy Lidstone pxviii; © antos777 p42; © aragami12345s p18; © Artazum p183; ©Artazum and Iriana Shiyan pxviii; © AtthameeNi p220; © auremar pp xi, 18, 45, 65, 75, 178, 204, 236, 238, 239, 277; © Baloncici p190; © Barry Barnes p41; © bikeriderlondon p139; © Bokic Bojan p46; © Bronwyn Photo pxv; © Chad McDermott pxv; © Christian Delbert p162; © Christopher Elwell p149; © Cynthia Farmer p18; © Dani Vincek pxxv; © Darkkong p15; © daseaford p41; © David Reilly p149; © DeiMosz p41; © demarcomedia p15; © DenisNata pp 22, 214; © DmitriMaruta p90; © Dmitry Kalinovsky pp 31, 60, 131; © eltoro69 p149; © endeavour p213; © ffolas p202; © Fireco Ltd p40; © Ford Photography p41; © fotoivankebe p149; ©Goodluz pxxii; ©gyn9037 pxxxi; ©haraldmuc p111; © Heather M Greig p148; © holbox p117; © Igor Sokolov (breeze) p3; © Igorsky p114; © IkeHayden p215; © imagedb.com p174; ©imageegami pxvii; © inxti p188; © Israel Hervas Bengochea pp xvii, 25; ©IVL p182; © Jahina_Photography p91; © Jamie Rogers p224; © Jan Gottwald p185; © Jesus Keller p97; © jocic p147; © John Kasawa p95; ©joppo pxviii;

288 THE CITY & GUILDS TEXTBOOK